14

AMERIGO

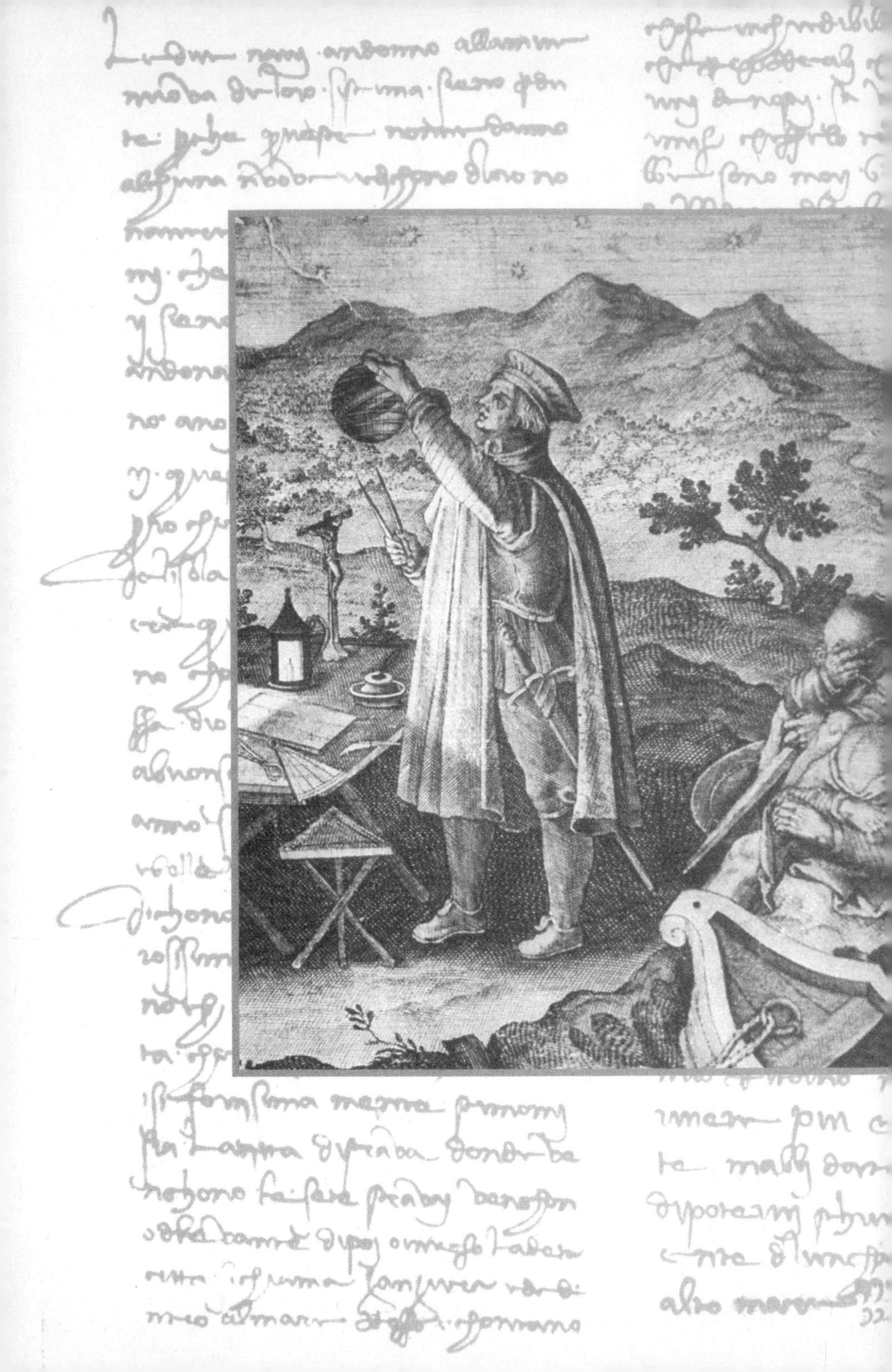

FELIPE FERNÁNDEZ-ARMESTO

AMERIGO

The man who gave his name to America

RANDOM HOUSE

NEW YORK

Published in the United States by Random House, an imprint of
The Random House Publishing Group, a division of Random
House, Inc., New York.

RANDOM HOUSE and colophon are registered trademarks of
Random House, Inc.

ISBN 978-1-4000-6281-2

LIBRARY OF CONGRESS CATALOGING-IN-PUBLICATION DATA
Fernández-Armesto, Felipe.
  Amerigo: the man who gave his name to America / Felipe
Fernández-Armesto.
      p. cm.
  Includes bibliographical references and index.
  ISBN 978-1-4000-6281-2
  1. Vespucci, Amerigo, 1451–1512.   2. America—Name.
3. Explorers—America—Biography.   4. Explorers—Spain—
Biography.   5. Explorers—Portugal—Biography.
6. Explorers—Italy—Florence—Biography.   7. America—
Discovery and exploration—Spanish.   8. America—Discovery
and exploration—Portuguese.   9. America—Discovery and
exploration—Italian.   10. Florence (Italy)—Biography.
1. Title.
E125.V5F47 2007   970.01'6092—dc22   2006051739
               [B]

Printed in the United States of America on acid-free paper

www.atrandom.com

9 8 7 6 5 4 3 2 1

FIRST EDITION

Book design by Simon M. Sullivan

The fool, of wisdom and reasón doth fail
And also, discretion, labouring for nought,
And in this ship shall help to draw the sail
Which day and night infixeth all his thought
To have the whole world within his body brought,
Measuring the coasts of every realm and land,
And climatés, with his compass in his hand.

He coveteth to know, and comprise in his mind,
Every region and every sundry place
Which are not known to any of mankind
And never shall be without a special grace.
Yet such follíes take pleasure and soláce
The length and bredé of the world to measure,
In vain business taking great charge and measure. . . .

For now of late hath largé land and ground
Been found by mariners and crafty governours,
The whiché lands were never known nor found
Before our timé by our predecéssours
And heré after shall by our successours.
Perchance more shall be found, wherein men dwell
Of whom we never before this same heard tell.

—ALEXANDER BARCLAY, *The Ship of Fools* (1509)

PREFACE

A MERIGO VESPUCCI, who gave his name to America, was a pimp in his youth and a magus in his maturity. This astonishing transformation was part of his relentless self-reinvention, from which sprang a dazzling succession of career moves and what the celebrity press now calls makeovers.

From his late twenties or thereabouts, he began to refashion his identity with a regularity that suggests self-dissatisfaction and a need to escape. First he deserted the service of the ruler of Florence, his native city, for that of a rival. A few years later, in 1491, he abandoned Florence for Seville and turned from his previous business—which was as a commission agent, dealing mainly in jewels—to organizing fleets that supplied Columbus's enterprise in the New World. In 1499, at the age of forty-five or so, Vespucci discovered a new vocation, taking to the ocean in person; and within a few more years, he had rebranded himself as an expert in navigation and cosmography. In the course of this last transformation, he shifted from Spanish to Portuguese service and back again. Notwithstanding his lack of qualifications and attainments, he was so convincing in his new role that he became a kind of official cosmographer, with a monopoly from the Castilian crown in the training of Atlantic pilots and the making of Atlantic charts. Some fellow experts hailed him as the new Ptolemy—a reincarnation of the greatest or, at least, the most influential geographer of antiquity. In the world of the Renaissance, there was no greater praise than to be acclaimed as the equal of the ancients.

Even without the extraordinary accident or error that bestowed his name on the western hemisphere, he makes an appealing subject of biography because of the amazing ease and perfection of these self-reshapings. He negotiated the narrows of life, conforming and reconforming fluidly, as if made of quicksilver. Yet no reputable scholar has ventured to write a biography in modern times. The nearest approach was Luciano Formisano's careful and well-informed biographical essay, included in 1991 as part of a coffee-table compilation of studies marking the approach of the five hundredth anniversary of Columbus's first Atlantic crossing.[1] The only full-length attempts at comprehensive biography are either partisan paeans, on which scholarship is squandered, or near-valueless vulgarizations that rely on romance, hero worship, and vacuous speculation to enflesh the evidence.[2] These are unnecessary strategies. The facts about Vespucci are stunning enough without elaboration. Yet the poverty of his biography has ensured that most of the facts, including those of the greatest interest and power to surprise, have remained unknown. I selected two for the opening sentence of this preface, not only because they are arresting in themselves but also because they are unmentioned in existing biographies and barely discussed—at least in print—by the handful of specialist scholars currently at work in the field.

The scholarly inhibitions are understandable. Peculiar, intense problems make the sources for Vespucci's life hard to handle with confidence. There is plenty of evidence. Indeed, we know more about Vespucci than any other explorer of his time except Columbus. But the comparison with Columbus is telling. Columbus poured out his soul almost every time he set pen to paper. Vespucci wrote little that survives, and although much of it is, in a broad sense, autobiographical, he never indulged in the sort of self-revelatory effusions characteristic of Columbus's work. Scholarship, moreover, has foundered on the problem of authenticity. Critics have impugned or endorsed all the letters ascribed to Vespucci or published in his lifetime under his name. Debate rages inconclusively. By general assent, the manuscript letters are now acceptable as genuine.[3] One of the greatest Vespucci scholars, Alberto Magnaghi, demonstrated that in the 1920s,[4] and subsequent work has confirmed his conclusions on that point. The question, however, of whether either or both of the two published letters should be in the corpus has remained unresolved. Some investigators reject both documents in their entirety,[5] endorsing the mid-nineteenth-century opinion of the *vizconde de* Santarém that they "bear upon their very face every sign" of forgery.[6] Others even more injudiciously accept them without cavil.[7] Still others—including all the leading scholars at work on the subject today—suppose that the texts are a mixture of real and feigned writings of Vespucci's but differ about where the balance lies. The doubts are paralyzing, for vital decisions depend on the letters in question: whether Vespucci was veracious—or, admitting that he was an inveterate liar, the extent of his mendacity; whether his claims to important discoveries are valid; whether he "deserves" to have a hemisphere named after him.

I believe we can now set the inhibitions aside. The undisputed documents give us a trustworthy set of Vespucci's "fingerprints" as a writer: his favorite images, his pet themes, his habits of thought, his mental tics. From the disputed materials, we can wrest a reliable match and see how much came from Vespucci's pen and how much from those of the editors responsible for the publications that bore his name. With the help of other sources—in particular, of surviving letters to Vespucci, which reveal the world in which he moved and the values that moved it—it is possible to reconstruct the phases of his life with reasonable certainty and even to penetrate his mind: to see the world as he saw it, to elicit his motives and ambitions, and to expose the reasons, or some of them, for his periodic makeovers. His life can be mapped with the hazy irregularity, vagueness, and distortions of scale of a typical map of the time. There are maddening gaps. I have tried not to fill them speculatively, like some medieval cartographer scattering empty spaces with hippogriffs.

Although I intend this book as a life story, and as an exploration of a mind, huge historical frameworks surrounded Vespucci. I try to sketch these into the background, because nothing he did makes complete sense except in their context. So the book follows him through the various milieus in which he belonged or to which he adapted: the Florence of Lorenzo de' Medici; the Seville of Ferdinand and Isabella; the ocean of Columbus; the new continent scoured by pillagers in Columbus's wake; the globe in which Vespucci's reputation resonated, grew, and ebbed. Some readers may find this tedious and yearn for the intimacies of a conventional biography of a subject more vividly visible in close-up. But the background-painting is necessary and, I think, revealing. For although Vespucci made no significant contribution to any art or science—as we shall see, his cosmography was amateurish, his navigation overrated, his writing feeble—he was an important figure in global history because he was one of the last in a series of adventurers from the Mediterranean who helped conquer the Atlantic and extend across the ocean the reach of what we now call Western civilization.

I am deeply indebted to scholars who preceded me and did the spadework on which this book is based, especially to Iliana Luzzana Caraci,[8] Luisa D'Arienzo,[9] Luciano Formisano,[10] Marco Pozzi,[11] and Consuelo Varela.[12] They have sifted the relevant archives to such a degree that we can reasonably confident no major new revelation will emerge from those sources. Not all the problems of the existing sources have been solved, but they have unraveled enough for us to trace most of the threads back close to their origins. Thanks to these same scholars, almost all the documents directly bearing on Amerigo's life are in print in good editions. The only exceptions are the archives of Amerigo's uncle's embassy in Paris, which the young Vespucci joined, and the scholar's copybook that lies in the Biblioteca Riccardiana.[13] For the former, which prove disenchantingly unforthcoming with unpublished data about our hero, I have relied on the microfilm copies in the Ilardi Collection of Yale University Library; and for the latter, I was able to examine the document, thanks to the kind invitation of Professor Anthony Molho to give a talk at the European University Institute. The brilliant and hospitable participants at Professor Molho's seminar gave me plenty of useful prompts, queries, and food for thought. I am grateful for the flawless help of the staff of the Biblioteca Riccardiana. I owe huge thanks to my colleagues at Queen Mary, University of London, where I began this book, and Tufts University, where I finished it. Both institutions have given me the best of company, the most attentive of students, the most generous of help, and the most stimulating of environments. Because I wrote bits of the book in London, Boston, Florence, and Madrid, I had to use whatever books were to hand and so the notes sometimes include references to more than one edition of a particular text; I have not bothered to standardize these except where one edition is particularly reliable. Where good translations in English are available, I have not hesitated to cite them and (sometimes with emendations) to quote them. Where such translations do not exist, I have made my own.

CONTENTS

PROLOGUE

AMERICA GOT ITS NAME on April 25, 1507. At least that was the day when printers finished typesetting the first book to suggest that the hemisphere should be named after the Florentine explorer Amerigo Vespucci. But the authors anticipated trouble. "Don't snub your nose when you read it, like a rhinoceros's snout" was the advice one of them added to the account they published of Vespucci's voyages. "Stay unprejudiced."[1] Indeed, some readers bowed before Amerigo's name. Other critics kept their noses sniffily elevated. Many—probably most—do so still.

The print shop that issued the book in question was relatively new, established around the mid-1490s in a place most contemporaries thought unlikely as a seat of learning. St. Dié was a little town of flax weavers, log sawyers, and brick makers, nestled in a woody fold of the Vosges—the low, stumpy, blue-ridged mountains that rise on the western edge of the valley of the Rhine, in the region known as Lorraine. It was then a sovereign duchy, later a frontier province, swapped between Germany and France. The Vosges at the time had a reputation for boorish, backward peasants, half-civilized highlands, and wild, bristling pinewoods. In Florence, where Vespucci had lived at the height of the intellectual and artistic movement we call the Renaissance, a famous academician expressed disbelief that such a remote and rural spot could harbor scholarship.[2] Yet the young ruler of the region, René II, duke of

Lorraine, had made St. Dié his home and attracted some ambitious and erudite men to his court.

An early edition of a great Vergilian-style poem about him, the *Nanceid*—named after the victory at Nancy that restored him, in his boyhood, to sovereignty in Lorraine—showed his triumphal entry into the city in 1477. In one of the woodcuts that adorned the text, the cross of Lorraine blazed on René's breast and another on his horse's flank as he rode proudly, baton in hand, on a heavily armored steed surrounded by the Swiss mercenaries who formed his army. The young duke and his horse both had glorious bunches of feathers at their brows. René turned in the saddle toward his followers, scorning the local patrician who knelt beseechingly at his feet. This evidence of ill feeling between the ruler and the town belied the caption: "The holy, God-given entry, to the huge joy of the citizens." The writer could be forgiven the pun. "Dié" is a corruption of the name of the patron saint of the place, St. Deodatus, which means "God-given."

René ruled a small, poor realm. But he had ambitions. He inherited grandiose titles—king of Sicily, king of Jerusalem—from ancestors displaced from their Italian possessions by Spanish invaders. He saw himself, rather overoptimistically, as a rival of one of the most powerful monarchs in Christendom: Ferdinand, king of Aragon and ruler of Spain, who controlled Sicily and also laid claim to the long-lost crusader throne of Jerusalem. The holy city remained the great cynosure of Western travelers: It was Columbus's professed ultimate destination. Prophets predicted that its conqueror would rule the world and inaugurate a new age that would culminate in Christ's second coming. Ferdinand, who fancied himself in the role, was Columbus's master and had been one of Vespucci's sponsors. As soon as a copy of an account of Vespucci's explorations reached St. Dié, it aroused lively interest—perhaps, in René's case, political as well as geographical.

René was the focus of the allegiance of the learned of St. Dié. They dedicated most of their works to him. When he died in 1508, the circle—or such of it as had not already dispersed, owing to lack of funds—broke up. Many of the scholars left to pursue careers elsewhere, and the town they had briefly glorified resumed a sleepy, modest, provincial air. But when the news of Vespucci's voyages arrived, a number of creditable writers, commentators, printing experts, and bibliophiles had gathered in St. Dié, thanks to the duke's patronage. There was Pierre de Blarru, who died in 1505, and who wrote those epic-style verses in praise of René. There were the ruler's secretaries, Simonin de Châtenois and Jean Lud, who produced a historical chronicle between them. There were Jean's brothers, Nicolas and Gauthier, who invested in the press and patronized the printing of works too erudite to make money, including, by Gauthier's own account, the text of Vespucci's voyages. The projects they favored showed that their interests were typical of the scholars called "humanists"—devotees of humane letters, the classics of Greece and Rome. Most of their publications concerned two standard topics in the humanist curriculum: Latin grammar, and ancient Greek and Roman geographical learning.

Gauthier's colleague in the cathedral chapter, Jean Basin de Sandaucourt, was a poet and grammarian who translated the Vespucci text. Other members of the circle included two poor scholars of obscure origins but brilliant promise: Martin Waldseemüller and Matthias Ringmann. They had been students together, educated in humanism. The former was a Swiss migrant, an engraver and typographer by training, with a genius for maps. The latter was a local boy made good: a student of grammar who, as an invaluable proofreader of classical Greek texts, was a welcome addition to Gauthier's circle. Gauthier, indeed, was the presiding figure in St. Dié's literary and scholarly life, proud of the fellow savants he helped the duke to gather in the town. In 1507, when Ringmann published *Grammatica Figurata*, in which he tried to illustrate, with images, all the principles of Latin grammar, like a classical Dr. Seuss, Gauthier could not resist adding a puff. "There is in the Vosges a place known the world over, called by your own name, oh St. Dié."[3] His town was not yet that famous, but by association with the name of America, it was eventually to become so. Today, in homage to the work of Waldseemüller and Ringmann, an annual international geographical congress meets at St. Dié.

Waldseemüller and Ringmann attracted some snobbish remarks from Gauthier, who seems to have thought of them as craftsmen or journeymen rather than gentlemen scholars of his own stamp. But they were the principal collaborators in a project that became the focus of scholarly effort in early-sixteenth-century St. Dié: the production of an updated edition, engraved with maps, of the work of the most renowned geographer of ancient Greece and Rome, Claudius Ptolemy, the second-century sage of Alexandria. While working on their edition, they received a work, purportedly by Vespucci, translated from Italian into French, recounting his adventures. Ringmann, as we shall see, already knew something of Vespucci's thoughts and deeds and admired them. He and his colleagues found the newly arrived text astonishing. As Ringmann wrote later to a scholar whom he called a bosom friend, Vespucci's voyages, with their tales of naked cannibals "situated almost under the Antarctic Pole," made Aeneas's journey to the underworld seem commonplace.[4] The sensational tone of the narrative might have excited skepticism: Ringmann seems to have realized that Vespucci would provoke incredulity, as his anxiety about the tilt of rhinoceros snouts suggests. But Vespucci's alleged achievements entranced Waldseemüller and Ringmann and members of their circle.

Jean Basin, who translated into Latin the text that had reached them, also likened Amerigo's wanderings to those of Aeneas and craved the eloquence of Vergil to chronicle them. (Vespucci, as we shall see, preferred to compare himself to Ulysses.) If Amerigo was equal to the ancients—in his admirers' eyes—as a traveler, so he was, they believed, in geographical learning. Waldseemüller placed Vespucci's portrait in a place of equal honor with that of Ptolemy. Beyond Africa, Ringmann announced, "lies a land unknown, oh Ptolemy, from your maps"—a land under the Tropic of Capricorn, bound by an immense ocean and inhabited by naked people. It had taken a Vespucci to discover it.[5] The sages of St. Dié adopted Vespucci as Ptolemy's modern equal—the man who perfected knowledge of geography by revealing the existence of a "new world" in the west. Calling America after him was their idea.

In some ways, one can understand their response. A superficially impressive text seduced them. It presented an opportunity for making their edition of Ptolemy revolutionary, by adding a new world to what the ancients knew. It appealed to the scholarly appetites of other members of the circle. It had political resonance for Duke René. But in an age of exploration, when the Western world resonated with the fame of Columbus, and when other adventurers of evident merit had contributed achievements almost as dazzling—including the transnavigation of the South Atlantic and the penetration of the Indian Ocean—why did Vespucci, in particular, fascinate them? What made his supposed adventures seem credible? What made his claims to peculiar renown so plausible and empowered him to eclipse rival explorers' credentials? Above all, who was this spellbinder who stamped his name on a hemisphere? Where did he come from? Where—and how far—did he really go?

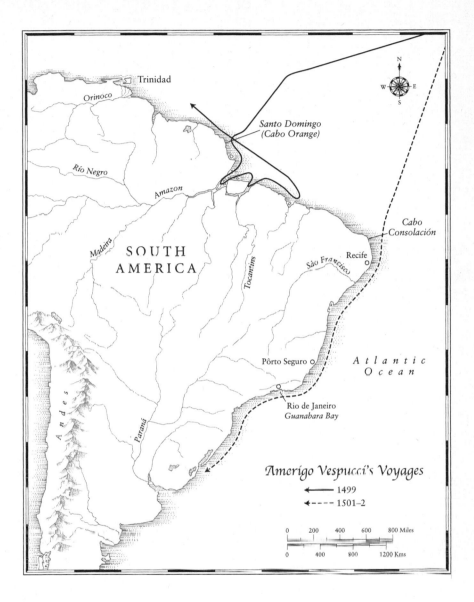

Trinidad

Orinoco

Santo Domingo
(Cabo Orange)

Río Negro

Amazon

Madeira

Cabo
Consolación

SOUTH
AMERICA

Tocantins

São Francisco

Recife

Andes

Paraná

Pôrto Seguro

Atlantic
Ocean

Rio de Janeiro
Guanabara Bay

Amerigo Vespucci's Voyages

◀——— 1499
◀----- 1501–2

0   200   400   600   800 Miles

0   400   800   1200 Kms

AMERIGO

CHAPTER ONE

THE SORCERER'S APPRENTICESHIP

Florence, c. 1450–1491 ∘ *Launching the quest for "honour and fame"*

HEROISM AND VILLAINY shade into each other. So do salesmanship and sorcery. Amerigo Vespucci was both hero and villain—but I expect readers of this book already know that. My purpose is to show that he was also both salesman and sorcerer. He was a merchant who became a magus.

This book tells the story of how that strange mutation happened and tries to help readers understand why. The naming of America was a by-product of the story: a measure of the success of Amerigo's self-salesmanship, an effect of the spellbinding nature of his sorcery. Salesmanship and sorcery require some of the same qualities: quicksilver tongue, featherlight fingers, infectious self-confidence. Vespucci began to acquire those qualities in the city of his birth and education. In Renaissance Florence, where life was fast-paced, flashy, competitive, consumerist, and violent, prestidigitators' skills came easily. That was just as well, because you needed them to survive.

THE MAGICAL CITY

In this city of forty thousand people, as much wealth was concentrated as in any spot in Europe. Florentine prosperity was a triumph against the odds, a classic response to a challenging environment. The city became a great riverside manufactory of fine wools and silks, despite having an unreliable river that habitually ran dry in summer. Florence became a great international trading state, with its own fleets, despite its location fifty miles from the sea, where enemies could easily control outlets and approaches. Fifteenth-century Florentines took pride in their peculiarity: They retained a republican constitution in an age of encroaching monarchies. The elite were unashamed oligarchs who celebrated the nobility of wealth rather than birth. In Florence, a prince could be a merchant without derogation.

In an age that worshipped antiquity, Florence had no historic pedigree, but most Florentines nourished their identity with myths: Their city was a sister of Rome, founded by Trojans. Closer to the truth was the origins narrative that Florence's historians proposed: Florence was a "daughter" of Rome, founded by Romans, "of the same stuff," only more faithful to republican traditions.[1] Florentines asserted their superiority over older, self-proclaimedly nobler neighbors by investing in civic pride: an ampler dome than any rival cathedral's, more public statuary, higher towers, costlier paintings, richer charities, grander churches, more sumptuous palaces, more eloquent poets. They claimed Petrarch as their own because he had Florentine parents, even though he hardly ever visited the city.

In consequence, Florence valued genius and was prepared to pay for it. Like classical Athens or fin de siècle Vienna or the Edinburgh of the Enlightenment or the Paris of the *philosophes*, the city seemed to breed talent, nurture genius, and deserve renown. The greatest age was over by the mid–fifteenth century, at about the time of Amerigo Vespucci's birth. The generation of Brunelleschi (d. 1446), Ghiberti (d. 1455), Fra Angelico (d. 1455), Donatello (d. 1466), Alberti (d. 1472), and Michelozzo (d. 1472) was aging, dead, or dying. The institutions of the republic had fallen under the control of a single dynasty, the Medici. But the tradition of excellence in arts and learning lived on. The sculptor Andrea del Verrocchio rented his home from one of Amerigo's cousins. Sandro Botticelli lived next door to the house where Amerigo Vespucci was born. In Amerigo's parish church, Botticelli and Ghirlandaio worked on commissions from his own family. At the time Machiavelli was an unknown twentysomething. Machiavelli's rival as an historian and diplomat, Francesco Guicciardini, was a small boy. Florence's fertility in the production of genius seemed inexhaustible. By the time Amerigo left the city in 1491, Leonardo da Vinci had already departed for Milan, and the revolution that was to overthrow the Medici in 1494 caused a temporary loss of opportunities for patronage. But the careers of the next generation—including that of Michelangelo, who was Ghirlandaio's apprentice—were already under way.

Could any of the greatness with which he was surrounded have rubbed off on young Amerigo? The opportunity was certainly there. His tutor was his uncle Giorgio Antonio Vespucci, who was one of the city's best-connected scholars.[2] From the mid-1470s at the latest, Giorgio Antonio belonged to a group of students and patrons who called themselves the "family of Plato." They made a kind of cult of the philosopher's memory, reenacting his symposia and burning a never-extinguished light before his bust. The group included the effective ruler of Florence, Lorenzo the Magnificent himself. Its focal leader—"father" of the "family"—was Marsilio Ficino, who was also priest and physician to the Medici. He called Giorgio Antonio "dearest of friends" and in letters to him used the language of "divine love" that was privy to the members of the circle.[3] Other members were with Luigi Pulci, Florence's most renowned poet at the time; Agnolo Poliziano, the leading scholar and no mean versifier; Pico della Mirandola, expert in the esoteric and even the occult; and Paolo dal Pozzo Toscanelli, the geographer who helped to inspire Columbus.

This atmosphere clearly had some—albeit slight—effect on Amerigo. The subject of one of the drafts jotted into his schoolboy exercise book is a letter explaining that the student has bought a text of Plato's for ten florins, as a present for his tutor; the writer begs pardon for the expense, as the book was worth only three florins.[4] Plato can hardly be said to have taken hold of Amerigo's young mind, which was not particularly well adapted to academic work. And the allusion in the notebook occurs in what may be an exercise rather than a real incident. It would be rash to infer that Vespucci ever read a line of Plato, but the mention places his education in the context of the intellectual interests common in his uncle's circle.

Because of the extraordinary constellation of talent in the city, which contributed so much to subsequent ways of looking at and thinking about the world, Renaissance Florence evokes sympathy and, in turn, a range of misleading assumptions in people who think back to it today. The city's popular image is as a place of enlightenment where antiquity was revived and modernity anticipated with classical taste, secular priorities, humanist habits of mind, and a high place for science and reason in the system of values. But every generation likes to spotlight its own modernity against the darkness of the past. We scan the past for signs of Europe's awakening to progress, prosperity, and values that we can recognize as our own. So we respond to the excitement with which Western writers around 1500 anticipated the dawn of a new golden age. As a result, if you are a product of mainstream Western education, almost everything you ever thought about the Renaissance is likely to be false.

"It inaugurated modern times." *No:* Every generation has its own modernity, which grows out of the whole of the past. "It was revolutionary." *No:* Scholarship has detected half a dozen prior renaissances. "It was secular" or "It was pagan." *Not entirely:* The Church remained the patron of most art and scholarship. "It was art for art's sake." *No:* It was manipulated by plutocrats and politicians. "Its art was unprecedentedly realistic." *Not altogether:* Perspective was a new technique, but you can find emotional and anatomical realism in much pre-Renaissance art. "The Renaissance elevated the artist." *No:* Medieval artists might achieve sainthood; wealth and titles were derogatory by comparison. "It dethroned scholasticism and inaugurated humanism." *No:* It grew out of medieval "scholastic humanism." "It was Platonist and Hellenophile." *No:* There were patches of Platonism, as there had been before, and few scholars did more than dabble in Greek. "It rediscovered lost antiquity." *Not really:* Antiquity was never lost, and classical inspiration never withered (though there was an upsurge of interest in the fifteenth century).

"The Renaissance discovered nature." *Hardly:* There was no pure land-scape painting in Europe previously, but nature got cult status in the thirteenth century, when St. Francis of Assisi discovered God outdoors. "It was scientific." *No:* For every scientist there was a sorcerer.

Even in Florence, the Renaissance was a minority taste. Brunelleschi's designs for the Baptistery doors—the project widely held to have inaugurated the Renaissance in 1400—were rejected as too advanced. Masaccio, the revolutionary painter who introduced perspective and sculptural realism into his work for a chapel in the church of Santa Maria del Carmine in the 1430s, was only ever the assistant on the project, supervised by a reactionary master. The most popular Italian painters of the age were the most conservative: Pinturicchio, Baldovinetti, and Gozzoli, whose work resembles the glories of medieval miniaturists—brilliant with gold leaf and bright, costly pigments. Michelangelo's design for the main square of the city—which would have encased the space in a classical colonnade—was never implemented. Much of the supposedly classical art that inspired fifteenth-century Florentines was bogus: The Baptistery was a sixth- or seventh-century building. The church of San Miniato, which the cognoscenti mistook for a Roman temple, was actually no earlier than eleventh-century.

So Florence was not really classical. Some readers may think that is too easy to say. After all, one could claim by similar logic that classical Athens was not classical, for most people there had other values. They worshipped Orphic mysteries, clung to irrational myths, ostracized or condemned some of their most progressive thinkers and writers, and favored social institutions and political strategies similar to those of today's silent majority: straitlaced, straight-backed family values. The plays of Aristophanes, with their lampoons of louche aristocratic habits, are a better guide to Greek morality than the Ethics of Aristotle.[5] Florence, too, had its silent majority, whose voice was heard at about the time Vespucci left the city, in the blood-and-thunder sermons of the reforming friar Girolamo Savonarola, and in the bloodcurdling cries of the street revolutionaries his words helped to stir a few years later. They made a bonfire of Medici vanities and outlawed the pagan sensuality of classical taste. After the revolution, even Botticelli gave up painting erotic commissions and reverted to old-fashioned piety.

Savonarola's Florence was not classical but medieval. Amerigo's was not classical but magical. I use the word advisedly, to mean a place where magic was practiced. There were two kinds of magic. Florence, like everywhere else in the world at the time, as far as we know, was full of popular spells and superstitions. Three nights before the death of Lorenzo the Magnificent, lightning struck the cathedral, sending stones from the famous dome crashing to the street. People said Lorenzo had a demon trapped in his ring and had released it as he sensed his impending death. In 1478, when Jacopo de' Pazzi was hanged for his part in a conspiracy against Medici rule, heavy rains threatened the survival of the cereal crop. Popular wisdom was that it was Jacopo's fault: His burial in consecrated ground had offended God and disjointed nature. He was dug up and dragged stinking through the streets, while rioters battered his remains before flinging them into the Arno.[6]

Superstition was not just a vulgar error. There was learned magic, too. The notion that nature could be controlled by human agency was a perfectly rational one. Promising approaches included techniques we now classify as scientific, such as observation, experiment, and the exercise of reason. Astrology, alchemy, conjuration, and sorcery had not yet proved to be false leads. As occultists in Renaissance Florence acknowledged, the difference between magic and science is narrower than most people think today. Both are attempts to explain and therefore to control nature. Western science of the sixteenth and seventeenth centuries grew, in part, out of magic. The vocations of scientists overlapped with those of magi—wielders of magical techniques for mastering nature. In the circles in which young Amerigo moved, magic was a common passion.

One of the long-abandoned or dormant notions the Renaissance recovered was that ancient people had possessed magic formulae that worked. In pharaonic Egypt, priests had supposedly brought statues to life with arcane talismans. At the dawn of Greece, Orpheus had written incantations that could cure the sick. The ancient Jews had a method of manipulating signs—the kabbalah—to invoke powers normally reserved to God. Renaissance research inspired these claims by supposedly unearthing magical texts from antiquity, which the piety of the Middle Ages had condemned as nonsensical or demonic. Marsilio Ficino argued that magic was good if it was used for healing or for gaining knowledge of nature. Some ancient magical texts, he contended, were lawful reading for Christians.

The most influential text of all was the work supposedly written by an ancient Egyptian known as Hermes Trismegistus, though actually it was composed by an unidentified Byzantine forger. It arrived in Florence in about 1460 among a consignment of books bought from Macedonia for the Medici library. It caused a sensation; the translator, who was a devotee of Plato, even gave it priority over the job of translating Plato's works.[7] Renaissance magi felt inspired to pursue "Egyptian" wisdom in search of an alternative to the austere rationalism of classical learning—a fount of older and supposedly purer knowledge than could be had from the Greeks or Romans. The distinction between magic and science as means of attempting to control nature almost vanished in the shadow of Hermes's influence.

As well as astrology, or instead of it, Florentine magi believed in and practiced astral magic—an attempt to control the stars and therefore to manipulate astrological influences. They also engaged in alchemy and conjuration with numbers. Pico della Mirandola added techniques based on the kabbalah, invoking divine power through spells with numbers. Astrology and astronomy were inseparable disciplines, commonly confused. When Pico turned against astrology in 1495, he had to begin by pointing out the difference between "the reading of forecoming events by the stars" and "the mathematical measurement of stellar sizes and motions."[8] Letters to Lorenzo di Pierfrancesco de' Medici, Amerigo's schoolboy companion and future patron, are full of stellar imagery. Ficino wrote him characteristically gushing, faintly homoerotic professions of love, strewn with allusions to the young man's horoscope. "For anyone who contemplates the heavens, nothing he sets his eyes upon seems immense, but the heavens themselves."[9]

Ficino wrote a follow-up letter on the same subject to Giorgio Antonio Vespucci, urging him to explain that the influence of the stars works alongside free will—"the stars within us."[10] An astrolabe, an instrument Amerigo Vespucci later used, or at least brandished, as a navigator, hangs in the background of a painting of St. Augustine that Giorgio Antonio commissioned from Botticelli.[11] Paolo dal Pozzo Toscanelli, who influenced Vespucci's geographical ideas, was a believer in astrology.[12] The study of the secrets of the world, the mathematical order of the universe, the relationship between the earth and the stars: These were the common ground of cosmography and magic. Magical thinking and practices surrounded young Amerigo Vespucci. Amerigo's education was, in a sense, the making of a magus.

Hermes Trismegistus numbered Lorenzo the Magnificent himself— the effective ruler of Florence from 1469 to his death in 1492—among his devotees. Lorenzo translated two of Hermes's pantheistic hymns into Italian.[13] The Medici were particularly susceptible to esoteric claims by scholars they patronized, because the family identified with the Magi of the gospels. They belonged to the confraternity in Florence responsible for keeping up the cult of the astrologer kings who followed Christ's star to Bethlehem. Benozzo Gozzoli and Fra Angelico painted leading members of the family in the role. The first painting lined the walls of the little private chapel in the Medici palace; the second was in Lorenzo's bedroom. When he died, the Confraternity of the Magi organized the pomp of his funeral.

THE GLUTINOUS FAMILY

Vespucci's family were, for the whole of his childhood and adolescence, clients of Lorenzo the Magnificent. The Medici connection was vital, for Florence is a knot of streets that seem tied tightly together, but in the fifteenth century the tangled topography enclosed emulous quarters with families who rivaled one another for power in the republic. If you roam the city today, you can still see the symbols of allegiance engraved on the corners of streets and facades of palazzi.

The Vespucci clan was a typical Italian extended family composed of clusters of cousins and uncles and younger sons who joined the throng of dependents or took their chance in the world. The family's part of Florence was in Santa Maria Novella—the quarter once dominated and beautified by the Rucellai dynasty, though their influence had dwindled by Amerigo's time. The Vespucci homes were concentrated along a stretch of street in the parish of Ognissanti. This was a modest part of Florence on the margin of the central area. It had started as a woolworkers' district. There was no shame in that, as the wool industry had been one of the foundations of the city's greatness. The Vespucci probably started in that trade when they first came to Florence from the nearby village of Peretola, only three or four miles away, in the thirteenth century. They still had or affected some interest in cloth making, although their main line of business was in silk.

Though some branches of the clan were prosperous, Amerigo's family members were classic "poor relations," dependent on wealthier relatives for patronage and loans. The tax return made by Amerigo's homonymous grandfather in 1451 shows a household in decline or, at best, treading financial water. They had sold property or lost it in dowries since their last assessment. The document lists a home in Ognissanti and a small house in the village of Peretola, from where the family originally hailed, inhabited by Amerigo Senior's poor brother Giovanni and his family, "who live in the country owing to their poverty." The house was part of the dowry of Giovanni's wife, so it must have become Amerigo's property as a result of Giovanni's indebtedness. Another brother, Niccolò, lived in the same village. In addition, Amerigo the elder had bought a vineyard from a monastery in the same village. It produced ten barrels of wine a year.[14]

The year of that tax return was an important one in the history of the clan, for it was then—as a result, presumably, of Medici patronage—that the Vespucci were selected as one of the lineages considered suitable for supplying the head of state, known as the *gonfaloniere*, or standard-bearer. The Medici controlled the board that elected families to this group. It was not a route to power, for it conferred no guarantee of office; in any case, the role for which it qualified those honored was purely nominal. But it was a public distinction that conferred prestige and impressed neighbors.[15] It mattered. Two members of the Vespucci clan did achieve the office of *gonfaloniere*. Another wrote candidly to Lorenzo the Magnificent admitting that he craved it. "You know I want to be *gonfaloniere*. . . . The electors are all devotees of yours and, because of your renown in the city, no one will oppose your will."[16]

The Vespucci clan had lifelines to the court. Simonetta Vespucci, the beauty of the age, was the object of ostentatious—perhaps affected— admiration from Giuliano de' Medici, the ruler's beloved brother. To know *la bella Simonetta* was to love her, and Florence united in her praise. She is the subject of a famous but unfortunately anonymous portrait that is one of the most bewitching and erotic images to survive from the Florentine Renaissance. She appears in perfect profile, bare-breasted, with a coiled serpent clinging to her neck, biting its own tail. The combination of sensuality and mystery is irresistible. What is the picture meant to suggest? The fragility of beauty? The immortality of love? It invites more than arousal; it begs questions about the meaning of its symbolism. It excites physical lust and intellectual intrigue. Who could want more in a woman?

Unsurprisingly, Simonetta's story has inspired a lot of romantic nonsense. Something about her makes historians' eyes goggle and their prose gooey. The vulgar assumption, for instance, that she was Botticelli's model for all his most famous beauties seems to be based on no better grounds than the feeling that the most beautiful woman of the day ought to have modeled for the most sensitive painter. Giuliano de' Medici wore her favors when jousting, and Agnolo Poliziano—one of the pet poets of the Medici ruling line—made rather a lot, in a coy way, of his sentiments in lines he wrote in celebration of a tournament. Though there is no proof, it is a fair bet that Simonetta was Giuliano's mistress. When she died young, he was supposedly inconsolable. Her husband and father-in-law made Giuliano a present of "all her garments and her portrait."[17] This betokens more than normal courtesy. But does it help to explain Amerigo's path in life? Rather, we should see the connection between Simonetta and Giuliano as further evidence of the ways in which the fortunes of the Vespucci and the Medici interlaced. More important than Simonetta's beauty—certainly for the advancement of Amerigo's side of the family—was Giorgio Antonio's learning. Thanks to him, the Vespucci family reveled in privileged access to the Magnificent One. They had access to his villa in Mugello in times of plague.

When Amerigo the elder died in 1468, he left a legacy of twelve denari a year for his and his wife's soul to the Ognissanti parish church.[18] Here, in the early 1470s, the Vespucci endowed a chapel and decorated it with a painting by Domenico Ghirlandaio before he became famous. The money came from more prosperous members of the clan than were found in Amerigo's immediate family. The belief that Ghirlandaio portrayed Amerigo among the family members depicted under the Madonna's cloak rests on an assertion that the chronicler of Florence's artists, Giorgio Vasari, made three-quarters of a century later. By then Amerigo's fame was enough to create a presumption in favor of the idea. But there is no good reason to believe it: We have, alas, no well-authenticated portrait of Vespucci from life and no description of what he looked like.

Amerigo's parents were still living in his grandfather's house when he was born. But when exactly was that? "Amerigo Vespucci was born in . . ." Biographers conventionally end such sentences with a date and a place. In Amerigo's case, although the place was unquestionably Florence, the date is less certain. Births of two infants of the same name, to the same parents, were registered at about the right time, within two years of each other. The first was presumably a victim of infant mortality—one of the innumerable little ghosts who died unmourned, ostensibly because their souls were innocent (and mourning was a penance designed to speed souls to heaven). Psychology suggests a further or alternative explanation: Infants died so often that parents' best strategy for escaping pain was to forget them as rapidly and completely as they could. The name of Amerigo had to be perpetuated in the family, for it was the name of the patriarch of the household. So the next son inherited it. His certificate of baptism bears a date in mid-March 1453, but Florentine official documents at the time, like those of many other parts of Europe, followed a calendar that began with the feast of the Annunciation on March 25. This was logical, for it was the date of Christ's conception, and the fashion for assigning a pagan date—January 1—in imitation of the practice of ancient Rome, had not yet taken hold. So, by today's reckoning, this Amerigo was born in 1454.

But was this our Amerigo? The probability favors this conclusion, because in a document four years later, his father gives his age as four years. Parents of the time were notoriously lax about birthdays though are unlikely to have lost count so early in their son's life. Amerigo, like everyone else at the time, was casual about his date of birth, and later documents attribute to him inconsistent ages. It is not impossible that he was not the newcomer of 1454, but a third, otherwise unrecorded Amerigo born to the same couple. If unconstrained by the absence of direct evidence, I should opt for a conclusion of that kind, for at every subsequent stage of his life, Amerigo seems young for his years. His formal education, if he was really born in 1454, continued into his twenties—indeed, it was apparently at its most intensive then—without his getting beyond the level of a good schoolboy. He may have been a late starter or a late developer or what people now call a perpetual student, but this is one of the most puzzling features in the chronology of Amerigo's life.

In any event, our Amerigo was born amid reminders of mortality. The family's preceding Amerigo was already dead. And it seems likely that the newcomer of 1454 had a twin: The certificate of baptism refers to Amerigo and Matteo. Unless this can be read to mean that both names were bestowed on the same child, Matteo Vespucci was another sibling who did not survive infancy. A sister, Agnoletta, was mentioned in the household's tax returns at the age of one, among what Florentine officialdom, with its practical values, called "mouths." Then she disappeared from the records.

Of the children who did survive, Amerigo had two elder brothers: Antonio, who was destined for the law; and Girolamo, who, after some hesitation in his youth, ultimately went into the church. To judge from some rather bitter asides ascribed to Amerigo in a surviving letter of Girolamo's, Antonio was the favorite and monopolized the affection of their mother, Lisa. "You tell me," Girolamo summarized, "that Mona Lisa is well and has devoted herself entirely to Master Antonio, and takes little interest in the rest of us."[19] No excursion into psychobiography beckons, however. Amerigo, if he felt any resentment of this sort, never mentioned it in any other surviving document. In the context of his letter to his brother, it is evidently an exculpatory device to explain why Girolamo should not expect to get what he obviously and repeatedly asked Amerigo for: money and help in his ecclesiastical career. It was normal for the eldest son to attract the most care, because he was being groomed for the greatest responsibility; and though Freudians might differ, I think that a childhood normal in its own cultural environment is unlikely to have a warping effect. Still, younger sons' prospects were inescapably limited by the choices their elder brothers made. Once Antonio had embraced the law and Girolamo the church, Amerigo and his younger brother, Bernardo, had few options left. Service in the state or a wealthy household were possibilities; war offered chances of advancement. The most likely outlook was migration abroad, probably as a merchant. As we shall see, both the youngsters attempted this course at different stages of their lives.

There is one other tantalizing clue to what would now be seen as a common form of psychological trauma. In an undated schoolboy exercise, Amerigo had to describe himself. "I am called Antonio," he wrote, "and for a surname I am called 'the Great,' no less. But I think myself small, and neither good nor learned."[20] Amerigo was probably not the originator but merely the translator of these lines, perhaps from an original composed by an elder brother. But in the same hand, there are doodles of signatures of "Antonio" and "Antonius" on the endpaper. Is this evidence of sibling rivalry, envy, even potential hatred? In fin de siè-cle Vienna, the conclusion would have been inescapable, but not necessarily in quattrocento Florence.

THE EDUCATION OF A MAGUS

Amerigo was educated on the cheap. His father's household was well-to-do and well connected but not wealthy. Nastagio invested heavily only in the education of his eldest son, who was to follow him in the profession of notary. It made sense for the future head of the family to be educated for prosperity, since his future was of privileged responsibility, charged with the support of less advantaged relations. The family was fortunate to have such a well-qualified tutor in its ranks as Giorgio Antonio, for Nastagio's brother was one of the most respected scholars in the city. He had inherited the vineyard in Peretola but sold it to his brother in 1464. The connection ensured that young Amerigo had access to scintillating company and to fashionable learning, not only in the poetry, rhetoric, history, and philosophy that humanists favored, but also in the cosmography, astronomy, and astrology that were particularly valued in Giorgio Antonio's world.

The bond between Amerigo and his tutor seems close. Expressions of devotion and gratitude apparently addressed to Giorgio Antonio: "By you I was guided and taught, as by a good and wise preceptor and therefore I will always obey and honour you and hold you higher in esteem than any other master."[21] Amerigo remained on close terms with Giorgio Antonio—at least all of Florence thought he did, and many correspondents closed letters addressed to Amerigo with remembrances to the sage. After Giorgio Antonio fell ill as the result of a grave accident, when Amerigo was out of town, friends rushed to communicate the news. But we teachers make friends with our pupils for all sorts of reasons and nonreasons, not all of them contingent on good performance in class. How good a student was Amerigo?

By his own confession, he was neglectful of his uncle's teaching, but that may be the sort of pious regret people conventionally utter when they look back on the lost opportunities of life. His one surviving attempt at unguided Ciceronian prose composition is tentative and inelegant, though not inaccurate. "I hardly dare write in Latin," he wrote—in Latin—but "to do so in the vernacular would make me blush somewhat."[22] Professional scholars evince shock at the fact that Amerigo, writing to a patron, once attributed to Pliny a self-deprecatory remark made by Catullus ("You used to think well of my trifles"); or they express incredulity at his tendency to confuse Stoicism and Epicureanism. Those do not seem to me to be uneducated or unpardonable errors; they suggest, if anything, an excess of confidence in the writer's familiarity with classical allusions. From all we know of the talents he displayed later, he was better at math than letters.

Though Amerigo remained a modest Latinist, his relationship with Giorgio Antonio gave him access to some of the great patrons and practitioners of vernacular literature. When Piero Vespucci was in Pisa, he relied on Amerigo to supply him with a Livy in translation and a Dante, and asked for the loan of books of poems by Pulci and del Franco. Amerigo fancied himself a poet and wrote verses—which have not survived—to potential patrons. Like all Florentines, he was well schooled in the vernacular literature of his native city. As we shall see, memorized snatches of the works of Petrarch and Dante came easily to him in later life, even in the middle of the ocean.

It is as certain as any inference can be that the informal curriculum he studied with his uncle included some cosmography. According to Vespucci's own later recollection, Lorenzo di Pierfrancesco de' Medici, who shared the same tutor, understood "something of cosmography."[23] It was a fashionable subject in Florence at least from 1397, when Manuel Chrysoloras brought Ptolemy's *Geography* to Florence, where he arrived to teach Greek.[24] Once the translation into Latin was complete, anyone who was anyone in Florence seems to have studied it. Giorgio Antonio Vespucci had his own copy, probably made by his own hand.[25] Amerigo's writings make at least a dozen allusions to the text.[26] Ptolemy implanted in Amerigo's mind some of the key notions that later guided his understanding of the world he explored: its supposedly perfect sphericity; its size—twenty-four thousand miles around at the equator;[27] its mapability on a grid of lines of longitude and latitude.

The study of geography was part of the humanist curriculum. The rediscovery of ancient texts revivified it. Of special importance in Florence was Strabo's *Geography,* a text of the late first century B.C. that stimulated debate over the size of the world and the existence of previously unknown continents. Strabo's ideas circulated widely from the time of the ecclesiastical council held in Florence in 1439, when scholars met to exchange cosmographical news as well as ecclesiological opinions. A complete translation of the *Geography* into Latin was available from 1458 and in print by 1469. Giorgio Antonio had a copy of it.[28] "It may be," Strabo speculated, "that in the temperate zone itself there exist two inhabited worlds or even more, especially on or around the parallel of Athens that is drawn across the Atlantic Sea." In the context of Strabo's thought generally, this observation sounds ironic, but irony is notoriously difficult to identify, and many fifteenth-century readers took the passage literally. It made the Atlantic seem worth exploring for new worlds and unknown continents. Classical geography also raised the possibility that if navigators could overcome the immensity of the Atlantic, "we could sail from Iberia to India along the same parallel." Paolo dal Pozzo Toscanelli, Giorgio Antonio's "brother" in Florence's "family of Plato," was a major advocate, perhaps the originator, of the theory that Asia was accessible by a western route. The notion that inspired Columbus's Atlantic crossing was debated in circles with which Amerigo was familiar in his youth. The connection to Toscanelli was the first of the links Amerigo shared with Columbus; those links would multiply for as long as both explorers lived, and would bind their reputations inseparably after their deaths.

Amerigo's moral education has left some trace in the evidence—not so much the evidence of his conduct, which could be shabby or slimy, according to his needs, but in the copybook apparently from his hand, for the most part, that survives in a Florentine library.[29] There is room to doubt the authorship, though a note in the back, in the same hand as most of the manuscript, says: "Amerigo son of Ser Nastagio Vespucci writes this little book." As a young man, Amerigo certainly made a book of moral precepts, apothegms, and advice: a "book of sentences," to give the genre the name it bore at the time. Amerigo's only surviving youthful letter to his father refers to it as a collection of his father's sayings: "I am occupied," he says, "in writing out rules of conduct [*regula*]—in Latin, indeed, if I may so call it," he modestly adds in parentheses, "in order that on my return I may be able to show you a little book in which those rules are garnered from your opinion [*ex vestra sententia*]."[30]

This does not sound like the surviving manuscript, which is almost entirely in Tuscan, with only a few Latin versions of some of the exercises. The Latin, moreover, which always faces the Tuscan translation, is in an older, freer, more accomplished hand. So it looks as if the tutor wrote out the Latin for young Vespucci to translate into the vernacular. Although composition in Latin was the main part of any curriculum of studies of the time, exercises of this type were commonly prescribed.

Some biographers call it an exercise book and associate it with Amerigo's formal education at Giorgio Antonio's hands. But it may have been in use over a long period of time. It bears no dates, but the hand of the principal writer, who was responsible for all but a few of the 170 folios, gets bolder, more fluent, and more mature as the work progresses. All the documents the book contains are drafts of letters, couched in general terms, appropriate for a wide range of business and family circumstances. But some of them are strong evidence of the nature of the education Vespucci received, while some even had clear personal resonance in his life.

The exercises reveal the values in which young Vespucci was coached. "Vehemently," he writes, "does my father desire that I should learn and understand all things by which I may acquire fame and fortune."[31] That was to remain the nearest thing to a consistent objective through all Vespucci's subsequent changes of career. Many exercises are in one way or another reproaches against laziness, inattentiveness, and ingratitude. Of course, if teachers are to be believed, these are normal student vices, and they made a common theme in masters' messages to pupils at the time. Vespucci's exercise book, however, is exceptionally rich in such injunctions. He resolves repeatedly to rise early, sleep less, arrive promptly for class, and avoid neglectfulness and sin by attending willingly to his master's precepts.[32] He endured constant injunctions to follow his father's example. "Whoever has lived well, as your father has, will doubtlessly make a good death."[33] The passionate rhetoric of family obligation resounds through the pages: "Never by me was a brother loved as much as you."[34]

The surviving exercises are also keys to the kind of religion in which young Vespucci was instructed. Some pieces are about the moods appropriate to the seasons of the Christian year: Lenten penance, Christmas joy. He absorbed the characteristic friars' piety of many late-medieval communities, with the accent on salvation by faith—a doctrine not yet suspected as heretical. Savonarola himself would have approved of the words with which one of the exercise-book pieces begins: "I do not believe so much in my own merits as in the grace of God." But the writer continues lightheartedly, ironically, drawing an almost blasphemous analogy between divine grace and a tutor's favor: "I have become as if elect and honoured among your company . . . all of which I own and attribute not so much to my own merit as to your generosity."[35] Religion, perhaps, never came very high on the scale of values in which Vespucci was raised. In childhood he learned little of the God he later largely forgot. Indeed, the evidence of his revulsion from religion is plain enough in his exercise book. In one of the most extraordinary pieces the book contains, he confesses that "in the end, I hold the things of heaven in low esteem and even come close to denying them." As for his fellow men, they seemed to him "more like the image of a brute beast than of that omnipotent deity."[36] He would come to see the native inhabitants of the New World in a similar light. In adult life, he hardly ever referred to God, except in general and conventional terms, whereas Columbus could hardly utter without invoking the Almighty and dwelling fervently on his personal relationship with Him.

PARISIAN INTERLUDE

The end of his youth left Amerigo well schooled but with uncertain prospects. In the late 1460s, when Amerigo was approaching manhood, the deaths of Amerigo the elder and his brother Giovanni left Giovanni's children still living in the modest house in Peretola and in the aura of poverty. Nastagio's household, by contrast, grew gradually more prosperous but never sufficiently so to provide independence for the next generation. Nastagio was a notary specializing in currency exchanges, and the profession ensured the means of comfort. An exercise in young Amerigo's schoolbook reconstructs or imagines lavish meals at Nastagio's table: "We lunched and dined yesterday at our father's house where were cooked many doves, little singing birds, capons and other fowl, which at the time our stomachs digested with ease. . . . We cannot even say how much there was to behold and how many sweets we ate."[37]

By the next surviving tax assessment, in 1470, not much had changed. The family still inhabited the house in Ognissanti. Giovanni, still "very poor," continued to occupy the Peretola property, where, his brother complained, he "does nothing" save "harm to himself and us." The family vineyard's capacity, however, had risen to fourteen barrels a year. And there was a new vineyard in the nearby village of Santo Martino a Brocci. In 1470 the family acquired a farm called Campo Gretti, in the village of San Felice a Ema, with a house for the owner and a farmhouse for a tenant or worker. In 1474 the family added a nearby property, letting it at a respectable rent, which exactly matched what they paid for a house they rented in Florence for an unspecified purpose.[38] In 1477 they bought some wheat fields and a small vineyard in San Moro. Meanwhile, they sold the vineyard in Peretola. By then Antonio had graduated as a notary and worked in the building that housed the city government. He could afford to marry and did so. For Amerigo, a job in one of the big commercial households or in the court of the ruler beckoned.

His first opportunity—or at least the first we know of—occurred in

1478, when his uncle, or, as we should say, cousin of an older generation, was appointed to fill a vacancy in the service of the republic, as a result of the death of the prospective Florentine ambassador to France. Guido Antonio Vespucci was the stopgap. He invited Amerigo to accompany him on his mission. This is perhaps the best indication of Vespucci's credit, or at least competence, as a scholar. There is, however, no evidence of why he chose his young nephew. Though Vespucci's biographers tend to speak of Amerigo as his uncle's secretary, there is no record of the capacity in which Amerigo traveled to France, or of what he did when he got there. It is tempting to speculate that he would hardly have gotten the chance of the trip if his tutor had been displeased with him. It was a huge opportunity. Without it, Amerigo might have shared his younger brothers' enforced idleness. In their tax returns of 1480, Girolamo and Bernardo were described as being in the wool trade but currently without work, whereas Amerigo "is in France with Messer Guidantonio Vespucci the ambassador."[39]

Amerigo made little or nothing of his chance. Two facts stand out: First, the embassy was a failure; and second, Amerigo never again enjoyed official preferment. Guido Antonio's later reputation has obscured the failure of the Paris embassy. His next mission, to Rome, attracted much praise. Machiavelli, whose history of his city achieved great éclat among later historians, lauded his skill.[40] But the mission Amerigo accompanied was abjectly disappointing. Its purpose was to secure French intervention on Florence's side in war against Naples. It was not a question of forging a new alliance with France, merely a case of making Louis XI respect undertakings he had already given. But the king was concerned with objectives closer to home: He was busy absorbing the vast domains of the duke of Burgundy, whom he had just defeated and killed, and securing them for his crown.

Louis made many cheap and chummy gestures. He forbade his realm to Lorenzo's enemies. He encouraged the ruler of Milan to take action, which was hardly a major risk on Louis's part, since Milan was already deeply imbroiled in the war on Florence's side. He used the pretext of support for Florence to cut the pope's income from and authority in

France. He threatened to invade Italy; perhaps he even dreamed of it. "If you refuse to make peace," he wrote to Ferrante, "we shall take care with our forces of armed men. . . . So to act that from that war peace will follow."[41] The Florentines authorized Guido Antonio to use the most extravagant assurances to get the king to act. "The Florentine nation is in your hand," they told him, "and will be as long [as] our walls remain standing."[42] But he did nothing. Lorenzo soon despaired of getting any real help from him.[43] Moreover, the embassy failed in two secondary assignments: seeking compensation for Florentine merchants whom French pirates had plundered and trying to keep Venice out of the Holy League, the pious postwar alliance in which France, Florence, Naples, Milan, and the Holy See all joined with the ostensible but neglected object of promoting a new crusade. When Guido Antonio was recalled to Florence in the summer of 1480, he had registered no significant progress in any of his tasks at the French court.

Amerigo took no further part in diplomatic life and never acquired an office of profit in the state. If he was the embassy's secretary, he was not cut out for the work. He never recalled Paris in his subsequent surviving writings. Biographers usually waste time speculating on whom he might have met in the French capital: Columbus's brother Bartolomeo is the most remarkable fantasy, though he was almost certainly not in Paris at the same time. Amerigo met no one who subsequently mattered to him. It looks as if he had had his chance and flunked it.

Over the next few years, he at least had means of livelihood. In 1482 Nastagio, shortly before his death, appointed his son to conduct business on his behalf. When his father died, Amerigo seemed relatively well set up, both in family affairs and in the favor of the ruling family. In February of the following year, Amerigo received a letter from one of the most prominent members of the clan, Simone Vespucci. The terms employed were intimate; evidently, Simone commissioned Amerigo to buy and sell gems on his behalf, notably a sapphire, which turned out not to be what was wanted. Simone asked to have his regards passed on to Giorgio Antonio and—more curiously—to "the Magnificent Lorenzo."[44] There is danger of confusion, since Lorenzo's cousin

Lorenzo di Pierfrancesco also attracted the epithet "magnificent," which Florentines did tend to bestow promiscuously. But in the context, and in view of the fact that Guido Antonio had taken Amerigo into the ruler's orbit, Lorenzo the Magnificent himself is probably indicated. If that is correct, this letter is the first intimation of Amerigo's personal closeness to Florence's greatest potentate. It is also the last. How did Amerigo get close to Lorenzo? Why did the relationship not endure? To understand what happened, an excursion into Florentine politics is needed and, in particular, into Lorenzo's unique world.

THE SHADOW OF MAGNIFICENCE

"I am not Florence's lord," Lorenzo wrote in 1481, "just a citizen with a certain authority."[45] This was strictly true. To be a lord was not a practical aspiration, where republican virtue was ingrained. Other Florentine communes had submitted to lords in the course of the late Middle Ages, but not Florence—or so Florentines kidded themselves. Leonardo Bruni, the great ideologue of the city in the early fifteenth century, was proud that while tyrants triumphed elsewhere, his hometown had remained true to its heritage as a foundation—so myth sustained—of ancient Roman republicans. The Florentines who plotted to kill Lorenzo in 1478 saw themselves as embodying the virtues of Brutus, sacrificing Caesar to preserve the purity of the republic. *"Popolo e libertà!"* were the rebels' recurrent watchwords—not to be taken too literally, as most rebellions were struggles of excluded families against those the Medici favored, and few conspirators were willing to sacrifice the blessings of oligarchy; they just wanted the freedom to exploit them for themselves. Alamanno Rinuccini, one of the most thoughtful supporters of the Pazzi family and faction, secretly denounced Lorenzo in an unpublished Dialogue on Liberty, but his main gripe was with the parvenues the Medici raised to eligibility for office.[46]

But the "certain authority" Lorenzo admitted to elevated him above all his fellow citizens. He never held any political office. He was never even a member of Florence's executive council, much less head of state, but that did not matter. The Florentine constitution was ironclad in republican principles and riveted with safeguards against tyranny. In consequence, the nominal officeholders could never get a grip on power. They rotated at two-monthly intervals and were selected by a mixture of indirect election and lottery from mercurial lists of eligibly rich or aristocratic families. They key to permanent power lay not in holding office oneself but in managing the system. Lorenzo ruled by stealth.

The first element in his system of management was the dexterous manipulation of institutions and networks. He joined everything, cultivated everybody. Unlike earlier Medici rulers, he chatted with fellow citizens in the cathedral and piazza. He belonged to far more confraternities, guilds, and committees than anyone could hope to attend regularly, but they extended his network of obligation and kept him abreast of what was going on in the city. The formal business of all the organizations he joined was reported to him as a matter of course. More important, perhaps, the gossip transacted at meetings fed back into his system. Ruling a republic was a matter of cybernetics. The entry codes were whispered, passwords exchanged in the private language of families or the argot of the elite. Power of control lay in manipulating the system of indirect election and selection by lot, which led to membership of the ruling council and other influential committees. Rinaldo Albizzi, for instance, who had briefly forced Lorenzo's father from power into exile, neglected to fix the elections, with the result that his supporters were ousted and his enemy recalled. The only way to be sure was to be crooked. Lorenzo used bribery and intimidation to fix the rules of eligibility, advance his own creatures and cronies, and make sure that the final lottery for office was always rigged.

As a result, though he had no formal right of jurisdiction—which, at the time, was considered the main attribute of sovereignty—he dispensed justice, in effect, according to his whim. On a notorious occasion in 1489, he ordered a peremptory public execution, with the scourging of bystanders who had the temerity to object. The only palliation one can offer is that his gout—which always tortured him—was peculiarly painful that day.[47] Effectively, the Medici were monarchs.

Lorenzo was the fourth of his line in succession to run the city. When he died, leading citizens lined up to beg his son to take over.

Second, Lorenzo relied on wealth. Largesse made him magnificent. The mob that rallied in Lorenzo's support when he survived an assassination attempt in 1478 hailed "Lorenzo, who gives us bread." He milked the state (the evidence, though not conclusive, is too suggestive to discount) and embezzled money from his cousins. He dispensed wealth corruptly to gain and keep power. He never solved the problem of balancing wealth with expenditure. As Lorenzo famously said, "In Florence, there is no security without control." But control cost money, and Lorenzo, like his predecessors, tended to overspend to buy it. He inherited a fortune of over 230,000 florins, by his own estimate. This was the biggest fortune in Florence, though depleted from its peak in his grandfather's day. Fraud leached it. A new enterprise—exporting alum— nearly proved ruinous. Lorenzo's personal extravagance made matters worse.[48]

Third, Lorenzo, though a mere private citizen of ignoble ancestry, affected sacrality almost as if he were a king. His love poems are justly renowned. His religious poetry was of greater political importance, which is not to say that it was insincere; to become a great saint, it is no bad first step to be a big sinner. Indeed, there is something convincing about Lorenzo's lines, with their yearning for "repose" with God and "relief" for the "prostrated mind": the intelligible longings of a heart bled by business and a conscience stirred by the responsibilities of power. Confraternities to which he belonged chanted his calls to repentance, or sang them—as sacred words were often sung—to profane tunes.[49] He invested heavily in adorning the religious foundations his family had endowed, and in boosting their prestige. In particular, he nurtured the Dominican house of San Marco in Florence: a nursery of greatness where Fra Angelico painted and Girolamo Savonarola thundered—the tub-thumping reformer who influenced Luther and helped remold the Florentine state after Lorenzo's death. But San Marco struggled to survive financially and recruit postulants until Lorenzo poured wealth into it. His motives were not merely pious. He saw San Marco as a venue for supporters—it was at the heart of the quarter of the city that had the longest associations with the Medici family. He tried to make it the dominant house for the Dominicans of Tuscany and a source of wider influence over the affairs of the Church. He also tried, albeit unsuccessfully, to organize the canonization of Archbishop Antonino of Florence, the pet churchman of Lorenzo's house in his father's day.[50] When Lorenzo died, his supporters portrayed him as a saint.

Finally, and hardly consistent with saintly aspirations, he made an art of intimidation. Wealth bought power in its crudest form: toughs and bravos to bully fellow citizens within the city; mercenaries and foreign allies to cow Florence from without. Lorenzo cultivated allies—sometimes the popes, sometimes the kings of Naples, always the dukes of Milan. Part of the deal was that they would send troops to his aid in the event of an attempted coup or revolution in his city. It was not just that everyone knew he could afford to crush any opposition with mercenaries or foreign troops if he wished. He practiced the politics of terror to subdue opposition. The city of the Florentine enlightenment was a cruel, savage, bloody place where the body parts of condemned criminals strewed the streets and revengers mimed ritual cannibalism to round off vendettas. Lorenzo impressed his enemies with horrifying displays of terror and implacable campaigns of vengeance. The participants in the Pazzi conspiracy suffered the most vicious—but not unrepresentative—violence Lorenzo ever unleashed. Normally, criminals died on gibbets just outside the walls, so as not to pollute the city, but Lorenzo had the conspirators tossed screaming from the windows of the palace of the governing council. The crowds in the main square watched them dangle and twitch, convulsed by their death throes, before slaking their vengeance by tearing the bodies to pieces when they hit the ground. Lorenzo made vindictiveness a policy, harrying his victims' survivors into beggary. For a while, the government of Florence even made it an offense to marry one of the Pazzis' orphaned or bereft womenfolk. This was equivalent to condemning the women to starve to death.

Lorenzo was magnificent, of course, in art as well as power. As art patrons, the ruling branch of the Medici were never leaders of taste. For them, art was power and wealth. Lorenzo was not, however, quite the boor that modern scholarship has made him out to be. He was a genuine, impassioned aesthetic. His poetry alone is ample evidence of replete sensitivity and a perfect ear. He had, perhaps, a less than perfect eye. His aim was to collect objects of rarity and stunning visual effect. The courtyard of the Medici palace was lined with ancient inscriptions—a display not so much of learning or antiquarianism as of fashion and wealth. By far his biggest expenditure was on goldsmiths' work, jewelry and small, exquisite antiquities; wealth that could be handled for tactile satisfaction and moved quickly in case of a change of political fortune: the potential solace of exile, such as befell Lorenzo's father and son.

Although he was not a builder on the lavish scale of his Medici predecessors—politics, perhaps, constrained him—he remained actively interested in all public building projects and quietly embellished many of the grand buildings and religious foundations his family traditionally patronized.[51] But there was a touch of vulgarity and ostentation about even the architecture he favored. He was a member of a committee that crowned the dome of the cathedral with a golden ball, the symbol prominent on the Medici coat of arms. The paintings he bought (a trait apparently heritable in the ruling line of the house of Medici) were old-fashioned by Renaissance standards: the hard, gemlike colors of the works of Gozzoli and Uccello, the rich pigments—gilt and lapis lazuli and carmine—that glowed like the fabulous collection of gems Lorenzo assembled. His taste for battle paintings was part of his pursuit of the cult of chivalry. Tournaments were among his favorite spectacles, and he assembled gorgeous ritual armor in which to appear in the lists.[52]

It looks as though, in his youth, Amerigo had the chance of employment, if not in the business of the state, at least in the household of the ruler. After February 1483, evidence of Amerigo's closeness to Lorenzo vanishes. Princely favor was always a precarious commodity. The theme of one draft in Amerigo's exercise book was of a man placed "under the lordship and command of a certain prince" who "always did him all the harm he could and knew."[53] That was how Amerigo came to feel about Lorenzo. To approach an understanding of what befell, we have to go deeper into the world of the Medici.

THE FIGARO OF FLORENCE

Poverty and the struggle to ascend unite families. Wealth and success tend to divide them. The two branches of the family shared the same house until 1459; their business interests remained inextricably connected long after that. But grounds of resentment were already accumulating. Cosimo, the elder cousin and effective ruler of the city, abused his position as head of the family during Pierfrancesco's minority, by using the entire wealth of the family for his own benefit. In 1451, when Cosimo retired and Pierfrancesco attained his majority, a legal settlement split the wealth of the house equally between the two branches. Lorenzo complained that his uncle got "half of all our possessions, giving him a gross advantage over us and all the best items . . . and at the same time he carried off a third share as a partner in all our companies, in which he has gained more than us through having fewer expenses."[54] This was a division of responsibilities as well as of spoils. Lorenzo, with his lean and hungry look, carried the burden and costs of keeping Florence under the family's thumb, while Pierfrancesco, with his reputation for idleness and obesity, dallied in his rural villas, hunting and riding, and watched the money roll in.

They preserved a united front in public until 1466, when Piero de' Medici was in power, and his cousin Pierfrancesco signed an opposition petition exalting—in obvious disavowal of the rulers' methods —"just and popular government by customary means." One of the ruling Medicis' techniques for consolidating their position was systematically to purge old, politically unreliable families from the lists of those eligible for high office; the object of the 1466 petition was the reinstatement of those excluded. It was a serious crisis that brought Florence to the brink of civil war and drove other petitioners, including the former Medici supporter Niccolò Soderini, into exile and poverty. Pierfrancesco regained his cousin's forbearance by lending him 10,000 florins, but he never held another office in the state for as long as Piero lived. When the latter died, Pierfrancesco withheld collaboration, supporting candidates for office whom Lorenzo—Piero's successor in power—found distasteful. He tried to keep his son Lorenzo di Pierfrancesco free of Lorenzo's influence by refusing to allow the youngster to go on holiday with his cousin.[55]

In 1477 Lorenzo made overtures of conciliation to his cousins. He betrothed a newborn daughter—one of many who did not survive infancy—to Giovanni di Pierfrancesco. Botticelli's *Primavera* was perhaps commissioned for the occasion.[56] The following year, the Pazzi conspiracy unleashed an expensive emergency that drove Lorenzo to some morally questionable expedients, including—so contemporaries alleged—raiding the state treasury to shore up his own power. He also helped himself to his cousins' money. Between May and September, he transferred to his own account 53,643 ducats belonging to Pierfrancesco's sons.[57] The cadet branch claimed that they had been "forced" into the loan;[58] when Lorenzo di Pierfrancesco and his brother came of age, they demanded its return, with interest: a total of 105,880 florins. Lorenzo repaid only a little over 60,000. The enmity between the two branches of the family could now be computed in coin. It amounted to hatred: The odium seeps from between the lines of the handful of private letters in which members of the two branches refer to each other. In 1489 Lorenzo publicly spurned his cousins' pleas for mercy for a condemned criminal. The mutual revulsion continued to grow. It climaxed in 1494, when the cadet branch abjured the name of Medici and adopted that of *popolani*, echoing the cries of the rebels.

Meanwhile, the Vespucci—or at least Amerigo's branch of that family—left Lorenzo's service and joined Lorenzo di Pierfrancesco's camp. The events surrounding this shift probably began as early as 1478, with one of the most traumatic events in Lorenzo's life. Assassins attacked him in the cathedral, during or perhaps just after mass. His brother Giuliano was stabbed to death in a frenzy; his corpse bore more than a dozen wounds. Lorenzo escaped. It was part of a broad conspiracy aimed at wresting the government of Florence from the grasp of the Medici. The leading conspirators belonged to the Pazzi family— guardians of the old traditions, representatives of an oligarchy that had been prominent in Florence for hundreds of years before anyone ever heard of the Medici. Other malcontents among the elite were impli- cated. The archbishop of Pisa was in the thick of the plot. Foreign pow- ers, hoping to prise Florence from political alignment with Milan, fomented the unrest. The pope, while urging a bloodless coup, encour- aged the plotters by promising to send troops. The king of Naples did the same. But the conspirators bungled. They failed to kill Lorenzo. They failed to take possession of the government buildings. And when the doyen of the Pazzi family, old Jacopo, led his retainers onto the streets with the cry of *"Popolo e libertà,"* the people shrank from him or rushed to arm in defense of the status quo.

The Vespucci had nothing to gain from the conspiracy and every- thing to lose. They owed their recent ascent, such as it was, to Medici favor. But republican values were so deeply etched in the minds of edu- cated Florentines that a conspiracy against a quasi-monarch had almost automatic appeal. Among the prose exercises young Amerigo wrote was a piece in praise of the leading conspirator in the assassination of Julius Caesar, who was murdered on the same pretext as the attempt against Lorenzo: His ambitions as sole ruler subverted the purity of the repub- lic. Most of the Vespucci were too prudent to emulate Brutus. One member of the family, however, broke ranks. Piero Vespucci, Amerigo's uncle, was the nearest thing the family produced to a beau ideal of chivalry. He was renowned in the joust, a talent that endeared him to Lorenzo, who loved chivalric frippery. Piero always denied that he was a plotter and insisted that he had acted out of charity. Nonetheless, he helped one of the conspirators escape. Napoleone Franzesi was an old friend, and Piero claimed to have helped him in ignorance of the con spiracy. But everyone in Florence seems to have taken Piero's guilt for granted. He confessed to rage "enough to make a man burst" at Lorenzo's parsimony with patronage.[59] He nursed a grudge against Lorenzo because he felt insuffuciently rewarded for his services to the ruling house: They were dangerous, dirty services involving espionage missions against Naples and in Milan. The murdered Giuliano had probably cuckolded Piero's son.

Piero was tortured for twenty days. The family disowned him. His daughter pleaded for his life, reminding Lorenzo of "the charity you used with me when you called me sister."[60] Lorenzo eventually released him into the custody and service of the duke of Milan. In 1490 Piero was murdered in Alessandria, executing a mission for his new master. His killers dangled him from the balcony of the government building— the same method employed to dispatch the Pazzi conspirators—before finishing him off with daggers when he crashed to the street.[61]

It is unlikely that Piero's indiscretions can have compromised the Vespucci family as a whole in Lorenzo's eyes. Piero had always been a maverick, at odds with his cousins. He had tried to drive a wedge between the Medici and Guido Antonio, whom he had accused—most improbably—of complicity in an earlier conspiracy.[62] Still, the guardian of the family escutcheon had blotted the family copybook. Meanwhile, with Giuliano dead, the allure of Simonetta Vespucci no longer counted politically, if indeed it ever had.

The new circumstances did not at first affect Amerigo's prospects. On the contrary, the war that the Pazzi conspiracy unleashed was an opportunity for him. It stimulated Florentine diplomatic activity, brought important postings for Guido Antonio, and created the opening that took Amerigo to Paris. The outcome of the mission, though—what we have called its failure—can hardly have done much for Amerigo's standing. By the time Simone asked him to pass on those toadying greetings, Amerigo may already have been past his point of greatest influence in the household.

Meanwhile, the opportunities for patronage with the Magnificent One were in decline. Lorenzo was withdrawing from commerce. Following a pattern increasingly common among Florentine grandees, he looked outside the city, choosing in 1485, as Poliziano remarked, a country villa "as relief from his civic duties."[63] He worked at increasing the profitability of his farms to make up for the shaky nature of his busi-

ness as a banker. These were not propitious circumstances for the viscer-
ally urban, commercially minded Amerigo.

It is not clear what exactly went wrong in Amerigo's relationship with
the Magnificent One. But something did, and it involved a withdrawal
of favor from the entire Vespucci family. According to Lorenzo di Pierfrancesco, Lorenzo deliberately let the Vespucci down and left Giorgio
Antonio exasperated. A letter of uncertain date gives us the unfleshed
bones of the event. Amerigo had called on him, Lorenzo di Pierfrancesco relates, to discuss the family's affairs. "I think that things are
going badly," Lorenzo di Pierfrancesco wrote, "because it seems to me
that Lorenzo is not inclined to help." After urging comfort for Giorgio
Antonio, "find out what he wants," Lorenzo di Pierfrancesco instructed
a henchman, "and offer him on our behalf everything, whatever it may
be, and tell him that while we possess anything, he will want for nothing, and that through God's grace we have so much that he will always
be well off despite him who wishes otherwise."[64] The ill-wisher was
undisguisedly Lorenzo the Magnificent. Partly to spite his cousin, it
seems, and partly to honor Giorgio Antonio, Lorenzo di Pierfrancesco
committed himself to supporting the Vespucci. When Amerigo needed
remunerative work, he found it with the cadet line of the Medici. What
he did not find was security of employment, and certainly not the
"fame" and "honor" his father had enjoined him to seek.

It is hard to resist the temptation to wonder about Vespucci's reliability in business. From the time he left the circle of Lorenzo the Magnificent, he revealed, as we shall see, a spivish, picaresque side, making
small profits in gutters and alleyways, in dodgy deals and shady company. Mendacity—which was habitual with Vespucci—sometimes ac
companies other forms of dishonesty. One of the draft letters in
Amerigo's exercise book anticipates a dispute with an employer over ac-
counting shortfalls: "I will never," protests the writer, "buy or sell anything of importance on your behalf, except in accordance with your
explicit instructions and expectations."[65] Was this merely an exercise, or
a preenactment of a potentially embarrassing encounter such as we all
practice in our heads? It is at least evidence that accusations of pecula-

tion were routine in Vespucci's world of work. But there is no evidence that Lorenzo dismissed him for wrongdoing. The Magnificent One's break with the Vespucci seems to be an episode in a history of progressive severance.

Vespucci's biographers have tended to project his later greatness back to his youth, and to use extravagant terms to express the degree of importance he assumed in Lorenzo di Pierfrancesco's employment. He was not the general manager or overseer of the business of that supertycoon, nor did he run the Medici bank. He was no wunderkind CEO of a big corporation. In any case, if he was really born in the early 1450s, his was hardly a case of unusual precocity. At first, to judge from the modest commodities mentioned in his letters, he was more of a major-domo, responsible for keeping his employer's household supplied with essentials.[66] This is the sort of job designated, until recently, as a butler's and now—at least by the socially squeamish or politically correct—referred to a house manager's. But he must have "given satisfaction" in the job, for his responsibilities gradually widened, and in 1488, when Lorenzo di Pierfrancesco was old enough and experienced enough to begin to handle business affairs himself, he used Amerigo for transactions of all kinds. In September of that year, Lorenzo di Pierfrancesco, calling him "most dear Amerigo," entrusted him with the sale of wine and the collection of debts.

Amerigo gradually acquired a wide circle of clients of his own. He continued to discharge business for members of the Vespucci and Medici families, shifting his allegiance to the cadet branch of the ruling house. He established himself as a fixer, mediating between Lorenzo di Pierfrancesco and his less amenable business partners. He purchased bibelots for Lorenzo's wife and advised on suitable business partners. He stood guarantor for debts and collected them on behalf of creditors. Inmates of the debtors' prison petitioned him for help from their cells in the stinks. He established what sounds like a corrupt relationship with one of the warders, who asked him for a pair of women's shoes "because we are preparing a masquerade. . . . Pardon me if I am too presumptuous."[67] This is the sort of language small-time blackmailers use. Amerigo checked the accounts of the Medici family's agents. Some obscure references in his letters to unidentified or obscurely identified women make one suspect that he worked a sideline as a pimp—to recall the word I used in the first line of this book. "Procurer" might be a more generous term. He certainly acted as a go-between for a colleague, who asked him to convey a ring to a "lady,"[68] and for his cousin, who asked him to intercede with a certain Mona B.[69] The same client also asked him to procure books.

Everyone trusted him, especially in the demimonde, but the honor he enjoyed was honor among thieves—not the kind his father had in mind. Amerigo had the quality that, according to Arthur Miller, a salesman must have: He was liked. He displayed amply an engaging amiability, a gift for making fair-weather friends; he projected reliability and could convince others of the sincerity of his service to them—rather in the spirit of the American comedian who said, "Always be sincere, son, even if you don't mean it." Petitioners sought his backing, and patrons valued his judgment. He was becoming the Mr. Fixit of Florence, a Figaresque *factotum della città*. He was dealing in wine, perhaps, and gems or jewelry on his own account: These commodities crop up periodically in letters his associates or customers sent him. His main work was as a commission agent, buying and selling gems for clients. He accumulated some capital in the trade, but probably not much. The only evidence is that when he left Florence, he placed a ruby and a pearl in Bernardo's keeping. He remembered them on his deathbed twenty years later and asked that Bernardo realize their value, if he still had them, and spend the proceeds for the good of his soul.[70]

Amerigo's real early vocation, in short, was for neither scholarship nor affairs of state but business. The same talent for calculating profit and loss, wheeling and dealing, wheedling and needling, served him well when, later in his career, a change in vocation turned him into a ship's pilot, navigator, explorer, and cosmographer. The switch in his way of life—the conversion of the man of business into stargazing adventurer—has always puzzled students and scholars, but continuities riveted the two phases of Vespucci's life: continuities of skill and continuities of mentality and mental habits. A man with a head for accounts may also have a head for astronomical lucubrations.

He acquired a mistress and a daughter. This was a routine vice for a younger son who could neither afford to marry at his own expense nor attract a rich wife. Young Amerigo's exercise book shows that his father had warned him about it and obliged him to imagine himself legitimately united to "a prudent lady of the right sort [*una donna costumata e savia*] such as I married myself."[71] We know that Amerigo disobeyed in this respect only from a reference in a letter of uncertain date from a Spanish business associate who asked to be remembered to the daughter and alluded to what sounds like a hapless intrigue of his own: "Let me know if Lessandra is well—not that I wish her well, but just to know if she is alive or dead."[72] Who was Lessandra? Another "business" woman belonging to Amerigo's string?

And who was the equally mysterious Francesca, to whom two of Amerigo's correspondents referred by name? She was not the mother of Vespucci's child, for the same correspondent who inquired after the daughter asked separately to be commended to "one called Francesca," as if with amorous intent. On the other hand, the only other reference we have to her implies an intimate and probably meretricious relationship with our hero. The circumstances were sordid. A letter of February 1491, from a colleague of Amerigo's, supplies intriguing details. The whole tone of the letter is raffish, the language streetwise and wisecracking. The writer had failed in a task his Medici employers had entrusted to him; he had skedaddled—left town in a hurry; he was stumped for an excuse; he owed money. The letter is full of ambiguities and obscurities. For present purposes, the interesting passage concerns the writer's unsuccessful effort to take leave of Amerigo and another friend before his precipitate departure. "And I had no luck," he explains,

> and if it were not for the love I bear him, and the obligation your love places
> upon me, and the fact that she is so good-looking, I would curse Francesca and
> whoever lives in that street, especially as it is so dark there men who go there

keep getting lost, and I think it well that she should be a source of great pleasure
for you etcetera.

The ribald, teasing tone is sustained right up to that final "etcetera."
How seriously should we take this sort of laddish raillery? It sounds as
if, when he wanted to find Amerigo in a hurry, one of his most intimate
friends went to look for him in a house of ill repute in a dark street.
Amerigo seems to have felt no loyalty, forged no lasting links, to the
friends he left behind when he quit the backstreets. He never referred to
his informal family and never, as far as we know, made provision for
them or recalled them after he left Florence for good.

CHAPTER TWO

THE PROSPECT FROM EXILE

Seville, 1491–1499 ° Taking to the sea

IROLAMO AND BERNARDO continued to be a drag on the family fortunes. Like so much of Florence's underworld and elite, they looked to Amerigo to handle their business, wheedle favors on their behalf, and fix their lives. Girolamo left the family hearth in about 1480, became a priest at an uncertain date not later than September 1488, and joined a community in Rhodes. This was an evasion of sorts; he could not buy his way into a respectable appointment in Florence. Away from home, he spent his time importuning the family to send him money or procure him a benefice, and exchanging with Amerigo claims to have written letters and gotten no replies. Bernardo, meanwhile, sought employment in Hungary, where numerous Florentines clustered to try to take advantage of the ruler's taste for Renaissance arts and learning.

Matthias Corvinus, king of Hungary, saw himself as a new Hercules. He began his palace at Visegrád in the Gothic manner but turned increasingly for inspiration to antiquity and, therefore, to Italy. In 1476 he married an Italian princess. Hungary became a land of opportunity for Italians barely employable at home, but especially for artists and engineers able to give the king's surroundings a Renaissance look and feel. The court humanist Antonio Bonfini described the palace—or perhaps his work was more literary confection than description, so perfectly was it modeled on a classical ideal of a country house. He led readers through loggias, high-vaulted spaces, and a bathroom equipped with a hypocaust. In "golden chambers" with beds and chairs of silver, undisturbed by the noise of servants, or the murmur of the sea, or the roar of storms, or the flash of lightning, the interiors were so well proofed against the weather that slumberers could "see the sun only through unshuttered windows." Trompe l'oeil enhanced the zealously contrived artificiality. In the library "the sky could be seen, painted on the ceiling." The books, however, were authentic: Matthias Corvinus had the princely total of over twenty-five hundred of them.

He was staking claim to fame as enduring as that of the Romans. "When you read that Romans created gigantic works that proved their magnificence, you do not permit, oh invincible prince, that their buildings should surpass yours in their magnificence, but you revive once again the architecture of the ancients." Matthias Corvinus called on all the resources of the Renaissance to project and perpetuate his self-image. "His triumphs over the enemy," Bonfini averred, "will not perish owing to virtue, bronze, marble, and the written record."[1]

Matthias realized that Florence was preeminent in the arts and tastes he craved. Ficino wrote to him and promised to visit Hungary himself, though he never got around to it. Francesco Bandini, who accompanied Matthias's first wife from Italy, was a Florentine, a colleague of Ficino's. Bernardo Vespucci, however, never adjusted to Hungary and never attracted royal favor or, it seems, any kind of valuable patronage. The king's marriage to a daughter of the duke of Milan briefly excited Bernardo's hopes, but his complaints to Amerigo reveal him in what he confessed to be "a bad way, . . . having often had to sleep in the woods or in hay carts." He was ridden with lice, despite bathing twice a week. He made some sort of living as a bookkeeper for an Italian merchant, on a year's contract, at the end of which he resolved, "I will try to return to Italy." His protestations are too much: self-underminingly vehement. Germans, he claimed, dominated the court. Florentines were out of favor (but, rather inconsistently, were resented for having "more power than the king himself"). All the Italians at court were in fear of their lives. The king's notions of justice revealed him, by implication, as a tyrant who put malefactors to death by garrote, burning, hanging, drowning, and breaking on the wheel. Every excuse for failure pours from the page.[2] Bernardo, like Girolamo, seems to have been a hopeless case, incapable of self-help. In Amerigo's generation, the Vespucci were, on the whole, a disappointing brood, ill equipped to obtain the fame and honor their father prescribed.

There is no evidence that Amerigo exerted himself on his brothers' behalf. His punctiliousness was most in evidence when it was most to his advantage. Despite their brother's promises, Girolamo remained without a job, Bernardo without a vocation. With Antonio, the relatively rich and successful elder brother, Amerigo was—as we shall see—attentive and solicitous. The habit of calculating his favors stayed with him for the rest of his life. Meanwhile, the fortune hunting that sent Bernardo eastward took Amerigo to the west.

THE MAGNET IN THE WEST

"Go west, young man" was good advice in fifteenth-century Italy. The booming Iberian markets were staging posts on the way to the Atlantic and northern Europe, as well as offering tempting commercial opportunities in their own right. For Florentines, Spanish wool was an important resource in their weaving industry, an activity in which the Vespucci family had interests of its own. The Pazzi family—the Medicis' greatest enemies in Florentine politics—had opened a branch in Barcelona in the 1420s, which helped to restore their fortune after a downturn that threatened to leave them out of the top rank of Florentine dynasties. The Medici had agents in Spain continuously, from that decade on, and employed Spaniards in their own entourage in Florence—including Fray Francisco de Aragón, who counseled Lorenzo de' Medici on princely behavior.[3] Spain, meanwhile, supplied Florentines with some of their fine horses and dogs.[4]

Vespucci's destination was Seville. It was one of the best places in Spain for a foreigner to do business in the late Middle Ages. The city had long attracted immigrants from Italy. Genoese had been among the first, arriving soon after King Ferdinand III of Castile added Seville and its region to his kingdom in 1248 by conquest from the Moors. In Vespucci's day, the Genoese still predominated among the foreign community and constituted the largest group of foreigners resident anywhere in Spain. Two of the richest and noblest families in the city, the Estúñiga and Boccanegra, had arrived from Genoa a few generations before. Among numerous new arrivals in the second half of the fifteenth century, there were many with surplus capital, on the lookout for adventurous ways in which to invest it. There were more than a hundred Genoese merchants in Seville, by a contemporary reckoning in 1474.[5] Between them, they paid over half the city's tax yield. More than thirty of them had the rights of citizens, divided between eleven merchant houses.

Alongside the Genoese, the rest of the foreign community was beginning to diversify and grow. There were at least twenty-one other Italians, about half of them Venetians. Burgundian and French taste predominated in the arts, and most immigrant artists came from northern Europe: In the 1470s Lorenzo Mercadante arrived from Britanny, and the dazzlingly omnicompetent Enrique Alemán from Germany. In 1478 Enrique installed new glass and altars in chapels in the cathedral. By then Italy's reputation as a nursery of the arts had reached Sevillan patrons, and Italian artists were increasingly welcome. The printing trade, which flourished in Seville, attracted Florentine artisans. Opportunities in commerce were even greater than those in the arts. In 1469 five Florentines were among the merchants who shipped grain in to meet the shortage Seville experienced that year.[6] But the Florentine businessmen were not yet settling in Seville in the way Genoese did. Only four Florentine merchants are known to have had rights of residence in the city at the time of Vespucci's arrival. The numbers of foreign settlers soared when the New World trade started, but Vespucci moved to the city just ahead of this new phenomenon. His presence cannot be explained merely as an instance of a large-scale migration. We need to try to identify, or at least imagine, his personal motives.

Seville had undeniable attractions. It is an inexplicable city: one of those places that, like Florence, seems to have been built in the wrong place for greatness and to have become a great trading center in defiance of geography. It is fifty-six miles upriver from the sea. A sandbar makes the Guadalquivir hard of access. So Seville was, for most of its history, more of a fortress city or regional market than an oceanic emporium. You can still see the outline of the city as Vespucci saw it—or at least as the citizens wanted it to appear—by looking at the model, made at about the same time, for the high altar of the cathedral. It is a cascade of golden roofscapes. The cathedral dominates, with the Almohad minaret of the former mosque that still provides it with a belltower; below the tower, arcaded palaces ripple to the double line of huge castellated walls and gateways that line the river's edge. Another survivor from Moorish times, the Torre del Oro, jutting from the model's foreground, is recognizable to any tourist who compares it with the real thing today. Shortly after Vespucci's arrival, the Nuremberg cosmographer Hieronymus Münzer surveyed the city from the cathedral tower, noting the fertile surroundings, sizable dimensions (double those of his own city), abundant water supply, and numerous rich houses of religion.[7] Seville was one of a mere handful of Spanish cities that Vespucci's fellow Florentine Francesco Guicciardini singled out for praise when he toured the country a few years later.

Castilian cities were part of a kingdom. None had republican ancestries or traditions of independence. Many were run by aristocracies with predominantly rural interests, others by royally nominated bureaucrats. Mercantile interests were rarely preponderant. It was impossible for the citizens to have the kind of pride Florentines felt for Florence. But Seville inspired its citizens with exceptional depth of feeling. It was an old city, with genuine Roman origins. It had long been the residence of kings—first in Visigothic times, and under a Moorish dynasty of its own, before becoming sporadically a Castilian courtly center. Its aristocrats did not disdain trade. Its clergy were lavish in patronage of the arts. Artistic opportunities grew with general prosperity. The city authorities took on the responsibility of paving the streets. Zealous aristocrats and religious communities bought up dwellings simply to tear them down and create public plazas.[8] There were still insufficient monumental spaces for the city's needs. In 1490 the jousts to celebrate the marriage of a princess had to be held outside the walls.[9]

Seville was the biggest city in the Spanish monarchy by the time Amerigo moved there, about the same size as Florence. The population roughly doubled during the fifteenth century, but in the small towns and villages of the surrounding countryside, growth was even faster: Here, numbers more than tripled. Near the gates, the piles of refuse grew as the city's population and productivity increased; they were useful pinnacles to retreat to in times of flood.[10] But Seville was essentially a regional center, dependent on a wealthy agricultural hinterland. No area of comparable size was richer than the kingdom of Seville, which contributed 15 to 20 percent of the tax yield of Castile in the fifteenth century.[11]

The olive oil, textiles, and raw wool of upper Andalusia came down the Guadalquivir on its way to the sea. Olive oil, above all, was the product that lured international commercial agents, but the country also specialized in wine, cereals, and cattle. Skins of wildcat and rabbit were particularly coveted. Pigs and pork products from the forested hinterland were famed. The city housed an important fish market. But long-range trade was still on a modest scale. Only twenty-six citizens were classed as merchants in the 1480s.

Industry expanded. In 1489 about 42 percent of the active population engaged in artisans' trades or retailing.[12] The local industries operated on more than workshop scale—the royal ironworks, huge soap factories, a shipyard. Potteries made storage jars for olive oil, which in turn made Sevillan soap highly sought after, exported as far as Germany and England. It used to be assumed that wine and Canarian sugar were the lures that brought English merchants to Seville in considerable numbers. It now seems that soap was, as much as anything, what they were after.[13] The mint was Spain's biggest, by a long way. Seville was already used to handling large amounts of gold and silver before the discovery of America.

Seville gathered the reins that linked the ports around the mouth of the Guadalquivir and Guadiana from Huelva to Cádiz. Bonanza and Sanlúcar de Barrameda, Moguer, Palos, Lepe, Puerto de Santa María and Portal de Jeréz, Gibraleón, Cartaya, and Ayamonte all depended on Seville's financial institutions—the bankers, the insurers, the markets. The fishing industry was the driving force behind the city's growing involvement in the Atlantic. The need for ever longer voyages in search of fishing grounds schooled mariners in long-range navigation. The demands of freight and war stimulated the shipping industry. Trade grew in all the important products Seville traditionally handled: gold and slaves from the trans-Saharan world, Maghribi leather and sugar from Sus, dates, indigo, and amber.

Despite Seville's long history of success, the immediate circumstances at the time of Vespucci's move there were mixed. The eighties and early nineties of the fifteenth century were a tough period. Plagues and famines struck. In 1484–85 the monarchs banned people from Seville from joining the front against Granada in case they spread plague in the army.[14] In 1494 the town council held its summer meetings outside the city for the same reason. Half the citizens were too poor to pay taxes.[15] These were routine problems for late-medieval cities. Seville's singular troubles were man-made and partly self-inflicted: religious intolerance, social conflict, and war.

Remarkably, all these disasters had equivocal effects and, in some respects, unpredictably benign consequences for those who survived them. Take the Inquisition. It had a chilling effect on any economy it touched. It was never as active as when it was first instituted. Chroniclers left conflicting tallies of the numbers of victims in the archdiocese of Seville: between three and five thousand investigated, many harried into leaving, and between three and seven hundred "relaxed"—that is, handed over to the secular authorities for chastisement, though not all, perhaps not even most, were actually put to death. Victims were often selected for corrupt reasons. In 1487, for instance, they included a *converso* who held a huge debt from the cathedral chapter, and a group of former Jews who were close to one of the town's most conflictive bosses, the duke of Medina Sidonia: Factional politics were always dangerous in Seville. Between 1495 and 1497, two thousand formerly Jewish families in the city effectively bought immunity from further persecution.[16] So the economic benefits of the presence of the rich, enterprising *converso* community were perhaps not altogether lost. Many took refuge nearby on the lands of hospitable aristocrats, who were glad of exploitable tenants. The Inquisition, in short, recycled golden eggs without killing the geese that laid them.

Meanwhile, the city's remaining Jews were expelled, on pain of death, along with those of neighboring dioceses, in 1483—nearly a decade before the same policy extended to the whole of Spain. The text of the decree has not survived, nor are there any records of the arguments adduced in favor of the move, but the kingdom had just launched a war against the Moors of Granada, and the fear of what we should now call a fifth column probably played some part. Moreover, the Inquisition confirmed a widespread source of anxiety: The presence of Jews imperiled the souls of converts from Judaism, seducing them into apostasy or immuring them in the culture of their former faith.

By the date of the expulsion, there were fewer than sixty Jewish households in Seville. Expelling Jews rarely confers economic benefits: An economically productive, fiscally exploitable minority is lost. In Seville's case, the move increased opportunities for newcomers and made real estate available relatively cheaply. Property speculators had been targeting Jewish homes even before the expulsion, as shown by a royal decree of 1478 protecting the Jews from harassment in that connection. The effects of the expulsion were immediate. Work on one of Seville's most famous aristocratic palaces, the Casa de Pilatos, or House of Pilate, belonging to the Enríquez de Ribera family (who had remote Jewish ancestors themselves), began in 1483 on a site vacated by a Jewish expulsee. The Jewish exodus was one of the reasons for the influx of immigrants, of whom Vespucci was one.

Seville was, for decades prior to Vespucci's arrival, a city at war: first a civil war in the 1460s, which was ruinous for commerce and arrested or reversed the growth of the city's tax yield; then war with Portugal in the 1470s, when the effects were equivocal. Many shipowners in the region took the opportunity to make fortunes and acquire experience, raiding Portuguese trade with Africa. The Florentine Francesco Bonaguisi was among those who shipped to Guinea aboard a raiding venture against Portuguese gold sources in West Africa in 1478.[17] The Portuguese took back all the gold in a counterraid, but the expedition demonstrated the available opportunities. In 1478, partly as a spin-off of the Portuguese war, the effort to conquer the Canary Islands resumed in earnest, after a long period, under the direction of the crown. Seville was the center of efforts to organize recruitment, shipping, and finance. Finally, in the 1480s war broke out against the kingdom of Granada, flinging chances of lucrative war-supply contracts to merchants with enough capital to exploit them. In 1487 the capture of Málaga, Granada's main port, switched vast amounts of business in Seville's direction. The contracts for grain fleets that formally operated from Málaga now enriched Sevillans.

It is fair to say, on balance, that Vespucci arrived in Seville at a propitious moment. Speculators and adventurers had invested heavily in exploration of the Atlantic from Iberia's western edge for nearly a hundred years; for most of the time the rewards were, at best, modest. African slaves were the most profitable commodity of commerce—or of kidnap. Madeira and the Azores were reasonably productive: Indeed, after the sugar industry of Madeira began to boom in the 1450s, the island became the home of a sort of medieval *Wirtschaftswunder.* But the Atlantic continued to have a bad reputation with investors. The conquest of the Canaries was a drain on the blood and treasure of everyone who undertook it.

Suddenly, in the 1480s the economic returns leaped into the red. The Portuguese opened a trading station at São Jorge da Mina, on the underside of the West African bulge, near the mouths of the rivers Pra and Benya. In reality, it was a humble place: The local chieftain professed disappointment with the poverty of the Portuguese residents. But it rapidly acquired a grand reputation in Europe, where cartographers depicted it as a many-turreted city, a sort of Camelot with blacks. Cheap gold was the basis of São Jorge's fame. It was not particularly near any major source of gold production, but traders from the interior did bring what, by Portuguese standards, seemed substantial amounts of gold with which to acquire the tin truck and wool cloth the Portuguese offered in return. This was a major breakthrough for European enterprise in the African Atlantic, where gold had long been the main target of explorers' efforts. Soon after, the Canary Islands at last turned profitable, with the opening of a sugar mill at Gaete in Gran Canaria in 1484. Moreover, Vespucci's arrival in Seville more or less coincided with the Catholic monarchs' commission to Columbus. If Columbus's promises proved true, and he found a shortcut to the riches of Asia, investors would make fortunes. In the atmosphere induced by the events of the 1480s, and the new profitability of Atlantic enterprise, the chance of getting a cheap cut of Columbus's schemes enthused several of the Italian bankers in Seville.

VESPUCCI GOES WEST

This context explains why Italian and, a fortiori, Florentine merchants were attracted to Seville. It does not explain why Vespucci in particular should have been among the handful of Florentines who made the move. Vespucci's trajectory resembled that of Columbus. The latter reached Iberia through serving the Centurione family business in Genoa as a buyer and seller of goods, especially sugar; Vespucci, similarly, got to know Spain on behalf of his Medici employers. The first whiff from the West that we know of reached his nostrils late in 1488, when he had some unsatisfactory dealings—the details remain unclear—with Tomasso Capponi, Lorenzo di Pierfrancesco's representative in Seville.[18] A few months later, Lorenzo di Pierfrancesco lost patience with Tomasso. According to Lorenzo, he was an unworthy agent who wrote nonsense and handled affairs badly. He was evasive, perhaps mendacious. A replacement was necessary: Would Amerigo report on the suitability of a recommended candidate?[19]

The name proposed was that of Gianotto Berardi, whose main place of business had been Seville from 1485 at the latest. He dealt at that time mainly in slaves, not just as a buyer and seller but also as an investor in slave raids or acts of piracy at sea, by means of which Castilians captured Portuguese shipments of slaves. This Florentine businessman has left few traces in the records and no writings from his own hand, except his signature on some humdrum contracts. Yet he deserves a prominent place in any account of the history of the world. Together with a group of Genoese bankers in the same city, and a few aristocrats, courtiers, and cosmographers, he was a central figure in the lobby that promoted Atlantic expansion as an objective of Spanish policy and raised Columbus to eminence at the court of the monarchs of Castile.

Amerigo's advice on the candidates for the Medici agency in Seville has not survived. We do not know how he compiled it, but it is a fair bet that he interviewed Lorenzo di Pierfrancesco's informant and Tomasso Capponi himself, both of whom returned from Seville to Florence at about that time.[20] It is also clear that Amerigo made a favorable assessment of Berardi's potential, for soon thereafter Berardi took over the handling of the Medicis' operations in Seville. There is no justification for the widespread—indeed, traditional—assumption that Vespucci made a personal voyage to Spain to verify Berardi's suitability. Clearly, however, the affair brought the two Florentines sufficiently close to make a favorable mutual impression. Vespucci not only recommended Berardi to Lorenzo di Pierfrancesco; he also, in effect, left the latter to become the former's employee. He still thought of Lorenzo di Pierfrancesco as his patron and kept in touch with him, and Berardi's firm discharged some work for the great Florentine house, at least for a while.

In some ways—taking all the circumstances of Seville at the time into account—the move seems unsurprising. Spain was a magnet for Florentine businessmen. Seville was already something of a boomtown. Medici business had introduced Amerigo to contacts in Spain and to Berardi in particular. On the other hand, there is something puzzling about this veritable turning point in Vespucci's life, which led him to a new circle and a new career. Traditionally, biographers have assumed that he was in a position of considerable trust and profit in the household of Lorenzo di Pierfrancesco de' Medici. If not the right-hand man of the head of the firm, he was, by most accounts, a confidant of great influence and experience. His place in Florentine society, though not honorable, was supposedly respectable and profitable. If this was so, why should Lorenzo wish to transfer him to what, for all its opportunities, was still a remote outpost of Medici business? We know of no forfeiture of trust, but it was rather like a command to "go and govern New South Wales"—the sort of switch that might follow a failure or a fall from grace. Away from Florence, Amerigo never ceased to look out for another patron, but that may have been mere routine prudence rather than a sign of dissatisfaction with Lorenzo, or vice versa. And why should Amerigo abandon a good berth in Florence for an adventure on a remote frontier? His place in Berardi's firm was important but not commanding: Berardi referred to him as "my agent."

If, on the other hand, as seems more likely, and as we have argued, Amerigo was merely a marginal figure in Lorenzo di Pierfrancesco's world who made his living mainly as a freelance commission agent, there was no particular reason for his employer to keep him at home and no particular reason for Vespucci to decline the chance of a new life in Seville.

Perhaps this is a moment to risk a speculation: The initiative that took him to Seville may have come from Amerigo himself—a first sign of the restlessness, the wanderlust, that would lead him first to the edge of the ocean, then beyond it. It would not be surprising if he had grown restive in the trammels of his relationships at home, with his illicit household, his dubious companions, his demanding clients, his importunate family. The move to Seville was a throw of the dice and an effect of frustration. Amerigo had failed in Florence to find the fame and honor his father demanded of him, or the fortune he sought for himself. The chance of employment with Berardi was a risk and proved, in the long run, a bad risk. But it was an escape from a world of restricted opportunity into a world where dreams could come true.

They came true, at about the time Vespucci arrived, for another Italian adventurer: Christopher Columbus. Berardi was instrumental in Columbus's enterprise of mounting an expedition to cross the Atlantic Ocean. Amerigo's new associate was deeply involved with a group of courtiers, bureaucrats, cosmographers, would-be missionaries, and financiers who had come together over the previous dozen years in connection with the funding of the conquest of the Canary Islands.[21] Berardi also took a leading role in the trade of orchil—the dyestuff unique to the Canaries that was one of the magnets for the conquistadores. His partners were Francesco da Rivarolo, a Genoese banker of Seville who was a mainstay of Columbus's, and the English merchant John Day, who doubled as a spy and was another member of Columbus's own circle.[22] Columbus had links of a different kind with another Florentine banker in Seville, Francesco de' Bardi, who married Columbus's sister-in-law and who also had repeated and prolonged dealings with Berardi.[23] One way or another, Columbus's and Berardi's paths crossed and converged.

The same group of backers clustered around Columbus. Berardi was in Santa Fe, the royal camp outside Granada, with some of the other financiers in March and April 1492, when the first transatlantic expedition was planned. No one in the circle was closer to Columbus. What attracted Berardi to the adventurer? Other members of the group supported Columbus because, like him, they were Genoese; others again were Franciscans to whom Columbus was linked by bonds of personal piety; others, without ever becoming Columbus's intimates, supported him because they saw further Atlantic exploration as a natural extension of the project that had brought the Canary Islands under Spain's sway—and had even begun to make them profitable. Berardi was exceptional in embracing Columbus and his project without any obvious prior interest or predisposition to do so. And he was an outstandingly tenacious supporter who never wavered when things went badly. When Columbus's hopes of a short route to Asia proved fallacious, Berardi went on investing in the hope of getting slaves, at least, out of the venture. When the monarchs banned the slaving, he carried on, hoping to make money out of shipping contracts for the fleets that would frequent Columbus's discoveries—and perhaps the Spaniards who would settle them. The basis of the link between Berardi and Columbus is irrecoverable, but once it was in place, Berardi grappled it to his soul. He was irrevocably and, as it turned out, fatally committed to the explorer.

Amerigo wrote his last surviving letter from Florence on November 10, 1491. Toward the end of 1491 or the beginning of 1492, he joined Berardi in Seville. By that time, Berardi's fortunes were growing ever more closely entangled with those of Columbus. Vespucci had committed himself to work in a business in flux: When he first met Berardi, there was probably enough flexibility in the business to withstand a change of fortune. By the time he joined the firm, the enterprise was in the process of becoming entirely dependent on the fortunes of a single client. On March 10, 1492, he signed himself "Amerigo Vespucci of Seville" as a witness to a contract with other Florentine merchants on behalf of Lorenzo di Pierfrancesco's firm. Other employees and associates of the firm also signed. So did Gianotto Berardi.[24] It was the beginning of a relationship that would change Amerigo's life.

Soon after Amerigo's arrival in Seville, Lorenzo the Magnificent died. Relations broke down entirely between the dead ruler's heir, Piero, and Lorenzo di Pierfrancesco's branch of the family, who left the city and went into active, hostile opposition. Even if Amerigo had wanted to return to Florence, his retreat was cut off. But he had no real cause to contemplate departure from his adopted home. He put down roots in Seville. Here he could marry, free of the constraints that made a bride hard to find in Florence.

His wife, María Cerezo, is a maddeningly shadowy figure. According to Amerigo's will, she was the daughter of Gonzalo Fernández de Córdoba. The only Sevillan of that name known from other records of the time was one of the great figures of the age: the "Grand Captain," as Spaniards called him, who, against the odds, drove the French out of southern Italy and conquered it for Spain. If María was his daughter, she was illegitimate. The fact that she is so elusive in the archives suggests that status: Bastards tended to escape record. Vespucci, who had left—one could fairly say abandoned—at least one informal sexual alliance in Florence, could have contracted another in Seville if he wished, so there must have been some advantage to him in marrying María. It is tempting to assume a sentimental attachment of some intensity, but there are plenty of romantic illusions at large in existing books on Vespucci, and it would be otiose to add to them. For someone of Vespucci's status, linkage with a distinguished family, albeit on the distaff side, might have been attraction enough; and María was a useful business partner who bore Amerigo's power of attorney when he was away from home[25] and brought an exploitable range of connections to the marriage. Among the men she employed to conduct business on her and her husband's behalf, a relative, Fernando, repeatedly stood proxy for Amerigo in deals. After her husband's death, she displayed some acuity—or chose representatives who did so—in securing her husband's back pay and obtaining a pension from the crown. She exhibited the same qualities a few years later, when a child slave in her house was killed in a traffic accident and she sued those responsible before obtaining an out-of-court settlement.[26] The fact that her signature does not appear on any document has raised suspicions that she might have been illiterate, perhaps another of Amerigo's lowlife contacts.[27] But the speculation needs more evidence to sustain it.

Berardi seems to have sunk all the firm's capital in support of Columbus. There was little left over for the business of Lorenzo di Pierfrancesco de' Medici. It is unclear how much of that business the firm of Berardi and Vespucci handled. Italian merchants in Spain sent newsletters to their principals. A fragment of one Vespucci wrote jointly with another Medici employee, presumably for Lorenzo, survives from January 1493, with news of an assassination attempt against the king of Spain the previous month. Unremarkable in itself, this letter is worth noting for the light it casts on the sustained relationship that led Vespucci to continue reporting to Lorenzo years later, long after leaving his service. It was a habit he could not or would not break: a way of maintaining a route back to his former master's service should the need arise. He also continued to attend to Medici business: In January 1493 his presence in Barcelona, where he heard of the king's escape, was on Medici business—shipping a cargo of salt to Florence.

However much he continued to think of himself as linked to Lorenzo di Pierfrancesco by past obligations or future hopes, Vespucci worked ever more closely with Berardi, on business that went far beyond the Medicis' concerns. The riskiest element in that business was the investment Berardi made in Columbus. And as Columbus's fortunes waned, so did those of his backer. At first the discoverer must have seemed like a golden opportunity for a speculator with an eye to a quick and glorious profit. In 1493 Columbus returned from his first voyage with astonishing proofs that he had landed somewhere exotic and exploitable: parrots, "Indians," tiny but exciting droplets of gold. Ferdinand and Isabella's court cosmographer hailed Columbus's achievement as "more divine than human." Plain Cristoforo Colombo, the Genoese weaver's son, was instantly transformed into Don Cristóbal Colón, admiral of the ocean sea, viceroy, and governor. He had acquired the seeming paradise of Hispaniola for his royal patrons and was to return to rule it, gathering its gold into Castilian coffers and its native people into God's Church. Like a preincarnation of Sancho Panza, Columbus seemed to have achieved a squire's dream: "an island with a little bit of the sky above it." No romance of chivalry ever ended on a more spectacular fade-out.

Berardi's story had many chapters yet to unfold. He won the contract to supply Columbus's lucratively large second fleet and to keep the colony on Hispaniola provisioned. But the deal soon proved bad. Columbus returned to a bitterly disillusioning experience in Hispaniola. He had left thirty men as a garrison. The natives whose docility he had praised had massacred them. The climate he had extolled for its incomparable virtues was deadly. Malaria and miasmas had killed off his colonists. He had to abandon the town he founded because of the unbearable exhalations from the swamps. The trades he imagined enriching the colony were chimerical. The island produced, naturally or in abundance, none of the goods for which he had hoped. The natives were incapable of mining gold in sufficient quantities to rectify the accounts. They had to be conquered and coerced, whereupon they disobligingly died. European diseases, to which they lacked any inherited immunity,

piled up hecatombs of victims. Meanwhile, Columbus's own men mu-
tinied. His efforts to extend the explorations only magnified his failure.
The lands he sought—China, India, Japan—continued to elude him. It
became obvious to everyone save him that he had stumbled not on the
riches of the Orient but on an obstacle course that lay in the way.

Even before his first voyage was over, Columbus seems to have realized that the only chance of retrieving profit from his enterprise was by
enslaving the natives. Berardi evidently relied—should all else fail—on
the returns from slaving to recoup his outlay in fitting out the fleet. Neither of the Italians reckoned with the equivocal Spanish attitude to slavery. During the conquest of the Canary Islands, Ferdinand and Isabella
had felt assailed in their consciences by clerical critics of the enslavement of the natives. In 1488, on the advice of a commission the monarchs set up to inquire into the question, they had ordered hundreds of
slaves to be freed on the grounds that they had been unjustly seized and
sold. Generally, Spanish law insisted on fulfillment of canon-law re-
quirements for the taking of slaves: Slavery was unnatural, so people reduced to it had to be captives of just war or must have forfeited their
rights by gross offenses against natural law, such as cannibalism or
sodomy. Columbus and Berardi's victims fitted neither category. They
had been unceremoniously seized or captured while exercising their own
natural right of self-defense. Cannibals were fair game, but no one
claimed that the natives of Hispaniola practiced cannibalism. Indeed,
Columbus explicitly exempted them from such a charge. If anything,
they were the prey of cannibals from neighboring islands, who were
proper objects of slaving, though the Spaniards could never capture
many of them. The Spanish monarchs therefore forbade the enslavement of their newly acquired subjects. Berardi's chances of making
money collapsed under the weight of a few royal scruples.

By 1495 it was obvious that Columbus's colony would need plenty of
nurturing before it turned a profit. Like many investors embroiled in expensive failures—or like many gamblers banking on a change of luck—
Berardi renewed his efforts. In April he signed a contract with the
crown, promising to send three convoys of four ships each to Hispan-

iola. It was an overambitious commitment. He was probably already fully stretched. He was able to muster only four ships in all. By June, the monarchs or their agent, the bishop and bureaucrat Juan de Fonseca, had despaired of Berardi and sent a fleet at the crown's expense. Amerigo supplied provisions "sufficient until they reach the Indies" and two pipes of wine.[28] He also dealt with at least some of the accounts on Fonseca's behalf.[29] The fleet foundered in a storm off Santo Domingo.

In October, Berardi reaped his first reward: in terms of the money of account used throughout Castile, nearly forty thousand *maravedíes'* worth of slaves from the New World, allegedly procured from the ranks of cannibals and lawful captives.[30] The capital obtained made it possible to renew the effort to get supplies out to Columbus. In December, Berardi was still working on the fleets when he suddenly died. "Suffering, lying on his bed," he made his will.[31] Columbus was in the fore of his mind. He called him "his lordship"—a title for which Columbus was indebted, indirectly, to Berardi's support. "He owes me," Berardi recorded,

> and is obliged to give me and pay me on his account as at present the sum of 180 thousand maravedíes—little more or less—as will appear from my books, and beyond that the value of the service and work I have done and performed for his lordship for three years gone by, in deed and with good will and intention, wherein to serve him I have left my trade and livelihood and lost and wasted my property and that of my friends, and have even sacrificed my own person, for if our Lord should take me from this world with this present sickness, it is the result of the travails and sufferings I have endured for the service of his lordship.

Berardi left his daughter, "orphaned and poor," to Columbus's keeping, "after that of our Lord God . . . because his lordship is a good Christian and servant of our Lord." He commended to Columbus a number of associates—"my special friends, servants of his lordship, who each according to his ability contributed amply to his lordship's service." Prominent among them was "Amerigo Vespucci, my agent," who was to be an executor of the will with responsibility for recovering the debt owed by Columbus, discharging in turn Berardi's outstanding obligations, including, in particular, those to a representative of the Medici.[32]

It is not clear what became of Berardi's orphaned daughter, but Vespucci was left holding the metaphorical baby. There was no hope of getting money out of Columbus: He never had any to spare. Shortly after Berardi's death, a payment of ten thousand *maravedíes* came through from the royal treasury for the fleet of four caravels that the firm had put together to send to Hispaniola, together with the advances due for the wages of key personnel of the fleet. But within a month, the fleet was wrecked in the Strait of Gibraltar. Amerigo ended up, by his own reckoning, 140,000 *maravedíes* to the bad.

Clearly, when Amerigo backed Berardi—first recommending him to the Medici, then joining him in business on his own account—the judgment for which he was renowned in Florence deserted him. If he had not quite descended to the level of the "pickle-dealer" of Ralph Waldo Emerson's imagination (below, p. 196), he was reduced to making a living as a glorified chandler, equipping, managing, and provisioning flotillas bound for the extremities of the world known to his contemporaries. The amount of available work shrank as Columbus fell into disfavor, and Ferdinand and Isabella cut their commitment to the Atlantic enterprise. Nor does Amerigo's relationship with Lorenzo di Pierfrancesco seem to have done him much good at this critical moment of his life. By 1497, at the latest, Piero Rondinelli seems to have handled the business of the Medici without reference to Amerigo. Rondinelli arrived in Florence in 1495, already well established as an associate of Medici employees. He dealt in slaves with Donato Niccolini, who had been decisive in persuading Lorenzo di Pierfrancesco to dismiss the Caponni. Competition within the Florentine community increased with its numbers. Still, other members of Columbus's circle continued to befriend Vespucci. Francesco da Rivarolo, the Genoese banker of Seville, and Gaspar Gorricio, Columbus's friend and confessor, went on doing business with him or bestowing charity on him. After Gorricio's death, Rivarolo applied for repayment of money he had lent him to pass on to Amerigo.[33]

FROM MERCHANT TO MARINER

So Vespucci's transformation from commission agent in Florence to long-range, large-scale merchant in Seville had turned out badly. He was no nearer to that elusive fame and honor. And instead of making a fortune, he was piling up debts. Even if he had not needed another change of vocation, he may have found the merchant's calling uncongenial. Merchant self-perceptions were equivocal. On the one hand, merchants tended to insist on the nobility of commerce. The handbooks some of them wrote for their profession resembled those for knights, with exhortations to meritorious conduct and assurances that trade was a training in virtue, because profit followed renown. One of the reasons why the theme of Tobias and the Angel is so common in late-medieval art is that merchants liked a subject that displayed one of their number in celestial company.

On the other hand, there was an unmistakable air of derogation about Vespucci's profession. Nobility remained associated in most people's minds with chivalry and the exercise of arms, or with blood and ancient lineage. In Spain the big new challenge to these old-fashioned notions came from the exaltation of education as a means of ennoblement. The growing ranks of university-trained bureaucrats and lawyers had an interest in developing the argument. But mere trade could not command in Spain the sort of prestige attainable in a commercial city like Florence. In general, until well into the sixteenth century, Spain was a bad country for a merchant who aspired to ennoblement.

Sevillan standards were not as ossified as those in the rest of the country. The dukes of Medina Sidonia had a small fleet, shipping salt tuna and supplying garrisons in Africa. The dukes of Medina Celi had a tuna-fishing and -processing business. But while an aristocrat could be a merchant, it was not easy for a merchant to become an aristocrat.

Some individuals, including Italian immigrants of former generations, managed it by accumulating great wealth and making socially ambitious marriages.[34] To Vespucci, in the circumstances of the late 1490s, the examples were remote and the opportunities unavailable. The really glowing prospects lay not in financing and provisioning fleets but in sailing in them. Columbus's example had proved it. When he launched his ships, Columbus launched his career. Not even his subsequent failures entirely reversed his fortunes. Even in disgrace, he still clutched his titles and grasped at wealth.

The way Amerigo's life and Columbus's entwined was an inescapable trammel for both of them. By 1499 Columbus was a source of disappointment to his patrons and exasperation to his friends. He had failed in all his promises. He had not found a short route to Asia, or certainly not to any commercially exploitable part of it. He had involved the crown in another expensive conquest of useless aboriginals, like that of the Canary Islands, without the same prospects of profit. He had found only small amounts of gold, of uncertain long-term potential. His promises that Hispaniola was a kind of paradise had dissolved in the odor of pestilence. His assurances that the natives were peaceful had presaged war and bloodshed. He had virtually abandoned his administrative duties and left Hispaniola in the hands of rebels and mutineers. He had made his men swear that Cuba was part of a mainland, whereas everyone able to express an independent opinion was sure that it was an island. He gave increasing signs of paranoia. His report on his third Atlantic crossing of 1497–98 sounded mad: full of visionary ramblings, paranoid laments, and speculations about a pear-shaped globe, with the earthly paradise at the tip of a nipple-shaped protuberance, which he had, he claimed, approached but not surmounted. In 1500 the investigator whom the Spanish monarchs sent to inquire into Columbus's conduct shipped him home in chains.

Yet Columbus left two reasons for optimism. First, his failure to find Asia could have been the result of incompetence rather than of any fundamental impracticality. Belief in the possibility of a westward route to Asia actually grew in the wake of Columbus's failure. At least the Genoese adventurer had shown that the western ocean was traversible and that there were ports of refuge on its western shore. Even if the world were too big for a one-hop route to Asia via the west, it was possible that one more effort might lead navigators there. Second, on his third voyage, Columbus found pearl fisheries richer than just about any local tribe, off what is now Venezuela.

Ferdinand and Isabella seem to have felt embarrassed to see the admiral appear before them in chains, but they made an unsentimental judgment about his abiding value. He could not be allowed to retain the monopoly of transatlantic navigation. Apparently, though not explicitly in any surviving document, they decided that he had broken his contract by failing to deliver his promises. They added a dexterous piece of floccinaucinihilipilification. Columbus had forfeited his right of monopoly on the coast discovered on his third voyage because ill health had prevented him from landing and taking possession in person.[35] They could therefore open transatlantic navigation to rivals. The combination of the lure of the East and the gleam of the pearls would ensure takers for the new opportunities. Amerigo was one of the takers. From May 1499, the monarchs authorized at least eleven voyages, eight of which took place, before they allowed Columbus to make another.[36] Amerigo sailed on the first.

Evidently, the pearls were the prize. Peralonso Nino, one of Columbus's disgruntled former shipmates, raced straight for them as soon as he got a license. Alonso de Hojeda, Columbus's strong-arm right-hand man in suppressing rebels and natives in Hispaniola, made for the place where the pearls were known to lie as soon as he reached the coast of the New World. Vespucci, for all his disclaimers, seized the same opportunity to stock up. As a former jewel dealer with long-standing interests in pearls, he knew a good specimen when he saw one.

One of the exercises in Vespucci's surviving schoolbook shows his early familiarity with the idea of voyaging in search of fame and honor. "Many of the men of this land," he wrote in Florence, "have departed without our hearing any news of them, nor has any eulogy of them been pronounced, for they are not dead, but are gone into perilous lands . . . and their desire is to take to sea and pass through many countries before they return home."[37] Vespucci now followed in their wake, as if their example had stuck in his mind.

Almost as soon as he arrived in Seville, exploration had spread a new ocean before him, like a magic carpet unrolled at his feet. The Atlantic of the 1490s was no longer the ocean sea of former times: untraversible, unexploitable, setting limits to experience. Columbus had shown that it could be crossed. Pedants often point out that Columbus did not discover the western hemisphere, except to the peoples of the Old World, who did not already know about it. But he did discover the way across it and back along commercially viable routes, linking the densely populated zones of both hemispheres and establishing permanent communications between Europe and the productive regions in and around the Caribbean.

He had cracked the code of the Atlantic wind system. Most history books contain too much hot air and not enough wind, for the wind systems of the world, for the entire age of sail, which occupied most of the recorded past, were among the most important determinants or conditions of long-range exchanges of culture. Columbus showed for the first time that by starting from Iberia, ships could quickly pick up the northeast trade winds to cross the ocean, then use the westerlies of the North Atlantic to find their way back. The discovery turned the Atlantic from a backwater on the edge of the world into an ocean of opportunity and an axis of global communications. Communities that had dwelled inertly on its shores for centuries or millennia, using it only for fishing and cabotage, now vied to launch missions of trade, colonization, and empire. Vespucci was in the right place at the right time.

If we focus determinedly on Vespucci's reasons for espousing a new vocation as an explorer, we run the risk of overestimating his agency. We change direction in life not always because we want to, but because we have to, or because we respond to new opportunities as a way of escape from existing constraints. In the late 1490s Amerigo was in difficult straits. He had lost much or all of the Medici business in Seville. Since Berardi's death, he had been encumbered with debts. Tempests and ill fortune had bedeviled his fleets. A change of occupation was just what he needed. The chance came because of Columbus. Vespucci was able to take it, perhaps, because of a deep-rooted aptitude implanted in his education. But, as so often, he was driven and drawn by circumstances into a new way of life like a mariner tacking against adversity who finds himself borne away by a sudden change in the wind.

In order to piece together a narrative of what Vespucci actually did at sea, and to retrace the thoughts that took shape in his mind as he did so, recourse to his own writings is necessary. As the reader knows, the authenticity of some of those writings is much disputed and widely doubted, with good reason. Chapter Four is a journey through those writings—to my taste, a journey more marvelous and eventful than any ocean crossing. Meanwhile, in retelling the story of his navigations, I shall adopt a simple and secure method: Whatever is common to the manuscript and printed sources, I take as authentically Vespucci's own work; whatever is peculiar to the printed sources, I set aside as suspect and subject to interpolation or alteration at editors' hands.

CHAPTER THREE

THE STARGAZER AT SEA

The Atlantic, 1499–1501 ∘ *Initiation in exploration*

ERDINAND AND ISABELLA chose Alonso de Hojeda to lead the first voyage in Columbus's wake because he was, they said, "reliable." As the son of an indigent nobleman, Alonso had been the monarchs' dependent at court for most of his life. He never cut much of a figure as a courtier, but he was an ideal enforcer: tough, ruthless, relentless. He was instrumental in preventing the Hispaniola colony from falling apart under Columbus's inept management. He had been Columbus's strongarm man, both in repressing the rebels and in terrorizing the natives into submission.

The story of his voyage suggests that these qualities did not necessarily make him suitable for independent command. He proved incapable of getting on with the other ships' captains, and in the end, his former shipmate and intended partner, Peralonso Nino, made an independent voyage. Still, a constellation of subordinates accompanied Hojeda, including Juan de la Cosa, Columbus's shipmate and mapmaker. Amerigo was among them.

SAILING WITH HOJEDA

Amerigo joined Hojeda's voyage in an unknown capacity. He wrote about it afterward as if he were sole commander of the fleet. Of course, this was untrue. No one would have been so rash as to entrust command to a landlubber like Vespucci, who had no experience of long-range navigation and no known qualifications for the job. Inexperienced figureheads were sometimes chosen to command expeditions. Vasco da Gama, for instance, was a mere up-country *hobéreau* when the king of Portugal summoned him to lead the first commercial fleet to India; still, he was at least a nobleman of sorts and had a military background. Similarly, the commander of the follow-up fleet, Pedro Álvares Cabral, was not a mariner, but he was an aristocratic courtier suited to the diplomatic role he would have to play at the fleet's destination. Vespucci had no corresponding advantages.

When not posing as sole commander, Vespucci contrived to suggest that he was an active decision maker aboard the fleet. At least he gave the impression that he was commander of his own vessel and conducted his own explorations independent of Hojeda. Yet no other document ascribed such a role to him; Hojeda himself testified on the matter after Vespucci's death, during the Columbus family's long lawsuit against the crown over the division of the profits of the admiral's discoveries. After ascribing the achievements of the voyage to himself alone, Hojeda added that he had "taken with him Juan de la Cosa, pilot, and Morigo [*sic*] Vespuche, and other pilots."

The context makes it sound as if Hojeda considered Vespucci a pilot—which is remarkable enough—but not a coleader. Perhaps the commander took his unlikely recruit at the recruit's own evaluation. It would not be inconsistent with Amerigo's character if he had—as we might say today— enhanced his CV and claimed expertise he did not really have. Or perhaps, after the passage of years, Hojeda classed Vespucci with other pilots on the basis of his later attainments. Meanwhile, though Columbus sued Hojeda for infringement of his privileges, and besmirched with accusations all the other leading figures of the expedition whom witnesses could be induced to name, Vespucci escaped without a mention.[1] This may be because Columbus had other obligations to Vespucci that exempted the Florentine from prosecution.

More probably, it implies that Vespucci's role on the expedition was too modest to be worthy of notice. It would not be surprising if he exaggerated it.

What was he really doing aboard ship? A useful precedent is that of Alvise da Mosto, a Venetian who had shipped as a passenger on a Portuguese expedition of exploration to the Cape Verde Islands and the Gambia in 1454–55, impelled, as he said, by love of travel and a desire to see the world. It was therefore, in principle, possible to take ship without having any useful role or contribution to make. But da Mosto's professed disinterestedness was a rare quality. To travel for mere curiosity was vanity. Amerigo later made claims to disinterested scientific curiosity; but in the circumstances of 1499, that was a luxury he could not afford. Though Vespucci never so much as hinted it, it is impossible to imagine his decision to sail with Hojeda except in connection with the pearls that Columbus had discovered. Across the Atlantic, they gleamed between half shells at greedy desperados who wanted to get rich quick. If there was any useful expertise involved in his shipmates' willingness to take him aboard, it can only have been Vespucci's knowledge of the pearl trade. It cannot have been expertise in navigation.

Amerigo's fellow voyagers were an unruly lot who left mayhem and complaints of piracy in their wake as they crossed the Atlantic, first off the African coast and then in the Canaries. Hojeda's choice of route across the Atlantic was clearly extrapolated from Columbus's experience. Columbus had shown that the fastest crossing led southward from the Canaries in the path of the northeast trade winds, toward the lesser Antilles. Hojeda set his prows a notch more to southward and made the coast of South America at a point he reckoned to be about two hundred leagues east of Columbus's mainland discoveries. The scholarly consensus is that his landfall was in the vicinity of Cape Orange.

Of surviving accounts made by participants at or near the time, the reports closest to Vespucci's sole authorship are two letters and one fragment of a letter. These never made it into print and do not survive in the author's own hand but were preserved by various copyists. The narrative these documents supply is markedly different from that given in all other sources, and no other evidence supports it. Therefore, they were long dismissed as forgeries. The first letter, however, datelined July 18, 1500, in Cádiz, can be regarded as of more or less guaranteed authenticity, since four contemporary manuscript copies survive from different copyists in widely scattered locations. The addressee is called simply "Your Magnificence" and, later in the letter, "magnificent Lorenzo." The Lorenzo who was once Vespucci's employer was now long dead, but the style remained appropriate for Lorenzo di Pierfrancesco de' Medici, the elder Lorenzo's cousin and Vespucci's rather inconstant patron.

The writer begins by excusing himself for not having written in some time, for want of any news worthy of report. The implication that Amerigo was resuming the habit of reporting his activities to Lorenzo di Pierfrancesco seems strong. He claims to presume that "your Magnificence" must already know "that I left with two caravels on 2nd May, 1499, by command of the king of Spain, to go to make discoveries in the western region by way of the Ocean Sea." This trick of assuming on the reader's part foreknowledge of information that the writer then goes on to convey is one of the oldest rhetorical devices around. It creates an atmosphere of complicity between the reader and writer. It flatters the reader with an assumption of knowledge while covertly supplying the knowledge in question. It inflates the writer's importance in the reader's perceptions. Instantly, Vespucci managed also to boost his image in the reader's mind by associating his activities with royal patronage and even giving the impression that he was the sole commander of the fleet.

Amerigo's description of the route is vague, as one might expect of a previously sea-shy passenger who probably had only a vague idea of where he was or where the ship was going. The only place-name he mentions is the Gulf of Parias, which Columbus had named on his previous voyage to the Venezuelan coast. Vespucci's tally of ground covered—at least 2,800 miles of coastline—seems hugely overestimated: more than double Hojeda's tally, if they were counting in the same sort of miles. Vespucci claims to have been much farther south than other records confirm, and adds just enough detail to make the claim plausible. In consequence, readers who want to know where Vespucci actually went end up baffled.

The historiography of the voyage tacks between extremes of credulity and criticism. Amerigophiles lap up every word and crush other sources to make them fit; skeptics reject Vespucci's account as an almost irredeemable fabrication. The most widely accepted synthesis treats Vespucci as if he operated in a kind of parallel universe, independent of the rest of the expedition. In the early history of European navigation to the New World, it was normal for ships to get separated by weather, or by the conflicting ambitions of their commanders, or in consequence of a rational strategy for maximizing the extent of their joint explorations. The sources contradict one another on the number of ships in Hojeda's flotilla, but there were at least two and perhaps as many as four, so it was perfectly possible for the fleet to divide. But this solution begs further questions: If Vespucci parted from the main expedition, who was with him? It is simply incredible that he should have commanded a ship of his own at this stage in his career. And if the fleet divided and registered important discoveries beyond those ascribed to Hojeda, why did no one except Vespucci ever say so? And why was the excursion unrecorded in official reports?

Various answers to these questions might be suggested. Hojeda had several companions who were well qualified to command a vessel, and although those known to us by name sailed with him, there were, by his account, "other pilots" in the fleet. So one of these unnamed others could have commanded the section or ship in which Vespucci sailed. Vespucci evidently strayed into waters assigned to Portugal under the Treaty of Tordesillas, so there may have been reasons for suppressing the news—except on Vespucci's part, since his pride could not be stifled—and it is worth bearing in mind that shortly after his return from the voyage, he entered Portuguese service.

The next question is how far did he reach along the South American Atlantic coast? This is unanswerable, but Vespucci's evasions do not necessarily mean that his voyage added nothing to previous knowledge of the coast. Although the discoveries Vespucci recorded appear in no other surviving report, they do seem to have influenced mapmakers. This is a tricky line of evidence to pursue, since maps are like the Bible: Devotees of particular doctrines can always find support in them, but they are so vulnerable to emendation and forgery that no historian should ever rely on them without supporting evidence from other sources.[2] Still, for what it is worth, the cartographic evidence does show that a lot more coastline of the New World was explored in all directions during the first decade or so of the sixteenth century than is apparent from explorers' official reports. And Vespucci, on this voyage or his next or both, could have contributed something to the accumulation of knowledge.

Which strains credulity more: to dismiss virtually everything in Vespucci's account as make-believe, or to accept that he took part in an excursion from the route traced by the flagship? Though Vespucci's imagination was fecund, his claim to have crossed the equator in 1499 rings with truth. A Florentine in Lisbon said as much in a letter home of 1504.[3] Most early-sixteenth-century commentators accepted that Amerigo had reached the "Land of the True Cross"—the name Pedro Álvares Cabral gave to Brazil when he made landfall there, well to the south of the equator, in May 1500. In the present state of the evidence, we have to proceed on the assumption that Hojeda's fleet divided when it reached the shore of the New World. The voyagers made their landfall probably in the vicinity of Cape Orange. Hojeda's section proceeded north and west, along shores already sailed by Columbus, toward the pearl fishery off the island of Margarita. The section in which Vespucci sailed turned south and crossed the equator, but we cannot say how much farther it went.

WHERE IN THE WORLD . . . ?

Although Vespucci's writings reveal nothing reliable about the extent of his navigations, they are unimpeachable in disclosing his mental image of the world. Where in the world did he think he was when he got to what would soon be called America? In his letter of July 1500, Amerigo quickly disclosed what he believed the voyage was all about. Like Columbus, in his mind, he was headed for Asia. "My intention was to round a headland which Ptolemy calls the Cape of Cattigara, which abuts the Great Gulf, which, according to my opinion, was not far from where we were, according to the degrees of longitude and latitude."[4]

Apart from its unwarranted but by now—to the reader—not unexpected self-importance, the most remarkable feature of this passage was its dependence on a worldview formulated by Columbus. Cape Cattigara, in Columbus's mental map of the world, lay at the eastern edge of the farthest arm of the Indian Ocean: the "Great Gulf," as cartographers called it at the time. According to Vespucci, the geographical results of Hojeda's voyage confirmed Columbus's findings. Amerigo's claims to have computed the longitude of his discoveries tallied—as we shall see—with Columbus's world picture.

Amerigo also accepted Columbus's hypothesis that the new land was part of, or close to, the eastern end of Asia: "another world," as Columbus called it, "which the ancients labored to conquer." Not only did Vespucci believe he was approaching the Indian Ocean, he also insisted that another voyage would present a chance to find "the island of Taprobana, which lies below the Indian Sea and the Sea of the Ganges, and afterwards I intend to come and return to my homeland and spend my old age there at rest."[5]

By "the Sea of the Ganges," Vespucci meant what we now call the Bay of Bengal. "Taprobana," which, he said, "directly faces the coast of India," was something of an obsession with him during his career as an explorer. It was Ptolemy's name for what was evidently the island later known as Ceylon and now called Sri Lanka. It was familiar to ancient Greek traders—of whom many frequented the Indian Ocean in antiquity[6]—because of its role as the world's major producer of cinnamon. Pliny ascribed stupendous longevity to its inhabitants. In medieval legend, Taprobana acquired a progressively exaggerated reputation as an island of great wealth. In maps inspired by Ptolemy, which Florentines made in large numbers during Vespucci's youth, it was always glowingly, conspicuously, centrally featured. Amerigo described a conversation he had with a traveler who knew Sri Lanka and Sumatra at first hand: "a reliable man called Guaspare," presumably one of the Italian merchants who worked the Indian Ocean, reaching it by laborious overland routes along the Nile and by caravan to the Red Sea, or via potentially hostile regions ruled by Turks and Persians, to the Persian Gulf.[7] Guaspare had visited many islands in the Indian Ocean

> *and especially one called Zilan. . . . He told me it was an island very rich in precious stones and pearls and spices of all kinds and drugs, and other riches such as elephants and many horses, so that I suspect that this must be the isle of Taprobana on the basis of the way he represents it to me. . . . Also, he told me that there is another island that is called Scamatara, which is as big as Zilan and very near it and just as rich. So that if Zilan is not Taprobana, Scamatara must be.[8]*

There is surely something disingenuous in these musings. "Zilan," or Ceylon, was well known and already identified fairly consistently with Taprobana in texts of the kind Vespucci surely knew, including the descriptions of the Indian Ocean by the most widely read travel writer of the Middle Ages, who called himself John Mandeville, and his inspirers, Marco Polo and Friar Odoric of Pordenone. Speculation that, alternatively, Sumatra might be Taprobana was also fairly common in medieval geographical writings. Vespucci wrote about his intellectual discoveries in the same way he wrote about his travels, representing them as his own independent achievements, omitting precedents and pioneers.

Vespucci's Taprobana fixation does help us reconstruct the mental image of the world he had while at sea. Like Columbus, he believed that if he could round or penetrate the long coast that lay athwart his proposed route to Asia, the riches of the Orient would lie spread before him. The mental map he superimposed on reality was based partly on Columbus's own views, partly on the sources that inspired Columbus.

The source of this image of the world is not hard to identify. Essentially, the picture was Ptolemy's. This is unsurprising. Vespucci could recall the cosmography he learned as a boy in Florence and use it to complement and perhaps to contradict the admiral's ideas. As a result of his education, he approached the New World with a head already stuffed full of Ptolemy. Indeed, there was something of a Ptolemy industry at work among Florentine scholars in Vespucci's youth. The most famous edition of the text of the time, which appeared in 1482, was prepared by Francesco Berlinghieri, a member of the "family of Plato." Mapmakers working in Florence in and after the 1460s produced dozens of maps based on Ptolemy.[9] Giorgio Antonio Vespucci, like most learned Florentines, possessed a copy of the *Geography* and probably copied it himself.[10]

But Amerigo did not have an unmodified Ptolemaic model in mind. Scholarship, speculation, and exploration all conspired to change the way Florentines read their Ptolemy in Vespucci's youth. In particular, in the late 1480s and 1490s, they grew in the conviction that the Indian Ocean was not landlocked, as Ptolemy had supposed, but open to the south and therefore accessible to navigators approaching from the east or west. In 1488 the voyage of Bartolomeu Dias, who rounded the Cape of Good Hope, strongly suggested this. In the early 1490s Portugal sent agents to Arabia and Ethiopia to confirm it. In 1497–98, Vasco da Gama's voyage to India around Africa proved it beyond cavil. Even before Vespucci left Florence, one of the cartographers who worked in that city, Henricus Martellus, produced a map that illustrated the Indian Ocean in this manner.

Martellus's map is probably as close as we can get to the world image with which Vespucci started on the nautical phase of his career. Near its eastern edge, where an island-sprinkled ocean washes Asia's farthest shore, a long peninsula tapers southward. Beyond it, to the west, lies the Malay Peninsula, or the "Golden Chersonese," as most people in the West called it. Whereas most of the late-medieval maps directly based on Ptolemy showed these peninsulas as jutting into a landlocked ocean, Martellus and other adventurous or well-informed cartographers placed them at the edge of Eurasia, partly athwart the entrance to the Indian Ocean or Vespucci's "Great Gulf." In the midst of that sea lay the island of Taprobana, centrally located and enormously exaggerated in size. Anyone matching Columbus's and Vespucci's experiences to the data on the map would draw obvious conclusions: The islands Columbus discovered were staging posts to Asia. The long coast Vespucci followed was, in his mind, Martellus's easternmost peninsula of Asia.

It was natural that Vespucci's views should have resembled so closely and depended so heavily on those of Columbus. Amerigo had worked for one of Columbus's most fervent admirers, Gianotto Berardi. He had plenty of opportunity to fall under the discoverer's spell. As a novice in navigation and cosmography, he was bound to defer to the man of experience and acclaim. By setting out on an Atlantic adventure of his own, Amerigo adopted Columbus as a role model, so it would be reasonable for him to adopt some of Columbus's opinions.

Moreover, Columbus had not yet quite used up the goodwill of cosmographers, which his first transatlantic voyage had stirred. In time, after a period of reflection and a chance to sift the evidence, most commentators rejected the notion that Columbus could have gotten anywhere near Asia, since the size of the globe precluded it. But in the excitement of Columbus's return, many contemporaries simply accepted his description of his findings without objection. The comment of the admiral of Castile was typical: Columbus had fulfilled all his promises. According to the duke of Medina Celi, he had "found all he was seeking very perfectly."[11] The pope—reflecting, apparently, the text of the first printed report of Columbus's voyage—accepted that the discoverer had found a wonderful and exotic land "towards India." In these circumstances, Amerigo could be forgiven for agreeing. He was not alone in maintaining faith in Columbus's vision. Until Magellan accomplished the project of finding a westward way to Asia in 1520, and demonstrated in the process that Columbus had been wrong about both the size of the globe and the ease of the voyage, most transatlantic navigators continued to dream of reaching Asia.

Both Columbus and Vespucci relied to some extent on the same sources of information. Both explorers shared partial dependence on the theories of Paolo dal Pozzo Toscanelli as well as on Ptolemy and Strabo. Although Toscanelli wrote virtually nothing that survives, he did leave an enormous reputation. Every contemporary who knew him or knew of him reckoned him highly as an expert in cosmography. Johannes Müller (known as Regiomontanus in the code of Latin names scholars gave one another), who compiled the best astronomical tables available at the time, hailed Toscanelli as a greater mathematician than Archimedes. In humanist circles, there could be no loftier praise.[12] In an exchange of letters with Toscanelli, Columbus received confirmation of the most precious of his geographical theories: that it was possible, at least in theory, to sail west to Asia across the Atlantic. Toscanelli claimed to have proposed such an endeavor to the Portuguese, and he sent Columbus a copy of a letter on the subject, with an illustrative map that he had sent to a correspondent in Portugal. Brought up as he was in Toscanelli's intellectual circle in Florence, Vespucci can hardly have escaped exposure to the same ideas.

In one respect, he dissented from Columbus's theories. He accepted the mainstream view on the size of the world: 24,000 miles around at the equator, bigger than the figure proposed by Columbus. Since Amerigo, when he endorsed this figure, thought in terms of Castilian miles, which were shorter than in most other systems, it was still relatively small by most contemporaries' calculations. Contemporary efforts to convert Ptolemy's figures on the subject into up-to-date measurements ranged from 22,500 to 31,500 Roman miles. Columbus also relied heavily on Ptolemy for his data but rejected the Alexandrian's estimate of the size of the world in favor of a smaller, rival estimate that Ptolemy mentioned only to refute. Stirring in some other, more or less arbitrary calculations, Columbus reckoned the globe at 20 or 25 percent smaller than its real size.[13] The nearest comparable underestimate— about 13 percent below the real figure—was proposed by Toscanelli and shared by the influential Nuremberg cosmographer Martin Behaim, who made Europe's oldest surviving globe in 1492.[14] Few experts took Columbus's figures seriously.

This is a curious fact. On the one hand, there was wide acceptance that Columbus had reached the threshold of the Orient after a relatively short trip: 750 leagues—roughly 3,000 miles—according to the pilot of his flagship, or a little over 1,000 leagues, by Columbus's own rather more generous and less reliable reckoning. At the same time, by almost universal agreement, the size of the world made such a feat impossible. Even by Toscanelli's reckoning, Columbus still would have been thousands of miles from the eastern edge of Eurasia when he made his landfall.

On this point, for Vespucci, Ptolemy was again the decisive influence. In common with most other readers of his day, Amerigo accepted Ptolemy's figures without modification. How, then, could he persist with Columbus's plan of sailing west to Asia when he knew that the size of the world made the voyage dauntingly long? A combination of wishful thinking and nautical naïveté seems to have been responsible. Perhaps he hoped that the figures would sort themselves out if he persevered in the quest, though he grossly overestimated the distance Columbus had traversed, repeating the admiral's wildly exaggerated reading of longitude as if he had made it independently. So, while not committing himself to a globe of a girth as tight as Columbus imagined, Vespucci assumed a relatively small world where Asia lay just around the corner—as it were—from Columbus's discoveries. Lacking any practical knowledge of the sea, he was wildly overoptimistic about how far and fast ships could go.

Yet no sooner did Vespucci get home from his ocean crossing than he began his campaign in favor of a new self-image. He became Amerigo Vespucci, celestial navigator, conner of the heavens, master of the art of reading latitude and even longitude: a Florentine *magus* in action. "Because," he wrote to Lorenzo di Pierfrancesco, "if I remember rightly, your Magnificence understands something of cosmography, I intend to describe to you how far we went on our voyage by means of longitude and latitude."[15] Vespucci's self-appraisal as a nautical expert appears surprisingly unannounced, as if a single sea voyage gave him an opportunity for self-education in a new art in which he emerged proficient, like Minerva leaping into life fully armed. How far was this image justified?

The Self-appointed Cosmographer

With plenty of conventional sneering at the "grossness" of seamen who did not understand the mysteries of the cosmos, Amerigo devoted much of his first report to cosmographical matters. Despite the aura of expertise, and an evident general familiarity with the look and feel of sea and sky in the low latitudes of the southern hemisphere, a lot of what he said made little sense.

Seeking to stress that his passage through "the torrid zone" took him beyond the equator, he said that at one point the sun cast no shadow in any direction, which was hardly possible in any out-of-the-ordinary way. Amerigo claimed that the expedition lost sight of the Pole Star at six degrees south and that the last two of the Guard Stars were barely visible, but this seems, at best, a gross exaggeration. According to Vespucci, forty leagues south of the mouth of the Amazon, the expedition encountered a tremendous adverse current, fiercer than that which stoppers the Strait of Gibraltar or rushes through the Strait of Messina. But there is no such current. He said that the fleet penetrated six degrees beyond the equator, but fixed the limit of their navigation at 60½ degrees south of the latitude of Cádiz, an error that can be explained only as the result of an aberration or a slip of the pen. He claimed that during July and August 1499, they were on the equator, or within four to six degrees of it, and that day and night were of equal duration, which clearly cannot have been the case.

Most absurdly of all, he advanced the theory that he sailed 5,466⅔ miles west of Cádiz. It was hard to keep a record of distance traversed on the open sea. Seasoned navigators did it by estimating their speed, essentially by practiced guesswork. They would throw a weighted, knotted line in the ship's wake and judge its motion against a fixed point or some bit of flotsam. The method was rough but ready. Vespucci, who had no relevant experience, was incapable of it, but he had shipmates to whom it came easily. Meanwhile, the navigator would time the ship's progress by means of a sand clock that a ship's boy turned, not always wholly reliably.

Speed multiplied by time gave the distance the ship made. Not surprisingly, estimates varied, commonly by up to 10 percent on long voyages when more than one navigator kept a log. But no qualified pilot, however incompetent, ever turned in an overestimate as egregious as Vespucci's.

Still, that Vespucci made so many mistakes and exhibited so clearly his lack of nautical expertise should not prejudice us against the possibility that he might have made some worthwhile observations or even a major scientific breakthrough. Such breakthroughs, after all, are often made by outsiders or laypeople who are unburdened by received wisdom and unbound by professional caution.

Vespucci made his most ambitious claims on this voyage not as a navigator but as an astronomer. His most startling reflections came to him while stargazing. A famous passage in his letter to Lorenzo di Pierfrancesco described his search through the sky for a southern equivalent of the Pole Star, a star sufficiently fixed in the firmament to steer a ship by. Vespucci was alerted, I suspect, to the quest by curious lines in the fourteenth-century travelogue known as the *Book* or *Travels* of the author who called himself Sir John Mandeville—a text that, as we shall see, was rarely far from Amerigo's thoughts when he was on his own travels. "You must understand," said the writer, recounting adventures he claimed befell him in the southern hemisphere,

> *that in this land, and many others thereabouts, the star called Polus Arcticus cannot be seen; it stands ever in the north and never moves, and by it seamen are guided. It is not seen in the south. But there is another star, which is called Antarctic, which is directly opposite the first star; and seamen steer by that star there as here they do by the Pole Star. Just as their star cannot be seen here, so our star cannot be seen there.*[16]

Vespucci's lines on the subject are worth quoting at length, partly because, in conjunction with the expectations Mandeville aroused, they convey a strong impression that he did penetrate the southern hemisphere, and partly because of another literary model they invoke:

*I, desiring to be the author who would first identify the star of the firmament
of the other Pole, lost many nights of sleep in contemplating the motion of the
stars of the other pole, to note which moved less and which went more rapidly in
the firmament. And, no matter how many bad nights I spent, or how many
instruments I used—which were the quadrant and the astrolabe—I could
not identify a star which moved within a circle of ten degrees around the
firmament. So I could not rest satisfied with myself, without saying that there
was no star that could be named the Pole Star of the south, because of the great
circle they made around the firmament. And while I revolved this matter, I
recalled a saying of our poet Dante, who makes mention of it in the first
chapter of the* Purgatorio, *when he imagines leaving this hemisphere and
finding himself in the other, and, wishing to describe the Antarctic Pole, he says,*

> *I turned to the right hand and my mind's span*
> *Towards the other Pole, where four stars gleam*
> *Ne'er seen before since humankind began.*
> *The sky appeared exultant with their beam.*
> *Oh, how bereft a northerner must be,*
> *Deprived of power these wonder-stars to see.*[17]

*It seems to me that in this verse the poet wishes to represent the four stars as
constituting the southern Pole, and I do not mistrust that what he says may
turn out to be true, because I noted four stars in the shape of a mandorla,
which moved little; and if God gives me life and health, I hope soon to return
to that hemisphere, and not to come back without discerning the Pole.*[18]

What are we to make of this? The passage captured the imagination of
everyone who read it. It was reproduced in every printed version, pirat-
ical or privileged, of Vespucci's voyages. It is hard to believe that someone who had stayed north of the equator could write it. The early
engravers of Vespucci's account spangled their pages with the stars. The
discovery was clearly recognized as a breakthrough in astronomy. Tradition has hailed Amerigo, on the strength of it, as the discoverer or at
least the prophet of the Southern Cross.

Before evaluating these claims, it may be helpful to set out the evidence for his other celebrated achievement on this voyage: making a reading of longitude at sea. Again, the influence of Ptolemy and of Vespucci's education in Ptolemaic lore are a vital part of the background. Ptolemy's proposed method of mapping the world on a grid of lines of longitude and latitude was impracticable, given the technology of the time, but it had long fascinated geographers. Even before Ptolemy's text was available in Florence, scholars knew of the method by report. A thirteenth-century cosmographer in the city, working on an obviously unreliable and speculative world map, proposed that Peking lay at 165 degrees 58 minutes to the east, at 46½ degrees north.[19] His method was sound in principle. He used timed eclipses to fix the relative longitudes of places at measurable distances from Florence, and worked outward from there, estimating remoter distances from the spaces they occupied on the map. Toscanelli extended the method, producing a table of estimated longitudes and latitudes with the aim of contributing to a new map of the world based on Ptolemy's principles.

The method Vespucci used to calculate longitude (though commonly said to have been of his own devising or, at least, never applied before his time) was well known in antiquity and the Middle Ages, at least in theory. This was how it worked: It is possible to predict the time at which two celestial bodies will coincide in the sky. Most commonly, observers use the moon and a planet, as these can be observed with the naked eye, and the rapid motion of the moon through the heavens means that such conjunctions occur relatively frequently. For centuries, astronomers amused themselves making tables of such predictions. Vespucci possessed printed copies of famous sets of tables of the kind, compiled at Nuremberg and Toledo. By recording the time when he observed the same conjunction at another place, he could calculate the time difference between that place and Nuremberg or Toledo. Effectively, this would give him his longitude, as difference in time is directly proportionate to difference in longitude.

Alternatively, or by way of confirmation, it was possible in theory to calculate longitude by measuring the difference in degrees between the

position of the moon and another celestial body, relative to the observer, at a given time. This method, which astronomers called the lunar
distance method, was effectively impossible with the technology
Vespucci had at his disposal. No instrument of the time was sufficiently
powerful or well calibrated, no timekeeping device sufficiently exact. In
any case, Amerigo grossly overestimated the speed of the moon's motion through the heavens, so no calculations he made on the basis of
lunar distances could have turned out right except by luck. And to make
matters worse, Amerigo seems not to have known the location for which
his printed tables were compiled. Those for Nuremberg, he took to
apply variously to Ferrara and Cádiz. No wonder, "as for longitude," he
wrote, "I declare that in knowing it I encountered such difficulty that it
was the greatest labour to know for certain the distance I had travelled
in terms of longitude."[20] Despite all these obstacles, some of which he
admitted, Amerigo claimed to be able to certify the distance between
the moon and Mars at a given moment.

That moment occurred on August 23, 1499. The time for the conjunction, according to his tables, was "midnight or half an hour before."
But he could not observe the conjunction directly, since at his position,
it occurred before sunset. So he measured the distance between the
moon and Mars at their first appearance and checked again at midnight,
local time. The measurements were mutually contradictory, yet Amerigo
admitted to no difficulty in reconciling them. He reckoned—on the
basis of these observations, he claimed—that the time difference between his position and that of the meridian of his tables, which at this
stage he associated with Ferrara, was about five and a half hours. He
concluded, rather oddly, that he had traveled, at that point, 82½ degrees
west of Cádiz, which was apparently not one of the places for which he
had tables and which is actually nearly twenty degrees west of the
meridian of the tables Vespucci was using.

Given that there were these alarming inconsistencies in his account,
what were his calculations worth? The method he claimed to have used
depends on exactitude of timing and observation. If he was on board
ship—as the context of the passage suggests—any motion would dis-

turb his timekeeping and his observation of the sky. No navigator who tried this or a similar method at sea before the development of the telescope ever succeeded in obtaining a result that was remotely accurate. Even in stable conditions on land, the method proved fickle and deceptive until well into the eighteenth century, when accurate tables, timekeepers, and telescopes made it practicable. To cap all the perils that would make Vespucci's efforts nugatory, serious inaccuracies by compilers and printers distorted the tables he used.

But where was Vespucci at the time of the conjunction? How did his real longitude compare with the longitude he claimed to have read? Hojeda arrived in Hispaniola on September 5, 1499. Whatever his divagations earlier on the voyage, at that stage, as far as we know, Vespucci was with him; so by that reasoning, on August 23, Amerigo was still on the Coquibacao Peninsula, or not far off it, in the vicinity of Cabo de la Vela. This is about sixty-two degrees, or a little less west of Cádiz. So he was about an hour and a quarter out in his timing. Of course, he may not have been in Hojeda's company at the time of the disputed observation. But even if he was at some other, unidentifiable spot, it can hardly have been much farther west. On the contrary, since he claimed to have spent August within about four to six degrees of the equator, he would, by his own account, have been even closer to the meridian of Cádiz, since the coast trends eastward as it approaches the equator. For Vespucci's figures to be correct, he would have had to be somewhere well out into the Pacific.

After unraveling this cat's cradle of uncertainties and errors, the reader will be relieved to learn that the mystery of how Vespucci arrived at his figures has an easy solution. All his claims to have struggled with the astronomy and mathematics of longitude are flimflam—the prestidigitations of a writer out to blind readers with science. The figure of 82½ degrees arose not from any observations or calculations: Vespucci got it from Columbus, who had miscalculated—grossly—the longitude of eastern Hispaniola by timing a lunar eclipse in 1494.[21] Columbus's figures were wildly inaccurate, but at least he had made some observations to base them on. Without using any readings he might have taken for himself, or perhaps without even taking any readings of his own, Vespucci plucked his figure from his predecessor on the assumption that he was in roughly the same part of the world.[22] The real mystery, it turns out, is not how Vespucci made his calculations but why people believed him. As a result of his claims, he attained the status he sought as an acknowledged magus. He became the most sought-after stargazer in Europe.

Technology accredited him—or, rather, the way he handled it impressed people who watched. Quadrants in Vespucci's day were great, clumsy, lolloping, crudely calibrated objects. There were astrolabes of delicacy and finesse, but they were not suitable for measuring lunar distances. They were designed to be suspended vertically and to measure the angle at which heavenly bodies were subtended above the horizon. To use one for the purpose Amerigo claimed, you would have had to hold it sideways while maintaining a constant point of view. His instruments were a conjurer's toys, useful, no doubt, for cowing impressionable sailors and conning impressionable historians, but of no practical use except display. Handling his quadrant and astrolabe, Vespucci resembled a conjurer rather than a magus—a stage magician distracting his audience with his props. He cannot have made any readings of longitude, and his romantic observations of the southern sky, though important and original, surely owed nothing to prowess in the use of instruments of celestial observation. He was not so much a geek as a pseudogeek, at ease with gadgets most people did not understand. He was the first person to claim to make a reading by the lunar distance method, and his purported attempt preceded the earliest known theoretical publications on the method by some years.[23] But to be meritorious, a claim has to be true.

Vespucci was like a character in a well-known literary conceit of the time: the Ship of Fools. In 1494 Sebastian Brant's famous poem of that name portrayed life as a voyage in a ship stuffed with fools. Hieronymus Bosch painted the scene at about the time Vespucci was at sea. Columbus's first report of his Atlantic crossing surely helped inspire the poet, who saw a German edition through the press. Early editions of Brant's doggerel showed the fools on the title page, about to set sail for Narragonia, the Land of Fools—the first dystopia inspired by the New World. Whatever one thinks of America as a name, it is perhaps as well that Brant's suggestion did not stick.

One of the voyagers in Brant's ship was a cosmographer. An engraving in the original edition shows him struggling to measure the earth with a pair of dividers, while a demon whispers instructions in his ear.

> *Who measures heaven, earth and sea,*
> *Thus seeking lore or gaiety,*
> *Let him beware a fool to be.*[24]

Brant's fool has a lot in common with Vespucci:

> *I do not deem him very wise*
> *Who energetically tries*
> *To probe all cities, every land,*
> *And takes the circle well in hand*
> *That thereby he may well decide*
> *How broad the Earth, how long and wide,*
> *How deep and large the seas expand,*
> *What holds th'extremest part of land,*
> *And how at ends of earth the sea*
> *Clings tight to each extremity,*
> *If round the earth a man can fare,*
> *What men live here, what men live there,*
> *If underneath our feet below*
> *Men walk the nether earth or no,*
> *And how they hold their ground down there,*
> *That they fall not into the air,*
> *And how with rule and compass you*
> *May cut the whole great world in two.*[25]

This satire might have been made for Amerigo.

Nonetheless, the fact that he was an inept navigator at the start of his seafaring career does not mean that he was incapable of improvement in the art. His first voyage was an opportunity for Amerigo to qualify. On his next voyage, he made a remarkably accurate estimate of longitude on land, reckoning the Cape Verde Islands at about six degrees west of the Canaries, which is not far off, if you take meridians through the approximate centers of both archipelagoes.[26] And he gradually accumulated real competence and an exaggerated but widely shared reputation for excellence in the art. Peter Martyr of Anghiera acknowledged him as a capable mariner and astronomer and as the author or inspirer of a map of the world beyond the line. After his death, Amerigo received similar plaudits from experts with no obvious interest in his reputation. Giovanni Vespucci, though his kinsman and protégé, might have been expected to distance himself from his mentor when he got the chance, but he attested that he had often seen his uncle read latitude, and he possessed logs compiled by his distinguished predecessor. Sebastian Cabot, who had no love for Vespucci, swore that Amerigo was "a man well versed in the reading of latitudes."[27] Both testimonies were recorded in pursuit of Castile's dispute with Portugal over the placing of the Tordesillas line.

So the merchant turned mariner became, at least by repute, an expert cosmographer and an authority on the science of navigation. Did he really undergo this sea change, or was it what we now call spin? He certainly displayed new qualities and added a new dimension to his life. His descriptions of his lucubrations with longitude on his second voyage are compelling:

> *Longitude is a harder matter [than latitude] and can be known to few, except to him who remains wakeful and watches the conjunctions of the moon with the planets. For the sake of the said longitude I have lost much sleep and cut ten years from my life. And I count it all well spent, because I hope to achieve long-enduring fame if I return safe from this voyage. May God not judge me proud, for all my travail is directed towards his holy service.*[28]

The seeds of his interest in cosmography were implanted, as we have seen, during his education in Florence. Life in Seville probably focused those ambitions. It is tempting—plenty of historians have succumbed to such temptations—to romanticize ambitions into dreams, as though Vespucci were a preincarnation of Humboldt or William Ernest Henley, led into golden lands by childhood reading. At some point he seems to have bought a map. That may sound unexceptional, but in a period when maps were rare and costly objects, this was an exceptional map. It cost 130 ducats: more than any of the precious paintings Lorenzo the Magnificent kept in his bedchamber. Moreover, it was a sea chart, made in Majorca—where some of the best mapmakers of the late Middle Ages worked—by Gabriel Vallseca, whose work is known from a number of surviving examples. And it showed the Atlantic—not just the Mediterranean or the Atlantic coast of Europe, like most charts of the time, but the broad ocean. Like all Vallseca's output, it was an attempt to depict the world realistically: the cartographic equivalent of a Renaissance painting, with an aesthetic—one could almost say—of realism. It incorporated news of the latest discoveries Portuguese mariners had made in the Atlantic at the time. It includes, for instance, the only surviving evidence of a voyage of 1427 on which a Portuguese pilot established for the first time the true relationship of the Azores to one another; previous efforts had depicted them strung along a north–south axis. It became famous later, when it was back in Majorca and George Sand spilled ink over it during a winter of dalliance with Chopin. But there is no evidence of when Vespucci acquired it. Indeed, the evidence that he did so at all is insecure: just an annotation on the edge of the map in a late-fifteenth- or early-sixteenth-century hand. The assumption that Amerigo bought it in Florence during his youth was a canard of a nineteenth-century biographer.[29] The map, if it can be linked with Vespucci, cannot be linked with the chronology of his career. But it does perhaps have a place in the context of his growing vocation for the sea, his growing ambition to explore.

TRANSFER TO PORTUGAL

After divagations beyond the equator, the section of the fleet Vespucci was in returned to rejoin Hojeda. The vague chronology of the surviving accounts does not permit certainty. But Vespucci's descriptions of battles with natives sufficiently resembled those of Hojeda and other participants to make it reasonably sure that they took part in these together. (The guarantee is not absolute, since Vespucci could have based part of his account not on his own experiences but on fellow travelers' reports.) Hojeda's concern, once he had failed to establish proprietary rights in the pearl fisheries, was to stake a claim on the discovery of Coquibacao, the coast from Cape Cordero to Cabo de la Vela. In 1501 the monarchs assigned him this area to explore further with the title of governor of Coquibacao. As a result of this dallying, by the time the vessels turned away from the coast, they were riddled with teredos and they had to take refuge in Hispaniola.

Vespucci does not seem to have stayed with Hojeda, who devoted some months, perhaps as many as six, to fomenting discontent among Columbus's outposts, squabbling violently with Columbus's men, and raiding for slaves. Vespucci went home to realize the proceeds of pearls bartered cheaply from natives—fourteen of them "which would greatly please the queen"[30] and at least 1,000 ducats' worth, which, by later admission, he obtained for himself. Though he contrived to do well for himself, not all of Vespucci's shipmates were equally lucky. The voyage had been cheap to outfit, but as a collective enterprise, it was still barely profitable: It yielded 500 ducats, divided among all the survivors, or— what amounted to almost the same total—190,000 *maravedíes* in the unit of account then current in Castile. This is Vespucci's estimate and seems consistent with the partial accounts that survive, which show returns of at least 120,000 *maravedíes,* and which are probably incomplete.[31]

This was insufficient to cover the costs of the voyage. The promoters therefore seized two hundred natives as slaves to recoup their costs. Crammed aboard the returning vessels, thirty-two died on the voyage. But the prospect of greater riches still beckoned in the form of more pearls, if a way of exploiting the fishery could be organized, to say nothing of the other gemstones Vespucci vaguely described, of bright but perhaps deceptive appearance. Amerigo paid a price of his own, for he ended the voyage stricken with fevers. But, he wrote, "I hope in God soon to recover, because they do not last long and I do not get the shivers."[32]

At the end of the report on his first voyage, Vespucci claimed that he was about to be entrusted with another mission, with three ships. Instead, we find him leaving Spain within a few months and taking service in Portugal. There was nothing dishonorable about this. Explorers, like scholars and artists, went wherever patronage was available. Vespucci's explanation was that he responded to an invitation from the king of Portugal. Since he was, as far as we know, the only participant in his previous voyage to report frankly the discovery of land in the zone of navigation assigned to Portugal by treaty, that is not an improbable claim. Moreover, Vespucci's account of the existence of such land was confirmed independently by Portuguese navigators in May 1500, when Pedro Álvares Cabral, bound for Calicut in India, penetrated deep into the South Atlantic in search of the westerlies that would bear him around the Cape of Good Hope. He stumbled on Brazil in the process.

Meanwhile, for Vespucci, whatever the attractions of Portugal, Castile was becoming a problematic haven. In 1499 a wave of revulsion against foreigners swept the kingdom. Columbus was one of the victims, for that was the year of the beginning of his disgrace—"blamed," he said, "as a poor foreigner." Others who suffered included many of the Genoese of Seville. Amerigo's old associate Francesco da Rivarolo was among those subjected to fines and more or less arbitrary confiscations of property.[33] While Vespucci was still away on his first voyage, the monarchs banned further participation by foreigners in Atlantic exploration. A voyage departing in August 1500 was forbidden to foreigners.[34] The belief that Vespucci was the intended victim of this measure surely overstates his importance. He was a bystander caught up in events greater than an individual could have caused.

In the circumstances, Portugal was an obvious place of refuge. The

Florentine connection helped. The colony in Lisbon was bigger and more influential than Seville's. When Vespucci inherited Berardi's business, Lorenzo di Pierfrancesco de' Medici's was not his only account. Berardi also represented Bartolomeo Marchionni, the biggest Florentine banker in Lisbon, who had been instrumental in arranging the financial backing for Portuguese ventures in the Indian Ocean.

So, toward the end of 1500 or very early in 1501, Vespucci headed for Lisbon. But the capacity in which the king took him into Portuguese service remains unclear. And the purpose, nature, and command structure of the voyage on which he set sail in 1501 are all uncertain. It is reasonable to suppose that the main object was to follow up Pedro Álvares Cabral's report of land he named Vera Cruz in what we now call Brazil. That was the assumption of most of the Portuguese chroniclers who had access to documents now lost. One of Cabral's pilots, moreover, recorded an encounter at sea on their way home, off the Cape Verde Islands, toward the end of May 1501, with a fleet that must have been Vespucci's, "which our king of Portugal commanded to explore the new land."[35] Vespucci himself reported the same meeting on June 4 to Lorenzo di Pierfrancesco and immediately noted the conclusion that the land Cabral had touched in the New World was "the same land that I discovered for the king of Castile, except that it is more to the east."[36]

Now, though never remarked, this is a most curious fact. Vespucci was on an expedition to reconnoiter land Cabral had discovered, yet he confided Cabral's news to his patron as if it were a newly released novelty. Can it be that he did not know the purpose of the expedition on which he was embarked? Or had he some deep and now inscrutable motive for alerting his patron to the discovery, while concealing the lateness of his report? Anyway, Vespucci's conclusion that "his" land and Cabral's were the same was correct, albeit riskily so, since he could not have known that the coast was continuous between the point at which he left it and the point that Cabral touched.

On this occasion, Vespucci did not claim to be in command. On the contrary, he took the opportunity in later writings to denounce the unnamed commander for incompetence. In another printed account of the voyage, published under Vespucci's name, the editors inserted a dramatic interlude in which the crew elected Vespucci to replace the commander: That was presumably a fantasy inspired by Vespucci's obvious contempt for his superior officer. Nor did Vespucci represent himself as a professional navigator. He went along as a passenger, like da Mosto in his day, or as the representative of some mercantile interest, such as that of the Florentine bankers in Lisbon who probably backed the voyage (most of the finance for Portuguese exploration in this period that we know about came from those sources). This time, however, when Amerigo flourished his quadrant and astrolabe, he did so with a little more practice than formerly, and therefore to somewhat more effect.

From independent evidence, we can be sure that the voyage happened. Its return was recorded—according to the Venetian ambassador in Portugal—on July 22, 1502. The ambassador packed a remarkable amount of detail into a few lines: "The captain says he has explored more than 2,500 miles of new coast, without ever reaching its end, and the said caravels arrived laden with brasil wood and cassia; nor did they find any other spices."[37] Brazilwood was the source of dye with which the coastal forest abounds. Cassia was an inferior condiment resembling cinnamon: It does not seem to have grown in the region the expedition visited. One can almost sense the relief the ambassador exhaled as he reported that the Portuguese had found nothing better, since Venice's prosperity depended on the city's privileged access to eastern Mediterranean markets in exotic spices traded across the Indian Ocean. If they were available more accessibly and more cheaply on the western shore of the Atlantic, Venice might lose business.

The rest of what we know about the voyage derives from Vespucci's own narratives and from chroniclers—and, some scholars believe, mapmakers—who seem to have depended on his information. As ever with material originating in Amerigo's mind, fact and fiction are hard to disentangle. The first version Vespucci wrote is clearly the most reliable. It was his report addressed to Lorenzo di Pierfrancesco, "my magnificent patron," as the writer says. Unlike subsequent versions, it was never printed and shows few signs of being prepared for the press. The surviving manuscript bears no evidence of interpolation or distortion by any editorial hand. But obscurities occlude it, and contradictions scar it. We have to make the best sense of it we can.

The expedition followed Cabral's route via the Cape Verde Islands. From there, it was a long crossing—sixty-four days—on a course west-southwest (*alla quarta di libeccio ver ponente*). If true, this would make it the most arduous crossing on record in the sixteenth century. Cabral took only twenty-eight days. Landfall occurred, by Vespucci's reckoning, 800 leagues from the islands. This was obviously another of the wishful overestimates of an explorer who wanted to believe he was getting close to Asia: 600 leagues, or 2,400 miles, is the maximum imaginable.

No attempt to place the landfall carries conviction. Cape São Roque roughly fits the latitude of five degrees south mentioned in a later version of Vespucci's account. Praia dos Marcos, near Três Irmãos in Rio Grande do Norte, has been suggested on the basis of otherwise unexplained markers that Vespucci's expedition might have erected there.[38] Some authors have professed to see nearby Punto Calcanhar as the place Vespucci describes. But his description was typically vague: The spot was full of inhabitants and "marvellous works of God and Nature."[39]

The expedition continued coastwise, entering, said Vespucci, "the torrid zone"—an unsettling turn of phrase, since by his account so far, he had been in the torrid zone, which lay between the tropics, throughout his crossing of the ocean. They crossed the equator and the Tropic of Capricorn, exploring the coast as far as what Vespucci reckoned to be thirty-two degrees south.[40] To know how far the explorers really got, maps are one recourse. But they are a snare and a delusion. There are, at most, five surviving maps of the New World that might have been made between Vespucci's return and the publication in 1504 of a fictionalized account of the voyage that plunged readers and interpreters into confusion. Only one map definitely dates from the right period. This is the beautiful Cantino map, purchased in Lisbon on November 19, 1502, by the ambassador of the duke of Ferrara. Even if all the maps could be dated securely to the right time, there is no guarantee that their representations of the coast of the New World were made on the basis of any independent information. They could rely, like many subsequent maps, on Vespucci's own accounts or data ascribed to him. The Cantino map does seem to include what, to the cartographer, was the latest information about Brazil, but it is based entirely, it seems, on Cabral's voyage.

The other maps are effectively useless for the present purpose. If they take account of Vespucci's claims at all, they simply illustrate the printed report of Vespucci's voyage and therefore cannot fairly be said to confirm it. By the time they were made, at least one more Portuguese voyage of reconnaissance had coasted Brazil and extended knowledge beyond the limits of the reach of Vespucci's expedition. In any case, once one corrects for the distortion that is pretty well systematic, none of the maps places the farthest south known to navigators on the South American coast—the spot called Cananor in most of the maps—much below twenty-five degrees south.[41] A credible solution to the problem of the relationship between the voyage and the maps is that the cartographers' work reflects access to another—perhaps official—narrative of the voyage, which included some of the same place-names as appear in the printed versions of Vespucci's account, but was less prone to exaggeration.[42]

The explorers reached even farther south on the open sea. They were out of sight of the Pole Star and the Great and Little Bear for nine months and twenty-seven days in all. Rhapsodical but unhelpful assurances follow from Vespucci about the beauty, clarity, and diversity of the stars in the southern sky. "In conclusion," he claimed, "I went to the region of the Antipodes, so that my navigation spanned one quarter of the world." He seems to have meant—to judge from the clarification offered in the *Mundus Novus*—that the distance between his farthest north and farthest south represents a quarter of the circumference of the globe. Lisbon, he said, was nearly forty degrees north, and he had sailed from there to fifty degrees south, making ninety degrees in all.[43]

The seeds of future errors are here. When Vespucci claimed to have "discovered a fourth part of the world," what he meant was that his navigations had covered ninety degrees of the earth's circumference. But as three continents—Europe, Asia, Africa—were known to geographers at the time, who called them parts of the world, a "fourth part" meant, to them, a fourth continent. For Vespucci, the claim to have discovered a new continent was a further, separate claim. In invoking the Antipodes, he was, as we shall see, joining an even more arcane and complex debate. Amerigo's zealous attempts to calculate how much of the circumference of the earth he had covered are recognizable as an innocent form of vanity. I expect many readers, like me, amuse and flatter themselves by marking their routes on street maps when they visit unfamiliar cities, in much the same spirit.

I suspect, too, that Vespucci was once again consciously imitating, and perhaps emulating, the achievements Sir John Mandeville proudly claimed. Mandeville explained that the world is divisible in two hemispheres. "Of the one part I saw a part to the north as far as sixty-two degrees ten minutes, under the Arctic Pole." This sounds impressive, but one must take the waywardness of his putative readings into account: By his calculations, he would have been in southern Belgium at this point in his supposed travels.

And of the other to the south I saw thirty-three degrees sixteen minutes. This adds up to four score and fifteen degrees and a half. So there want only four score and four and a half degrees, for me to have seen all the firmament. The quarter of it contains four score and ten degrees. And so I have seen three parts of it, and nearly five and a half degrees more.[44]

Still, even if literary tradition influenced Vespucci in this connection, his judgment that he had penetrated to fifty degrees south is also striking. If we are right in dismissing as a slip or a wild assertion his claim to have exceeded sixty degrees south on a previous voyage, no other navigator got so far until Magellan in 1520. Even Mandeville, who also affected expertise with an astrolabe but recorded exclusively nonsensical readings, claimed to have reached only thirty-three degrees, and we may suspect that Vespucci was out to break his supposed record.

How reliable was Vespucci's assessment? He was on the open sea at the time he took the relevant reading. This fact, strongly implied in his earliest surviving narrative of the voyage, was explicitly confirmed in a later letter.[45] He did not explain how he took this reading. Perhaps it was an extrapolation from the position of the sun. It cannot have been another copyist's error, as the printed tradition, which was based on manuscripts now lost, repeats the claim; furthermore, the claim was echoed—indeed, exceeded—by a celebrated Moravian geographer in Lisbon, known to the Portuguese as Valentim Fernandes, who, in a deposition of 1503 or 1504, mentioned a Portuguese fleet that found and baptized numerous inhabitants along 760 leagues of coastline in the region discovered by Cabral. "At length turning south it reached as far as 53 degrees towards the elevation of the Antarctic pole, and, having found extreme cold at sea, returned to the homeland."[46] An interesting and unremarked feature is that although Vespucci never claimed to have baptized anybody on his second voyage, such a claim is associated with his first voyage in a fictionalized printed version.[47] So although Valentim Fernandes may have gotten the details wrong, he clearly had access to some information, now lost, generated by Vespucci's voyages.

The only explanation that makes any sense—admittedly, not a great deal—is that, having explored part of the coast, the fleet turned southeast and headed for the depths of the South Atlantic. It sounds an odd proceeding and was incompatible with Vespucci's project of finding a westward route to Asia. Vespucci, however, was not in command. Whoever was in command knew that at the place mapmakers called Cananor, he had reached the limit of navigation assigned to Portugal. That may be enough to account for his failure to explore more of the coast. Alternatively, the decision to strike into the Atlantic was consistent with the usual Portuguese approach to the Indian Ocean.

If, as Vespucci claims, they lost sight of the Great Bear, they must have been beyond twenty-six degrees south. But the fleet can hardly have gotten as far as fifty or, much less, fifty-three degrees south: It would have encountered the Roaring Forties on the way. As for Valentim Fernandes's picturesque detail about the cold, it can suggest only that the sailors were, in that connection, oversensitive, or that a literary topos was at work. As we shall see, Vespucci would know or expect from his reading that the extreme south of the world would be cold.

To judge from the report Vespucci wrote for Lorenzo di Pierfrancesco de' Medici at the end of the voyage, he expected to go on working for the king of Portugal. Instead, he quickly returned to Spain in evident dudgeon. Why? One of the oddest myths about Amerigo is that he was a disinterested explorer. In a sense, it was a myth he believed in, or at least professed, himself. Mindful, perhaps, of Dante's Ulysses, who "burned with desire to become knowledgeable about the world,"[48] Vespucci traveled simply, as he once put it, "to see the world."[49] Or, on his second voyage, he claimed, "we journeyed for the sake of making discoveries, and not to seek any profit."[50] He also admitted to the lust for fame. Of course, there was more to it than that. He remained a salesman even when he became a sorcerer, an exploiter even while he was an explorer. He never lost sight of the hope of reward or the chance of profit. He moralized at need about "profit, which is that which nowadays people esteem so much, especially in this kingdom [of Spain] where inordinate greed rules without restraint."[51] He remained hardheaded, businesslike, with an eye to the main chance.

Piero Rondinelli, a former competitor of the firm of Berardi and Vespucci, recorded some of Amerigo's self-revelatory gossip in a letter from Seville in October 1502. It is the first in a series of documents that reveal Vespucci as, in one respect, a typical explorer of the period. Like Columbus, like all the many adventurers who plied the Castilian and Portuguese courts with claims for rewards, Vespucci was a whinger, jealous of the profits of his endeavors. Rondinelli absorbed his hard-luck story; later, Columbus would endorse a similar story. Vespucci was down on his luck. He had "endured hardships enough and got little recompense." He deserved better. The king of Portugal had farmed his discoveries out to Jewish converts—this was a term, rather like "fascists" nowadays, invoked to invite disapproval. The Jews had only a minimal rent to pay. They could take slaves and "perhaps will find some other source of profit."[52]

Some whingers can get mired in their own sense of failure. Vespucci was one of the other kind: those whose dissatisfactions inspire them to change. That, I think, is why he was a permanent makeover candidate, always making wild and risky career moves. In returning to Spain, he made another. Before we follow him there, we need to pause to look at the career as a self-publicist that he pursued in tandem with his life as an explorer. For as far as possible, we have seen what Vespucci did on his Atlantic travels. More interesting, perhaps, from a biographical point of view is what he thought he did: what he saw, how he perceived it, and what was going on in his mind. Those are the subjects to which we have to turn. They require, first, a fairly laborious excursion among the sources.

CHAPTER FOUR

THE SPELLBINDER'S BOOKS

Inside Amerigo's Mind, 1500–1504 ∘ *Literary peripeties*

ORRUPT SOURCES BEDEVIL the history of exploration. More than any other kind of history, the genre depends on maps and autobiographical narratives: documents peculiarly prone to distortion, misrepresentation, emendation, and forgery.

The structure of the book and map trade favors modern forgers, who have made fortunes by cunning falsification. The Vinland map, purportedly a fifteenth-century record of Norse Atlantic crossings, deceived some of the leading authorities when it first came to light. Yale University spent an undisclosed fortune to acquire it. Yet in retrospect, it seems incredible that anyone could have been deceived by the map or that there are still parties who believe in its authenticity. Its provenance is unverifiable and its form inconsistent with every genuine, known cartographic product of the period. The case of Columbus has generated some of the most spectacular and silly scams of all time, including a logbook he supposedly wrote in English, which appeared mysteriously just in time for the vendor to cash in on the four hundredth anniversary of Columbus's first transatlantic voyage. The fact that it was headed "My Secret Log Boke" did not stop the publisher who handled it from producing an edition on imitation parchment, bound in imitation sheepskin.[1] A map of Hispaniola, supposedly from Columbus's own hand, which the duchess of Alba bought at about the same time as the logbook scam, has continued to appear as an illustration in most picture books about the admiral ever since, in sublime indifference to the fact that it was forged. A long series of forgeries purporting to be manuscripts of Columbus's first account of the New World were already in circulation. When the New York Public Library rejected one, the vendor tore it up and flung it in a bin, from where the retrieved fragments, carefully reconstituted, became a curiosity of the collection.[2] Just in time for the five hundredth anniversary, the Spanish government paid a Barcelona bookseller 67 million pesetas for a previously unknown manuscript—purportedly a copy of a collection of documents from Columbus's hands. The provenance of this document has still not been made public, and though many reputable scholars rushed to hail the supposedly new source, there is every reason to be suspicious of it.

Modern forgers are, in a sense, in a respectable tradition. Explorers themselves, and their contemporary editors, publishers, and translators, have always been notoriously cavalier with facts. Self-interest, self-obsession, self-recommendation, self-delusion, and outright lies warp explorers' narratives, because they are autobiography, and autobiography is the most impassioned, poisoned kind of art. Exaggeration is the least of the common sins of the genre.

No one except a fool, as Dr. Johnson said, writes for anything except money. Travel literature suffers from the vice of all popular writing: It has to be sensational if it is to sell. Inside every travel writer lurks a Baron Münchhausen, tempted to tease and test his readers' credulity. Publishers cluster at his elbows, like imps of mammon, making editorial "improvements." In the late Middle Ages and the early modern period, these often consisted of gross distortions designed to make books more salable: what would now be called "dumbing down"—the editing out of anything deemed too learned—accompanied "writing up": the inclusion of imaginary or plagiarized episodes to add spice to a narrative excessively inhibited by truth.

The Sirens in the Sources

Tradition hallowed distortion. Medieval travel books were hardly complete without what readers, writers, and publishers called "mirabilia"—prodigies, monsters, enchantments, fabulous people and places, freaks of climate and topography. This was especially true from the twelfth century onward: Paradoxically, perhaps, the revival of classical learning restored faith in monsters, which Greek and Roman writers celebrated but some Christian authors in preceding centuries had doubted. Pliny the Elder, the most copious ancient writer on natural history, helped create an atmosphere of prejudice in favor of belief in the existence of monstrous "simulacra of humankind." "Where people who live far beyond the sea are concerned," he argued reasonably,

> *I have no doubt, that some facts will appear monstrous, and, indeed, incredible to many. For who could ever believe in the existence of black people, before he actually saw them? Indeed is there anything that does not seem marvellous, when first we hear about it? How many things are judged impossible, until they are judged to be facts?*[3]

A long list of monsters followed these wise remarks, including the Arimaspi, each with one eye in his or her forehead; the Nasamones, all of whom were hermaphrodites; the Megasthenes, whose eight-toed feet were turned backward; the dog-headed Cynocephali; the single-footed Sciapods; the Troglodytes, with "no necks and eyes in their shoulders"; the hairy, barking Choromandae; the mouthless Astomi, who took nourishment by inhaling; tailed men; and men who could enfold themselves in their enormous ears. Pliny also endorsed belief in various races of giants and anthropophagi, which Vespucci would later claim to confirm from personal observation. "Nature," Pliny concluded, "in her ingenuity, has created all these marvels in the human race, with others of a similar nature, as so many amusements to herself, though they appear miraculous to us."

Mythical marvels worked their way into fictional travelogues. Readers expected and therefore demanded them. To keep up with the appeal of fiction, the writers and publishers of real travel literature had to borrow some of the same material or embellish their work with inventions of their own. Mythic episodes common in medieval versions of the story of Alexander the Great included discoveries of the Fountain of Youth and the Earthly Paradise and encounters with griffins, Amazons, and mouthless folk. All occurred as embellishments in otherwise essentially factual narrative. They appeared, for instance, as fanciful additions in the reminiscences of Marco Polo, one of the most commercially successful travel writers of the age. Marco was largely veracious, but critics called him *Il milione*, which might perhaps be translated as "Mr. Million" or "the man of a million stories," because of exaggerations that he or his editors incorporated to make the work more appealing. Even the real marvels of China seemed incredible to Western readers, but most surviving versions of Marco's book included accounts of dog-headed men, islands of bald people, and isles inhabited respectively by men and women who came together only to breed. Fables from the Alexander romances recurred alongside what may be factual episodes in the most successful travel book of the Middle Ages, and one of Vespucci's personal favorites: the fourteenth-century *Travels of Sir John Mandeville*, which is so full of tall stories, sensationalist prodigies, ironies, jokes, and rhetorical tricks that most modern readers think it must all be fiction.

In short, the genres of romance, travel, and hagiography were so interpenetrated that it was hard to tell fancy from fact. Readers believed romantic elements in real travelogues and mistook fictional for historical work. We know this because they sometimes included passages from fiction in what they supposed to be accurate accounts, on a par with reliable documents, and occasionally reproduced whole fables as true narratives. The English Elizabethan magus John Dee mistook romances of King Arthur, in which that legendary monarch conquered Russia, Greenland, Lapland, and the North Pole, as evidence of the existence of an ancient British maritime empire. His Portuguese contemporary António Galvão was so convinced of the veracity of a fourteenth-century novel about an Atlantic navigator that he included it in his history of the Portuguese empire, and it has remained embedded in authoritative works of reference ever since.[4]

Delusion and self-deceit also played a part in inspiring travel writers. Reading and fancy distort the perceptions of well-read and inventive travelers. They see things that are not really there except in imagination or memory. Columbus was a rude autodidact by comparison with Vespucci, but his writings were still full of artifice—a diviner's fire aflame with fantasy and visions. When he described his discoveries, he cataloged hybrid trees that never existed anywhere, and a profusion of flora and fauna such as Eden can hardly have contained. He heard song-birds in midocean and glimpsed a ghostly, white-robed figure flitting between the trees of a Cuban forest. Historians have driven themselves to distraction by reading his narratives of his voyages as if they were precise logbooks that describe a real route, and trying to use them to work out where he made his first landfall in the New World. The writings are better understood as a kind of poetry that does not yield exact data.

Much of the misunderstanding that vitiates readings of such sources arises from three errors. First, it is a mistake to distinguish history from literature. History is a kind of literature; literature is a source for history. Second, once you err by dividing history from literature, you compound the error by assigning the explorers' narratives to the former category. They usually fit better into the latter. Finally, it is vital to remember that writing on the sea comes soaked in its own traditions, in which the ocean is a divine arena where fortune changes with the wind, and the stars, according to astrological lore, are divine messengers.

It is not that seafarers are particularly unreliable in reminiscence. Everyone's memory is an impure medium. Whenever we record or retrieve memories of real experience, the fire of the synapses brands our brains with extraneous images from art and letters; the flood of proteins washes in exaggerations and errors from outside.[5] And we tend to fuse what really happened to us with what we have read or dreamed or heard. That happened to Vespucci. When he related his experiences, he filtered them through his reading.

THE MELDER OF TALES

To sort out the fact from the fiction in Vespucci's writings is therefore a work of critical literary exploration. Like a discoverer striking out—as Vespucci did, say, on one of his voyages—into forbidding, stormy, and chilly seas, we have to make an excursion among the sources. Readers with no stomach for this stage of the journey do not have to jump ship. They can simply skip the chapter. But I urge them to stay on watch. Navigating a channel among the documents is, after all, the only way of getting ahead, and though I cannot make this odyssey as exciting as the best seafarers' yarns, there are plenty of whirlpools and sirens and spectacular rocks—in the form of forgeries, misreadings, historic confusions, and misleading prejudices—to keep passengers engaged along the way. The subject is inseparable from the quest to know what Amerigo was like. The most dangerous rocks in his wake are those he strew for the unwary scholar, and the most enticing, bewildering whirlpools are those of his own mind.

When we read Vespucci's accounts of his escapades, we should have his literary education and leanings in our thoughts. In his own mind, he was a writer, and it was the province of a writer to embellish the truth with artifice. He was not bound by an historian's conscience: The tradition in which he wrote valued rhetoric above information. When, for example, Vespucci or his editor indulged in prurient accounts of sexual hospitality, we should willingly believe that a writer of Vespucci's background and sensibilities could be that gross. The texts here followed a convention established by Marco Polo, who filled many readers' minds at the time.[6] Marco Polo was a sort of male Scheherazade whose role, when he lived in China, was to collect entertaining tales about the empire for the delectation of the Great Khan. As we shall see in the next chapter, the *Travels of Sir John Mandeville* also seems to have gone on echoing inside Vespucci's head, especially when he encountered people in his New World.

As well as the travel literature, chiefly represented in Vespucci's reading by *Mandeville* and Marco Polo, three kinds of literature are worth considering for their possible influence: chivalric romance, hagiography, and poetry. Although, unlike Columbus, Vespucci made no clear allusions to chivalric romance and hagiography, the genres were ubiquitous in his day. The best procedure is to look in turn at each of the three types. The poetry, which was most obviously influential, is the place to start, for works of Petrarch and Dante were well known to Vespucci, and he quoted them or dropped allusions to them readily.

Dante was the source of many of the mirabilia Amerigo recorded. Or rather, in the tradition Vespucci received, Dante handed them on from models originating in antiquity. At one point in his travels, Amerigo reported an island of giants off the coast of Brazil. In describing giants, he recalled the myth of the giant Anteus—not, solely or principally, one suspects, the classical story of Antaeus, the compulsive homicide whose strength derived from the earth, but Dante's elaboration of the tale, in which the giant, "tall as a ship's mast," guarded the ninth circle of hell and urged Dante's narrator on to the discovery of a sea of ice.[7] So Vespucci may well have felt the cold Valentim Fernandes attributed to him as he sailed deep into the southern hemisphere—but perhaps, in his mind rather than in his body.

The island of women, which Vespucci also reported, was a common enough topos. Presumably, the notion derived from an episode in the tale of Jason and the Golden Fleece. When the Argonauts arrived at Lemnos, they found that the women had murdered their menfolk in revenge for their husbands' adultery with women of a neighboring island. The story blended with that of the Amazons, who were not generally regarded as island dwellers in antiquity, but whom Diodorus Siculus, in the first century B.C., located on an island. The inference that there was a parallel island of men, with whom the Amazons periodically got together in order to breed, goes back at least to the Muslim geographer al-Idrisi, who worked in Sicily in the twelfth century. Marco Polo claimed to have heard of such a pair of islands. So did Columbus. Mandeville gave one of the most comprehensive accounts available, calling the Amazons "noble and wise," even though they had, he admitted, achieved independence by slaughtering their menfolk and preserved it by abandoning or killing their male children. Misogynistic irony was surely intended in this black-comic account.[8] When Vespucci mentioned the story, it perhaps recalled Penthesilea, the fabled Amazon queen whom Dante met in *Purgatory,* and who also provided Amerigo's model for describing the women on the island of giants.

Dante's versions of myth evidently stuck in Vespucci's head. No myth meant more to the explorer than that of Ulysses, the model seafarer. Dante's Ulysses was different from others. The poet made him say, for instance, that there were no people beyond the pillars of Hercules.[9] In Vespucci's mental world, this echoed conventional, ancient geographical orthodoxies that he was proud to have helped disprove. But Dante's Ulysses was a far richer, more significant, and deeply ironic figure for Vespucci. As so often with Dante's adaptations of classical figures, his Ulysses traveled further than tradition took him. He made a new voyage, eerily prefiguring those of Vespucci, beyond the pillars of Hercules, turning southward beyond the equator. His presumption incurred divine wrath. "Out of the unknown land there blew foul weather, / And a whirlwind struck the forepart of the ship."[10] Just before he died, he glimpsed the Earthly Paradise.

He died on a quest resembling Vespucci's, in an imaginary geography Vespucci carried with him in his mind. Amerigo could never escape its influence, even had he wanted to. He kept hearing echoes and seeing images of Dante, and especially of Dante's depiction of Ulysses's voyage, as he sailed under the southern sky and along previously unknown coasts. When he left Seville, he was reenacting the lines

> *da la man destra mi lasciai Sibilia,*
> *da l'altra già m'avea lasciata Setta,*

> *O frati! dissi, che per cento milia*
> *perigli siete giunti a l'occidente,*
> *a questa tanto piccola vigilia*
> *di nostri sensi ch'è del rimanente*

non vogliate negar l'esperienza,
di retro al sol, del mondo senza gente.

To starboard I left Seville gliding by,
While on the portside Ceuta slid by me.

"O brothers, who a million risks," said I,
"Have braved to gather on the western sea,
The voyage of life is brief. So dare
to add experience of something more:
Of lands beyond the sunset's glare
Where none have ever gone before."

When he was south of the equator, Vespucci relived Ulysses's vision, glimpsing stars of the "other pole" while the familiar sky sank below the horizon.[11] And the whirlpool that sucked Dante's Ulysses to his death struck just when the hero was in sight of the Earthly Paradise— the mountain beyond experience, "rising to endless heights."

Petrarch, whom Vespucci also cited, and whom every educated Tuscan read, relished Dante's conceit and turned the metaphor of the quest beyond the pillars of Hercules into a motif of his own life. "Ulysses," he declared, "travelled no more and no further than I."[12] Petrarch meant that metaphorically. Vespucci could echo the same sentiment in earnest and with pride.

Petrarch was an armchair traveler. But his work was saturated in brine. His life—as he wrote of it—was a voyage. Shipwrecks happen repeatedly; drowning threatens, though the poet never quite goes under.[13] When Vespucci cites Petrarch's crusading poem, "O aspettata in ciel," it is just what one would expect from Vespucci and more. The phrase he quotes concerns the missile weapons of barbarous people Petrarch postulates on the eastern edge of the inhabited world: "*colpi commette al vento*"—literally, "blows sent on the wind"—comes embedded in a passage that is programmatic for the course of Vespucci's career:

ecco novellamente a la tua barca,
ch'al cieco mondo ha già volte le spalle
per gir al miglior porto,
d'un vento occidental dolce conforto;
lo qual per mezzo questa oscura valle,
ove piangiamo il nostro et l'altrui torto,
la condurrà de' lacci antichi sciolta,
per drittissime calle,
al verace orïente ov'ella è volta.

Una parte del mondo è che si giace
mai sempre in ghiaccio et in gelate nevi
tutta lontana dal camin del sole:
là sotto i giorni nubilosi et brevi,
nemica naturalmente di pace,
nasce una gente a cui il morir non dole.
Questa se, più devota che non sòle,
col tedesco furor la spada cigne,
turchi, arabi et caldei,
con tutti quei che speran nelli dèi
di qua dal mar che fa l'onde sanguigne,
quanto sian da prezzar, conoscer déi:
popolo ignudo paventoso et lento,
che ferro mai non strigne,
ma tutt'i colpi suoi commette al vento.

Feel how at last your boat has turned its back
decisively upon the world that's blind,
to make its track
with solace sweet, borne on a western wind,
which, soaring through the midst of this dark vale,
where we lament how we and others sinned,
will bear us, blowing all that we bewail—

no need to tack—
to our true East, which this wind's bound to find.

There is a region of the world that lies,
in darkness wrapped and swathed in frozen snows,
forever far removed from sunshine's rays:
the days are short there, under cloudy skies.
And peace is natural enemy to those,
born there, whom deadly perils do not faze.
If faith transformed their unenlightened ways,
if taught, like Teutons, to inflict sword-blows,
we soon should know how highly to appraise
Turks, Arabs, Persians, all the pagan crew,
who all from sea to sea with blood bedew;
or idle, fearful peoples, all bare-skinned,
who ne'er with iron weapons cut or hew
but shoot their missiles through the gusting wind.

The first of these stanzas provides sailing directions to the Earthly Paradise. The second is presumably based on some romantic source about the Lapps or Finns: Tacitus sketched them into his account of northern peoples in mythic terms, stressing their savagery and innocence.[14] In the eleventh century, Adam of Bremen, the best-informed medieval writer on Scandinavia, fortified the myth, praising the moral qualities of hardy northerners who "despise gold and silver as dung."[15] Vespucci could reasonably expect to find similar peoples in corresponding latitudes in the southern hemisphere. In claiming that some natives were baptized on one of his expeditions, he or his editors echoed Petrarch's program of converting such people to Christianity and recruiting them for crusades.

Petrarch addressed the Holy Spirit. The voyage he described was obviously, glaringly metaphorical. But metaphors resonate in the mind and reemerge as projects. Real and spiritual journeys mutually elide. Every voyage is an opportunity at least for self-discovery, even if it yields no geographical novelties. In many mythologies, the soul is a ship or is

Lettera di Amerigo vespucci delle isole nuouamente trouate in quattro suoi viaggi.

The printer of the *Soderini Letter* recycled the title and title-page picture
from a 1493 edition of the first printed report of Columbus.

Pietro Vaglienti, who collected news of commercially exploitable discoveries
for one of the merchant houses of Florence, compiled materials concerning
Vespucci within two or three years of the explorer's death, including this
copy of Amerigo's letter written off the Cape Verde Islands while on his
way back from Brazil, in June 1501.

The most influential sixteenth-century image of Vespucci shows him
as a magus, equipped with cosmographical instruments, his eyes fixed,
Christ-like, on the heavens while his crew slumbers, like the disciples
at Gethsemane.

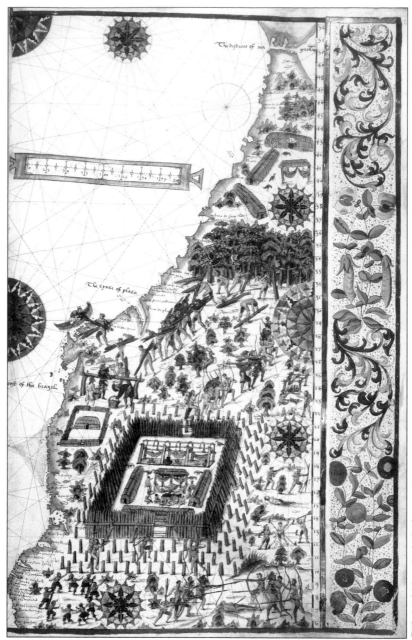

A map made in Dieppe reflects the accurate reports of Tupi life that
French woodcutters brought home in the years after Vespucci's visit
to Brazil.

An illustrator in 1525 assimilated Vespucci's cannibals into the dog-headed monsters fabled in classical antiquity that were sought—and sometimes supposedly sighted—by medieval explorers.

"Here are the new-found People." The Leipzig 1505 edition of *Mundus Novus* emphasizes the nudity and bellicosity of the people Vespucci described, but not their cannibalism.

Though originally published as a stand-alone picture, this woodcut of 1505 clearly illustrates Vespucci's version of Tupi life.

The 1507 world map of St. Dié displays an image of Vespucci at the top, in a position equivalent to that of Ptolemy, reputedly the greatest geographer of antiquity. The image Amerigo displays shows a continuous American land mass—contrasting with the main map, in which the New World is punctuated by a strait leading toward Asia.

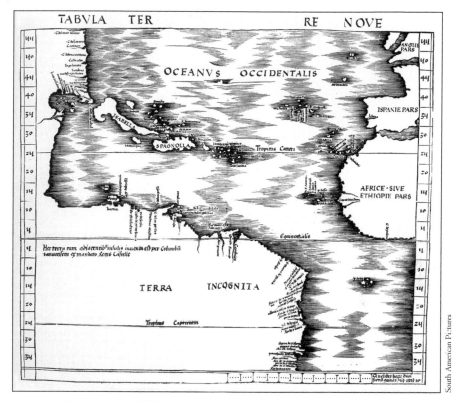

In his 1513 map, Waldseemüller withdrew his endorsement of Vespucci, renaming the New World "Unknown Land" and attributing its discovery to Columbus.

"All this province was found by command of the King of Castile":
Waldseemüller's cartouche of 1507 shows the strait Columbus sought
bisecting the New World.

shipborne to its resting place. Even a mind like Vespucci's, which seems in adulthood to have preserved no trace of the piety his tutor labored to instill, was susceptible to exaltation by the experience of the sea.

The most sea-soaked saint's life widely read at the time was the *Navigatio Brandani*, a hagiographical work that survives in scores of versions from the tenth century onward, and which probably goes back to a sixth-century prototype. It purports to tell the story of the sea wanderings of a group of monks in search of the Earthly Paradise, or "promised land of the saints."

Irish monks went to impressive extremes in self-imposed penitential wanderings or in search of deserts in which to imitate the isolation of John the Baptist and the tempted Christ. They used vessels constructed along the lines of traditional Irish fishermen's curraghs, made with materials characteristic of a pastoral society: ox hide stretched over light frames and waterproofed with fat and butter, rigged with ox-hide strips. They hoisted only a single square sail to catch the wind, for they traveled in a spirit of penitential exile and consciously entrusted themselves to God. Like Abraham, they were bound not for a target destination of their own choosing but for "a land that I shall show thee." Because they were willing to abandon themselves to wind and current, the monks were inherently more likely to go farther and find more than more purposeful navigators.

Of course, they were also more likely to come to grief or get stranded without hope of return. It seems amazing that their crafts could endure the high seas of the North Atlantic, but the indefatigable explorer Tim Severin tried a reconstruction in the 1980s and reached Newfoundland from Ireland without mishap.[16] It seems possible, at least, that some of the early turf dwellings that archaeology has revealed on Greenland and even on Newfoundland were the work of Irish hermits. Construction methods and materials were common to both the Norse and Irish traditions.

Brendan's voyage, however, is evidently a fable. It mixes Irish traditions of the land of the fairies with commonplaces from Christian ascetic literature. Brendan meets Judas in his place of torment; he lands on a whale, which he mistakes for an island; he encounters pillars of fire, cloud, and ice; he expels demons, escapes monsters, converses with fallen angels in the form of birds, and ascends by penitential stages to the state of grace in which the Earthly Paradise is revealed to him. Some of the details reveal the imagination of the writer: An island of sheep fatter than oxen suggests a monkish fantasy of Mardi Gras. But at the same time, the *Navigatio* describes the sea in terms that reveal the influence of real accounts, related from direct experience. The discovery of an island inhabited by a solitary hermit was an episode such as might really have happened on the rovings of Irish monks. The text includes a passable description of an iceberg.

Brendan directly inspired later voyages from Europe into the Atlantic. St. Brendan's Isle appeared on many charts and atlases of the fourteenth and fifteenth centuries. Bristolian navigators, to whose activities we shall return in the next chapter, actively sought it in the 1480s. Columbus alluded to the legend on his own last transatlantic voyage.[17] Atlantic cloudscapes, which often give a false impression of land at hand, reinforced the myth. In the sixteenth century, a chronicle of the conquest of the island appeared, modeled, perhaps with satirical intent, on real conquistador narratives.[18]

I am aware of no direct evidence that Vespucci knew the legend. The nearest we get is a mention in a text attributed to him, but of dubious authenticity, that the Canary Islands were formerly called the Isles of the Blest. This could have come from a map that bore the influence of place-names from the *Navigatio,* of which there were many in the late Middle Ages. But Brendan was so popular that it would be surprising if Vespucci were unacquainted with his story. The Mediterranean equivalent, the story of St. Eustace, was familiar from devotional art, as well as from many written versions. The *Golden Legend,* the most popular hagiographic compendium of the Middle Ages, made it universally familiar. The saint's travails involved seaborne flight from persecution, shipwrecks, storms, encounters with every kind of robber and pirate the sea throws up, traumatic separation from his family, and a series of calamities. The family was reunited just in time to experience martyrdom. The tale seeped chivalry, for Eustace was a knight of impeccable nobility, of blood as well as of soul, and therefore an excellent model for explorers; a popular elaboration of the story, the *Libro del caballero Zifar,* recast it in the form of a wholly secular chivalric romance.

Vespucci was less amenable to chivalric self-fantasies than Columbus, whose aspirations for social ascent were distinguishable from the fame and honor Amerigo sought. One way of characterizing the difference might be to say that chivalry was a medieval value, whereas those of fame and honor were of the Renaissance. That would be an oversimplification, because chivalry has remained influential in modern times, whereas fame and honor, in one form or another, seem to be near-universal quests that crop up in every culture with a socially influential aristocratic model. Still, it would probably be fair to say that the language of fame and honor gradually displaced that of love and war in aristocratic self-descriptions in the modern West. And Vespucci illustrates the trend: Free with fame's lexicon, he never borrowed directly—if I read him rightly—from the literature of chivalry.

Yet he could hardly escape its influence. It was everywhere around him in his day. And many deeds of knightly derring-do had seaborne settings. Vespucci's younger Portuguese contemporary the poet Gil Vicente could, without incongruity, liken a lovely woman to a ship and a warhorse: The comparisons were meant to be flattering. We must imagine the ship star-set and sail-girt, with streaming pennants, and the horse richly caparisoned with flowing livery.

> *Sailor, declare*
> *If ship or sail or star*
> *Can be as fair!*
> *Soldier, declare*
> *If horse or arms or war*
> *Can be as fair!*

The association of ships with chivalry was inescapably strong, as if waves were there to ride like jennets and warships bucked and plunged like warhorses. Typical storylines of chivalric fiction included tales of destined heroes who, frustrated by the trammels of life, took to sea, discovered islands, dispossessed the monsters, giants, and savages they found there, wooed princesses, and ended as kings. Real-life sea heroes modeled themselves on this appealing trajectory. The ruffians who served Prince Henry the so-called Navigator, and who explored the African Atlantic or scoured its islands from the 1420s to the 1460s, called themselves knights and squires and gave themselves such storybook names as Lancelot and Tristram. Count Pero Nino was one of the most celebrated Castilian naval commanders of the fifteenth century; his squire wrote his life in the style of chivalric romance. Columbus imagined himself as a "captain of cavaliers and conquests" and emulated in his own life the heroes of fiction. Of a slaughtered scion of the Peraza family of Seville, who conquered the tiny island of Gomera from its aboriginal inhabitants in a sordid little war in the mid–fifteenth century, poets lyricized,

> *Weep, ladies, weep, if God give you grace*
> *For Guillén Peraza, who left in that place*
> *The flower, now withered, that bloomed in his face.*
> *Guillén Peraza, Guillén Peraza,*
> *Where is your shield, where is your lance?*
> *All is undone*
> *By fatal mischance.*[19]

All the conventions of the genre are crammed into these lines: the invocation of ladies, the romantic sentiments, the equipage of knightly combat, the appeal to fortune. The same "fictional devices of an adventurer's yarn," in Luciano Formisano's phrase, infected Vespucci's writings.[20]

THE PROBLEM OF AUTHENTICITY

The author was not the only party with a financial interest in the dissemination of an explorer's experiences. At the time of Vespucci's voyages, Columbus's adventures had already unleashed a sensation and whetted public appetite for more of the same. Publishers hungered for copy. Propagandists rushed into print, eager to establish claims to some share in the potential profits of exploration on behalf of their patrons or nations. The first document to announce Columbus's discoveries to the world was a confection, purportedly from his own hand, and closely related to materials he produced himself, but processed with modifications by servants of the Castilian crown.[21] The admiral's literary executor edited his papers so heavily that it is sometimes hard to distinguish the original voice from the editor's agenda.

Much of the travel literature of the sixteenth century concerned entirely fictional voyages. Sometimes these were explicitly and candidly fictional or with undisguised satirical purpose, but sometimes they came mischievously masked as true accounts of discoveries, for instance, of new Canary Islands, Eldorados, Amazon lands, fountains of youth, and straits leading to arctic passages. Some of them deceived real explorers, who wasted lives and fortunes trying to follow them up. Similar features of the tradition lasted for centuries. Captain Cook was outraged at the embellishments his accounts of his voyages suffered on their way into print. The beginnings of the penetration of New Guinea in the late nineteenth century inspired extraordinary real-life Münchhausens. Even today few travel writers could fairly be put on their honor to tell the unembroidered truth. Falsehood was part of the fabric of an explorer's life. I do not mean that explorers necessarily lied—though Columbus and Vespucci, I believe, were both congenitally or pathologically mendacious. Falsehoods of which you have convinced yourself, and which you genuinely believe, are not lies when you pass them on to other people.

In partial consequence, Vespucci's career generated the most problematic narratives in the entire history of this corrupt genre. Historians have treated them as some theologians treat scripture: selecting items that suit their theses, and giving these the seal of authenticity, while rejecting other matter as fraudulent. We shall make sense of the documents in question only if we begin by accepting that none of Vespucci's writings—any more than those of any other self-interested writer, including me—are sacred, pure, or agenda-free. The distortions began when Amerigo first laid pen to paper.

Some sources of distortion are common to explorers' writings of the time and are well illustrated in the case of Columbus. They include promotional distortions, compelled by the need to recruit manpower and raise financial and political backing. Other warping or wheedling agendas include self-aggrandizement, for almost everyone who ventured the risks of an explorer's life was in it for enhanced status or wealth or fame. Part of the object in writing was to claim rewards. That was especially true of servants of the Portuguese and Castilian crowns, whose reports were also their *probanzas*—the statements of merit on the basis of which royal patronage was bestowed or renewed, rather like the self-appraisals executives have to write nowadays for their line managers. And, of course, literary and rhetorical conventions shaped the perceptions of writers confronting previously unsampled discoveries, not because the writers were dishonest but because they were surprised. Vespucci and Columbus alike struggled to make sense of the unexpected worlds they beheld, and they turned to tradition for help. Finally, each explorer had objectives and obsessions of his own. Columbus was concerned with portraying himself as a chivalric figure of natural nobility, and as a divine appointee or instrument of providence. Vespucci's agenda was more secular, more practical, and more modest, but no less powerful in shaping what he wrote: He sought to project himself as a magus in touch with the powers of nature, and he frankly wanted enduring renown.

Unsurprisingly, the distortions grew with writing, as appetite increases with eating. Broadly speaking, Vespucci's accounts of his voyages got progressively further removed from reality as time went on. I do not mean to single him out for criticism, for the same is flagrantly true of Columbus and, no doubt, of other, lesser explorers. As Columbus's disillusionment accumulated, he got ever more shrill and unconvincing in his claims. As the world disappointed him, he became ever more absorbed in messianic delusions and religiously inspired readings of cosmography. To some extent, the writings of Hernán Cortés follow the same pattern. He began the conquest of Mexico with a coolly secular mind and ended it in a state of febrile exaltation, dreaming of founding in the New World a church on apostolic lines to redress the evils of Old World Christianity.

In one key respect, Vespucci's writings are unlike those of Columbus and Cortés: He wrote little—or, at least, little that has survived—whereas Columbus was a victim of verbal incontinence whose irrepressible loquacity tired his correspondents, and Cortés had a fluent pen and a need to provide his king and his public with detailed accounts of his deeds. Vespucci, by comparison, has left frustratingly little. The writings published in his lifetime were obviously, sublimely romanticized, but by whom?

Allowing for editorial interpolations, it has to be acknowledged that Vespucci himself contributed to the gap between his real experiences and the narratives he authored. He craved fame and sought to ensure it by doctoring the record. He reminds me of the well-known anecdote about Winston Churchill, who, asked if he expected history to judge him favorably, replied that he did and it would, since he intended to write it himself. In an unquestionably authentic manuscript letter, Vespucci avowed his intention of writing his adventures up for publication: "All the most notable things that happened to me on this voyage I have gathered in a little book of my own, because, when I am at leisure, I shall be able to devote myself to leaving some fame behind me after I die."[22] He added that he had given the only copy to the king of Portugal. That work, if it ever existed, has not survived, but what Vespucci said about it declared plainly enough his motive in writing. It was the sort of motive that leaves marks.

Only six accounts of his voyages survive from his hand or under his name. This makes critical evaluation of their authenticity hard, because the scope for comparative study of imagery, say, or vocabulary or the tics of style is relatively restricted. Even so, it is possible to detect a clear pattern of development in three stages.

THE FIRST STAGE: MANUSCRIPTS ON THE VOYAGES

Two of Vespucci's manuscript narrative reports of his own navigations survive, with a brief résumé of what he had learned, in the course of a voyage of his own, about a rival expedition. Additionally, a letter known as the Ridolfi Fragment, after the scholar who discovered it in 1937, which Vespucci wrote in defense of the contents of his reports, confirms many points in the texts. All the reports were written between July 1500, the date the first bears, and the summer of 1502, when, from internal and external evidence, the third, undated document must have been written. None, as far as we know, is in Vespucci's hand, but in those of copyists who had a legitimate interest—commercial or diplomatic—in the material, with no known reason for wishing to modify, embroider, or censor it. The first document survives in no fewer than six effectively identical manuscripts, and the third in two virtually identical copies. This is an irreproachable mutual guarantee of the approximate accuracy of the texts and unquestionable evidence of derivation from a common source. No reasonable critic would suggest anyone except Vespucci as the author of the original. The exculpatory Ridolfi Fragment exists in only one manuscript, again not in Amerigo's hand, but its contents and those of the other texts of the first phase are, to a great extent, mutually corroborative. No reader can reasonably doubt Vespucci's authorship.

In this first phase of Vespucci's life as a raconteur of his own deeds, there is plenty of evidence of the way tradition and the natural prejudice of an autobiographer edge the writer away from a purely factual account. That will have been obvious to the reader of the previous chapter, where my analysis of Vespucci's routes is based on these writings and where the conflicts with other sources and with inherent probabilities are made plain. We shall return to these manuscripts in the next chapter, to sift the evidence they contain concerning Vespucci's perceptions of the New World and its people, with similar mixed results. Despite their difficulties, these documents are what historians normally consider good primary-source material. Much of their contents can be independently verified by comparison with other sources. The accounts they contain were written close to the events, with purposes and agendas we know about or can be reasonably confident of eliciting accurately. Above all, these accounts are at least perfect evidence of what was going on in Vespucci's mind, if not necessarily in any other area of his life.

With the Ridolfi Fragment, a distinct new agenda intrudes into the sequence. It is a defense of some of Vespucci's claims, almost all of which occur in the earlier surviving narratives, against challenges, queries, and denunciations from unnamed readers. The comparison with Columbus is again irresistible. Instead of being uniformly lionized for his discoveries, the explorer found himself suspected, disbelieved, and even vilified by skeptically minded critics. Vespucci responded, as Columbus did, with indignation verging on paranoia.

The letter contains no clue to the identity of the recipient, but the context is obvious. Vespucci's correspondent had collected objections from a number of different readers, so he must have been a member of a circle. The queries are not all sensible or wise, but they are all more or less learned, so the circle was one of savants. The learning involved was broadly humanistic, relying on Ptolemy and Aristotle as sources of queries. It reminds me of the exchanges common in academic circles nowadays between authors and publishers' readers, who are supposed to certify a manuscript for publication and who, when helpful comments are exhausted or elusive, sometimes feel driven to justify their fees by scraping together objections and queries of variable quality, with an air of desperation. Alas, in Vespucci's day, publishers were not that fussy, and the Fragment cannot be read as evidence of a work in the press.

Vespucci's answers have the hectoring, injured tone all too common in academic disputes, with a good deal of combative rhetoric, including sarcasm and intended humor. So the correspondent must have been well known to Vespucci to take this language in the spirit of banter. Vespucci makes no attempt to affect patience. He was confident in his correspondent's goodwill and indulgence. The letter is in Tuscan, so it must have been intended for Italy and probably for Florence. Vespucci could have written in Latin or Castilian, and probably in Portuguese, had he so wished, for appropriate audiences. In short, though we do not know the identity of the correspondent, we can profile him with some confidence. He was a learned, well-connected Florentine humanist.

Underlying his academic criticisms were doubts about the commercial viability of the enterprise on which Vespucci was engaged. By the end of his second voyage, Vespucci's project, like that of Columbus, whose undertaking it so closely resembled, was evidently failing. On his way out on his second voyage, Amerigo met returning vessels from the voyage of Cabral. Shortly after he got back, he faced—from his point of view—even worse news. Vespucci's voyage came home empty-handed, so abjectly so that he felt obliged to disown any profit motive and emphasize the scientific objectives of his work. João da Nova, meanwhile, went east by the established Portuguese route and brought home a fortune. Investors in Lisbon rushed to put money into more such voyages. Vespucci was left desperately defending an apparently doomed enterprise. Not for the first time in his life, he seemed to have made the wrong choice, and in this case, he had evidently committed himself to seeking Asia in the wrong direction. His impatience showed as he answered his critics' objections one by one.

First, doubters questioned whether he had really encompassed a quarter of the globe. In reply, Vespucci admitted that he was at sea when he made his reading of the latitude of his farthest south, and his result was, by implication, subject to error induced by the motion of the ship. But he insisted that his position was 1,600 leagues south of Lisbon in a straight line. If the world was 24,000 miles in circumference, that would amount, he said, to one-fourth of the world. Since he normally reckoned four miles to a league, the calculation seems rather wild. The obscure passage about the Antipodes raised queries in readers' minds,[23] as well it might, which perhaps explains why Vespucci subsequently went into more detail on the matter and attempted to illustrate it with a diagram (which, however, clarifies nothing, as Vespucci's view on this matter was literally nonsensical). Some of the other queries on cosmographical matters that critics addressed to Amerigo merely aroused his impatience. There was no point, he spluttered, in asking whether he had crossed the Tropic of Capricorn: That was clear from his text. The reasons for the reversal of the seasons in the southern hemisphere had already been explained.

He offered an indignant rebuttal of readers who challenged his claim to be able to determine longitude. "And to exempt myself from what the ill-intentioned have said, I say that I found it out in the eclipses and the conjunctions of the planets," checked against well-known published tables. He reached, he adds, 150 degrees west of Alexandria. This was a new claim.

> *And if any invidious or malign person refuses to believe it, let him come to me, and I will declare it to him, with authority and with testimonies. And let that be enough for you concerning longitude. And if it were not for the fact that I am very occupied, I would send you the manifest of all my many observations of conjunctions, but I do not want to get involved in all those convolutions [*tanta pasta*], for this seems to me to be the objection of an armchair intellectual [*un dubio di literato*].*[24]

It is worth pointing out that this was a slightly different claim from the one he made in his account of his first voyage, when he suggested that he had calculated longitude by lunar distances. The latter, as we have seen, was quite impossible with the means at Vespucci's disposal. He could, however, at least have attempted to use eclipses and lunar-planetary conjunctions, but without any serious chance of success using the technology available in his day. Others tried it. All failed miserably.

Many doubters challenged Vespucci's descriptions of the people of the New World. Almost all the queries focused on a single theme: Vespucci had not provided a realistic account, but rather rehearsed a series of literary conventions designed to represent the inhabitants of the new continent as denizens of a golden age of silvan innocence, or as implausibly superior savages—moral exempla for the implicit chastisement of civilized vice. To a great extent, these charges were justified. But they are best examined in the next chapter, in the context of Vespucci's perceptions of the natives of the New World.

The Ridolfi Fragment fits perfectly into what we know of the course of Vespucci's life and the trajectory of his thought. It exceeds Vespucci's earlier known writings in tone, but only in one matter of substance. This matter is important, because a further question depends on it. How many voyages did Vespucci claim to make?

"It is certain," he says in the relevant passage, "that I have navigated or taken part in three voyages—two of which I made westwards through the Ocean Sea, taking always a course to the southward with the northeast wind, and the third in a southward direction through the Atlantic Sea."[25] By crushing the text, or squeezing from it a meaning the writer can hardly have intended, it might be possible to argue that Vespucci here refers to only two prior voyages—those narrated in his earlier manuscripts and attested in other records. On this interpretation, the "third" voyage "southwards" could be a reference to either of two events. First, it might be simply the latter phase of the second voyage, in which Vespucci left the coast and headed deep into the open sea on a southerly course. But in other places, Vespucci specifies that the king of Castile commissioned both "westward" voyages, in which case the "third" voyage might be the excursion we believe Vespucci made from Hojeda's fleet across and into the mouth of the Amazon. Yet the plain and obvious meaning of the text is that he made—or claimed to make—three Atlantic crossings. This is the first mention in his surviving works of such a claim. And it was more than a slip of the pen or a momentary lapse of memory or a copyist's error: Later in the letter, he again adverts to two voyages.[26]

This is an issue of critical significance—on it rests the case for or against Vespucci as an honest claimant to honor in discovery. If he claimed to make three voyages, he was a liar or, at least, responsible for a claim unverifiable by other evidence. If such a claim was advanced on his behalf in edited versions of his work, without his authorization, he emerges innocent of the charge of falsifying the record—in this respect, at least. The appearance in the Ridolfi Fragment, a source apparently undoctored by any editorial hand, of a claim to have made a third voyage is strong prima facie evidence against Amerigo.

Taken as a whole, the writings of the first phase of Vespucci's authorial career establish criteria by which to judge the authenticity of works that appeared in print under his name. Authentic writings of Vespucci are self-laudatory; they tack between bombast and defensiveness; they are egotistical and belittle or sideline other individuals. They are full of exaggerations and distortions. They contain echoes of previous writers, especially Dante, Petrarch, Ptolemy, Mandeville, Marco Polo, and Columbus. They never fail to vaunt the author's pretensions as a cosmographer and navigator. Specifically, they all contain references to the use of quadrant and astrolabe and to the problems of longitude. They all deride practical and primitive navigators who do not make use of the instruments of which Vespucci claimed mastery. And they tend to exalt observed or experimental knowledge over the authority of books while remaining pretty well enslaved to reliance on the writer's favorite texts. So we have a checklist of Vespucci's characteristics as a writer with which we can approach the works of the second and third phases: the works of disputed authorship. Their authenticity can be measured by the extent to which they exhibit the items in the checklist, and, with the same method, passages by Vespucci can be distinguished from interpolations by other hands.

THE SECOND STAGE: *MUNDUS NOVUS*

The fact that the Ridolfi Fragment includes Vespucci's claim to have made an otherwise undocumented voyage tends to change our perception of the next work to occur chronologically in the series of writings attributed to Vespucci: the pamphlet known as *Mundus Novus*, which makes the same claim. This work of few pages but enormous impact on the world appeared in print under Vespucci's name in numerous editions from 1504 onward. As it is addressed to Lorenzo di Pierfrancesco de' Medici, it must date from before his death in May 1503, unless the author was improbably ignorant of the event. The work's fame derives from its name, which neatly summarizes the author's argument: Vespucci has discovered a new, previously unrecorded continent south of the equator.

There can be no doubt that *Mundus Novus* is not the work defended in the Ridolfi Fragment. It does not include all the passages cited or alluded to, and in some respects, it does not fit. For instance, critics who derided Vespucci for saying that the New World's inhabitants were white might have had his manuscript account of his second voyage in mind, but not *Mundus Novus*, where their skin is said to "incline towards redness."[27]

In most respects, *Mundus Novus* is unexceptionally a characteristic work by Vespucci. It reads like Vespucci's own work. The themes, the language, the obsessions are all the same as in his indisputable writings. It has his fingerprints all over it: the characteristic obsessions with celestial navigation, the egregious self-importance, the sustained quarrel with received wisdom on behalf of fresh and direct observation; almost all of its content overlaps with other work known or universally accepted to be Vespucci's own. Yet for over three quarters of a century (as I write in 2006), the scholarly consensus has been overwhelmingly against it, treating it as an inauthentic or fraudulent product or a confection with little input from Vespucci. Partly, this is the result of what one might call fallout from other notorious cases of fraud, including at least one manifest confection ascribed to Vespucci but utterly convincing, which we shall turn to in a moment. But, prejudice of this kind apart, there are essentially three reasons worth weighing for rejection or caution toward *Mundus Novus.*

First, it is a printed work. This alone raises the presumption that editorial hands must have intervened in its preparation for the press, with the object of making it more salable. It is worth pointing out that, although this is probably true, and consistent with the habits of publishers at the time, it does not preclude the possibility that at least one of these editorial hands may have been Vespucci's own. The book was clearly intended for the press. The exordium, addressed to Lorenzo di Pierfrancesco, refers to an account already tendered to him in person and labels *Mundus Novus* a "succinct" version. So it was clearly and candidly not intended for the dedicatee's personal perusal. It was a vulgarization destined for a large public. It includes the usual publisher's tease about a possible sequel. Most of the innovations in the text (apart from simple errors, which are evidence of nothing except the haste or humanity of the compiler) were of kinds calculated to appeal in the marketplace.

Second, the text is in Latin, whereas Vespucci's other travel narratives are in Tuscan. This makes it hard to judge the authenticity of *Mundus Novus*, for we have only two other brief texts in Latin by Vespucci, both written when he was a student. So there is, in this respect, nothing suitable with which to compare *Mundus Novus*. But the mere fact that it was published in Latin does not make it inauthentic. Vespucci was unquestionably capable of writing in Latin, and a work intended for wide circulation was best composed in that language for access to an international market. The Latin of *Mundus Novus* is not learned—that is, it is not the pedantic, fastidious Latin of humanist scholars who disdained anything unanticipated in the work of Cicero.

In any case, the Latin may not be Vespucci's own. A sort of colophon at the end of the book declares it to be a translation. This should not necessarily be taken literally. Authors often represented original works of the time as translations, to cover imperfections, strew mystification, and introduce distance between writer and audience—in a manner analogous to the effect modern dramatic theory calls *Verfremdung*. In the first Latin edition, *Mundus Novus* is said to be a translation from Italian. In the first Italian edition, it is said to be a translation from Spanish. In both, the translator is called "the jocund translator," which makes the whole thing sound like a joke on the author's part, though this could be a pun on the name of a real translator called Jocundus or some such name. Indeed, some early readers assumed this was a reference to the Veronese architect Giovanni del Giocondo. An otherwise unrecorded Giuliano del Bartolomeo del Giocondo is mentioned in another text ascribed (almost certainly falsely) to Vespucci. Other, later scrutineers have identified Giuliano del Giocondo, a Florentine merchant, as the translator. To quote the Latin version:

> *The jocund translator has turned this letter from Italian into the Latin language, so that all who understand Latin may understand how many*

things worthy of wonder are to be found in our days, and in order to crush the
temerity of those who presume to discern the heavens and their majesty and to
know more than it should be lawful to know, when, in all the vast time that has
unrolled since the world began, the vastness of the Earth and the things that are
therein have remained unknown.

This is obviously, richly ironic. The presumption of the closing claim is itself an example of the temerity the writer abjures. It would be risky to take anything in the paragraph *au pied de la lettre*. It would be like believing that *The Name of the Rose* was really a medieval work, or that Dr. Watson was the real author of the adventures of Sherlock Holmes.

Finally, there is the matter of the third voyage. The pamphlet alludes to "two voyages I made for the King of Castile." As far as we know, there was only one such previous voyage, but the Ridolfi Fragment had already introduced a mention of a third. The reference to three voyages in *Mundus Novus* is more clear-cut than in the Ridolfi Fragment. It admits of no cavil. The author says unequivocally, at the start of his summation, "These were the more noteworthy things that I saw in this my last voyage, which I call my third expedition; for there were two other expeditions, which by order of the most serene king of the Spains I made towards the west."[28] The next publication to appear under Vespucci's name went into great detail about this otherwise unknown voyage, claiming that it achieved landfall on the mainland of the Americas before Columbus. The author of *Mundus Novus*, therefore, was guilty of complicity in a notorious imposture. *Mundus Novus* also looks ahead to a prospective fourth voyage that never happened. In the next publication released by the Vespucci industry, both these putative voyages are treated as realities. So, from the point of view of his admirers, the main reason for excluding the letter from the corpus of Vespucci's writings is to exempt him from calculated and self-serving deceptions.

Yet self-serving deception was characteristic of the man (as it was, in slightly different ways, of Columbus). In any case, the reference to a third voyage in *Mundus Novus* is more of a fib than a lie. It is self-aggrandizing but does no explicit harm to anyone else. It is only in con-

nection with the subsequent elaboration—for which Vespucci, as I hope
to show, was not responsible—that it assumes sinister dimensions.

The letter follows Amerigo's manuscript report to his patron quite
closely. Apart from a passage of cosmographical theory, which we have
already considered, and some trivial changes of detail, the main additions are obviously designed to appeal to the taste of the sententious,
the sensationalist, and the salacious—the same combination that char-
acterizes the appeal of mass-circulation media today. In the original version, Vespucci mentions that his Atlantic crossing was a long one of
sixty-four days. *Mundus Novus* expatiates:

> *But what we suffered on that vast expanse of sea, what perils of shipwreck,*
> *what discomforts of the body we endured, with what anxiety of mind we toiled,*
> *this I leave to the judgement of those who out of rich experience have well*
> *learned what it is to seek the uncertain and to attempt discoveries, even though*
> *ignorant. And that in a word I may briefly narrate all, you must know that of*
> *the sixty-seven* [sic] *days of our sailing we had forty-four of constant rain,*
> *thunder and lightning—so dark that never did we see sun by day or fair sky*
> *by night. By reason of this, such fear invaded us that we soon abandoned*
> *almost all hope of life. But during these violent tempests of sea and sky, so*
> *numerous and so violent, the Most High was pleased to display before us a*
> *continent, new lands, and an unknown world. At sight of these things, we*
> *were filled with as much joy as anyone can imagine usually fall to the lot of*
> *those who have gained refuge from varied calamity and hostile fortune.*[29]

The printed version also adds a lot of self-important flummery;
Vespucci was never reticent, but print seemed to obliterate all modesty:

> *. . . if my companions had not heeded me, who had knowledge of cosmography,*
> *there would have been no ship-master, nay not the leader of our expedition*
> *himself, who would have known where we were within five hundred leagues.*
> *For we were wandering and uncertain in our course, and only the instruments*
> *for taking the altitudes of the heavenly bodies showed us our true course*
> *precisely; and these were the quadrant and the astrolabe, which all men have*

come to know. For this reason they subsequently made me the object of great
honour; for I showed them that though a man without practical experience, yet
through the teaching of that marine chart for navigators I was more skilled than
all the ship-masters of the whole world. For these have no knowledge except of
the waters to which they have often sailed.[30]

These passages capture Vespucci's authentic voice: the egregious self-recommendation; the contempt for traditional pilotage; the insistence on the superiority of navigation with instruments; the incantatory invocation of quadrant and astrolabe.

So *Mundus Novus* is essentially Vespucci's own work. This does not mean there was no editorial intervention. There are, most obviously, significant interpolations about sex. The passage best calculated to boost sales by injecting comforting horrors follows Vespucci's description of cosmetic self-mutilation among the natives.

They have another custom, very shameful and beyond all human belief. For their
women, being very lustful, cause the private parts of their husbands to swell
up to such a huge size that they appear deformed and disgusting; and this is
accomplished by a certain device of theirs, the biting of certain poisonous
animals. And in consequence of this many lose their organs which break
through lack of attention, and they remain eunuchs.[31]

In the original letter, Vespucci confines his account of native sexual practices to a modest outline, stressing the informality of sexual contracts and the relaxed rules governing incest. In the *Mundus Novus,* these become matters of taste rather than culture, ascribed to the lustful appetites of the women, and "when they had the opportunity of copulating with Christians, urged by excessive lust, they defiled and prostituted themselves."[32]

None of the arguments against the authenticity of *Mundus Novus* is compelling. It is not a veracious work, and it includes input by other hands, such as those of a jocund translator, perhaps, or other members of an editorial team. Where it departs from the manuscript accounts of

Vespucci's voyages, the changes seem calculated with an eye to the market, but it is still a product close to its origin in Vespucci's own work, and thoroughly representative of the rest of his authentic oeuvre. It is, to use a phrase of Luciano Formisano's, "not pseudo-Vespucian but para-Vespucian."[33]

THE LAST STAGE: THE *SODERINI LETTER*

Formisano thinks the same can be said of the so-called *Soderini Letter,* the last and ostensibly most complete narrative of the voyages attributed to Vespucci himself. But it is a work of an entirely different kidney. The first printed version—which must date from 1505 or perhaps late in 1504, when the printer first set up shop[34]—bears the title *Lettera di Amerigo Vespucci dell'isole nuovamente trovati in quattro suoi viaggi* (*Letter of Amerigo Vespucci Concerning the Islands Newly Found in His Four Voyages*). This sounds like a blatant attempt to cash in on the popularity of Columbus's work. The first printed report of Columbus's first voyage, in its most successful edition, bore the title *The Letter of the Islands That the King of Spain Has Newly Found.* And Columbus, as was well known, had made four transatlantic voyages.

The *Letter* ascribed to Vespucci is implicitly addressed to Piero Soderini, head of the Florentine state at the time of publication. The first two of the voyages it narrates are, in effect, different versions of the single voyage Amerigo made under Alonso de Hojeda's command. The third is the voyage of 1501–02 to Brazil under Portuguese auspices. Finally comes an account of an otherwise unrecorded and vaguely narrated fourth voyage and an account of a visit to Sierra Leone.

The *Soderini Letter* is the work that would mark Vespucci, if he really wrote it, as a fool or knave or both. I Iere, fantasy largely displaces reality, and travel writing crowds out genuine reportage. In fairness to historians who cling to belief in the authenticity of this text, it has to be said that not all the arguments commonly advanced against it are watertight.[35]

First, some readers are surprised to find the letter full of Hispanicisms and conclude that Vespucci—with his Florentine upbringing and knowledge of Dante and Petrarch—would not have written such corrupt Italian. One of the most ingenious suggestions is that the Hispanicisms arose from the influence of Columbus's writings on the compilers of the text.[36] But there is no mystery about them. The text was translated from Spanish or (I suspect) Portuguese. There are a good many Portuguese idioms and imports.[37] As Amerigo admitted to handing the king a version of his exploits crafted to perpetuate his own fame, it would not be surprising if it were written in Portuguese. In any case, Hispanicisms did creep into Vespucci's Italian: There are very few in the earliest of his surviving narratives, written in 1500, rather more in the report of his second voyage, and rather a lot in the Ridolfi Fragment. In other words, the longer he spent away from Florence, the more his Italian came under the influence of the languages of his host communities. That was surely an unsurprising effect: As the *Soderini Letter* was evidently written years after Vespucci's surviving Italian-language output, it would be surprising if it were unaffected.

Second, challenges to the authenticity of the text have been linked to the claim that Vespucci would not have written anything so crude. It is true that the inflation of sensation, which, as we have seen, introduced a good deal of prurient material into *Mundus Novus*, continued and intensified in the *Soderini Letter.* A revoltingly scatological passage can illustrate the point. "They are people neat and clean of person," says the author, referring to the natives he met, "owing to the constant washing they practise." So far, so familiar. But an interpolation follows immediately, with jarring effect:

> *When, begging your pardon, they evacuate the bowels, they do everything to avoid being seen, and just as in this they are clean and modest, the more dirty and shameless they are in making water, both men and women. Because, even while talking to us, they let fly such filth, without turning around or showing shame, that in this they have no modesty.*[38]

There are other passages equally sensational in different ways and therefore equally unreliable. The writer accuses native women of deliberately aborting their children in order to avenge themselves on husbands who displease them.[39] They kill off the moribund by exposure in the forest.[40] Interpolations of this kind do not necessarily undermine the claims to authenticity of other passages. Nor does the presence of errors and contradictions. This tells us nothing about the identity of the compiler. Vespucci was not above errors or contradictions or vulgar sensationalism in his well-attested works. Few, if any, writers are.

A further argument is connected with the claim that ripples through the *Soderini Letter:* that Vespucci, ahead of Columbus, deserves the credit for what we call the discovery of America. Vespucci, the argument goes, would not have been admired in Castile, or promoted—as he later was—to the rank of chief pilot of the kingdom, or honored by Columbus and his heirs, had he been identified as the author of a crude and unconvincing work that attempted to strip Columbus of the glory of his discoveries. Moreover, if Spaniards had taken seriously the claim that Vespucci had preceded Columbus on the mainland of the New World, the crown hardly would have resisted using it in the long lawsuit against Columbus's heirs.

This argument's whiskers need a trim with Occam's razor. To grant force to the case, we have to suppose that Spaniards knew about the works printed under Vespucci's name, but excused or ignored them because they also knew that Vespucci was not the real author. How could such a thing be possible? What media could have circulated so subtle a message? How come no one escaped the web of information that exempted Vespucci from responsibility for texts issued in his name?

The real explanation for Vespucci's abiding reputation in his adoptive country lies in the nature of the book trade there. The *Soderini Letter* was never widely known in Spain, one of the few countries in Europe where neither *Mundus Novus* nor the *Soderini Letter* was ever translated or published. *Mundus Novus* would not in any case be harmful to Vespucci's reputation. Its vague claim that he made an otherwise unrecorded voyage was an indifferent matter; the text does not say that Vespucci preceded Columbus across the Atlantic. Furthermore, the Spanish and, I think, the Portuguese book markets were relatively discriminating in their handling of travel literature. Even of Columbus's first published report on his first voyage, only two of the twenty-two editions from 1493 to 1522 were Spanish, and these do not seem to have been popular. They are certainly rare, as both are now known only in unique copies. In the second decade of the century, Peter Martyr's learned and unsensational book dominated the market to the exclusion of almost every other work on the New World. Vespucci could be known or suspected to be the author of self-romanticizing fictionalizations, but pardoned for it without comment by readers to whom the genre was obviously distinguishable from real narratives of exploration—just as no one mistakes the fiction of Edwina Currie or Douglas Hurd or Saddam Hussein for genuine political memoirs. Columbus's own son Hernando had Vespucci's printed work in his library, but he allowed it to pass without comment. Vespucci could plausibly—and, I believe, truly—disclaim all responsibility for the *Soderini Letter* as a forgery issued in his name. But he was never called on to do so, since the question never came up.

Traditional critics of the *Soderini Letter* also say that Soderini himself was an impossible addressee for Vespucci, because a client of the Medici would not write for one of their enemies. This does not follow. Considerations of loyalty never constrained Vespucci from seeking approval, support, patronage, and pay wherever he could get it. As titular head of the Florentine state, Soderini was a worthy recipient of the work. The assumption that he was indeed the intended reader arises from evidence in the body of the *Letter*, which invokes the "magnificence" of the patron and presumes him to be running the government of a "sublime republic," explicitly identified a few lines later as Florence. The closing lines of the account of the last voyage reinforce these references: "May Your Magnificence pardon me, whom I beg you to retain in the number of your servants," says the writer, commending to God "the condition of your lofty republic and the honor of Your Magnificence."[41] However, the printed version of the *Letter* is not explicitly addressed to Soderini. It is not explicitly addressed to anybody. Soderini's name appears in manuscript copies of the work, but it is impossible to say whether these preceded or followed the printed text. Indeed, the printed version seems likely to have come first and perhaps to be the source of the manuscripts.

How did Soderini's name get associated with the *Letter*? According to one theory, the publisher Giovanni Battista Ramusio added it. He did change the dedication of *Mundus Novus* to Soderini.[42] But Ramusio's edition appeared only in 1550, and the *Letter* had long been associated with Soderini. The possibility remains that the dedicatee was insignificant and that references to him appeared in obedience to a literary convention—as when the author of *Lazarillo de Tormes* or *Justine* addressed a mysterious but obviously fictional patron in an attempt to open intriguing distance between writer and reader.

There are, moreover, some points in favor of the *Soderini Letter*. It is only fair to mention these. Its language resembles Vespucci's short account of Cabral's voyage and may derive in part from that source. It echoes the Ridolfi Fragment on the change of course Vespucci claims to have made on his second voyage at thirty-two degrees south on the American coast and on the expedition's shift to midocean. The compiler was well informed about aspects of Vespucci's life. He knew about Giorgio Antonio Vespucci and his role in Amerigo's education. Addressing the unnamed dedicatee, he writes,

> *I recall how in the time of our youth I was your friend, as now I am your servant; and we used to go to hear the rudiments of grammar under the good example and teaching of the venerable religious of San Marco, Brother Giorgio Antonio Vespucci, my uncle. Would to God that I had followed his advice and teaching! For, as Petrarch says, "I should be a different man from that which I am."*

The reference has the ring of truth and calls to mind the self-reproaches of young Vespucci's exercise book with their confessions of inattentiveness. Of course, a clever fraudster could concoct a passage like this one, and the pious yearning to retrieve a misspent youth can be dismissed as a rhetorical device. Nonetheless, how like the real Vespucci is the wheedling tone, how characteristic the allusion to Petrarch! The compiler also mentions Amerigo's brother Antonio by name. Although these passages do not prove Vespucci's authorship of the *Letter,* they do place the work in a context close to Amerigo himself and draw our attention to passages the compiler might have taken from genuine works. The statement that follows also reveals that the compiler knew facts about Vespucci that were not available from any source at the time, except the explorer in person:

> *Your Magnificence doubtless knows that the reason of my coming to this realm of Spain was to engage in commerce, and that I persisted in this purpose for about four years, during which I saw and experienced the varied turns of Fortune, and how she kept changing these frail and fleeting benefits . . . and deprives one of that wealth which may be called borrowed. So when I had come to know the constant toil which man exerts in gaining it, by subjecting himself to so many discomforts and perils, I resolved to abandon trade, and to aspire to something more praiseworthy and enduring. So it came about that I arranged to go and see a portion of the world and its marvels.*[43]

Allowing for the rhetorical flourishes—the wielding of the image of fortune, the appeal to the reader's sympathy, the disavowal of base motivation—that seems to me a remarkably exact statement of Vespucci's career, as we might reconstruct it from reliable sources. And though the image of Fortune does not occur elsewhere in Vespucci's oeuvre, the peripeties of life and the insistence on disinterested travel are themes familiar to his readers.

So the traditional case against the authenticity of the *Letter* is inconclusive; there are points in its favor to be taken into account; and it contains some passages that sound like Vespucci's real ipsissima verba. Still, I find it impossible to read it without growing unease amounting to certainty that it is a confection in which relatively little input can be traced to the alleged author. A reader can almost hear the slash of the scissors and the splash of the paste. You can see the joins between passages lifted and adapted from other works of Vespucci and other sources. They are as plainly visible as in the work of any undergraduate plagiarist corrupted by the Internet.

For instance, the *Letter* takes the account of the first voyage and splits it in two, ascribing the first to 1497. Passages from the manuscript narrative of the second voyage are transferred to the first and decked out with elaborations concerning native customs that are taken in turn from classical speculations about Asia and Africa, or from other travelers' accounts of the New World, especially those of Columbus. The *Letter* includes the otherwise unrecorded "fourth voyage": The brief passage consecrated to this subject is evidently lifted from some other source. The compilers seem to have raided the travel literature of the time for picturesque matter in a way that, although not incompatible with Vespucci's methods as a writer, greatly exceeds anything of the sort he had perpetrated before. A passage, for instance, in which natives express their fear of cannibals closely echoes Columbus.[44] The writer lifts an episode of Columbus's third voyage from April 1499, concerning "serpents in the shape of crocodiles" or, in the *Soderini Letter*'s version, a creature resembling "a serpent except that it had no wings," which the explorers found, trussed, or butchered in an Indian camp; the Spaniards, deterred by fear or disgust, left it undisturbed.[45] The episode had appeared in print on April 10, 1504, in Venice, in the form of an extract from a translation in preparation of work by Peter Martyr.[46] The same text was the source for the *Soderini Letter*'s description of an attempt to capture a canoe, which had happened on the voyage of Cristóbal Guerra and Peralonso Nino,[47] and perhaps for the story of Indians chewing grass, which Peter Martyr's account of the Nino Guerra voyage reported as a method of cleaning one's teeth. Though new details on native diet are of uncertain provenance, the book's story of natives who drink only dew was drawn from chronicles of the conquest of the Canary Islands, where conquerors encountered the *dragonero* tree, which, by collecting heavy dewfalls, supplied the natives with water.

Clearly, none of this material originated with Vespucci, though he might have been responsible for borrowing it from other writers. And a few foundations dug from his earlier writings insecurely underpin the ramshackle edifice. Many of the additions are lurid and therefore selected for reader appeal. An inprecedented passage, for instance, narrates an episode in which cannibals devour a young sailor. His companions had put this personable individual ashore to establish friendly relations. Women crowded around him, touching him with every display of curiosity. It was a trap. Distracted by their attentions, he was felled from behind while archers covered his captors' retreat. The explorers could do nothing but watch "the women cutting the Christian to pieces" and taunting the onlookers by exhibiting the morsels as they roasted them.[48] The sensationalism hit home: This became one of the most quoted and pictured episodes in the Vespucci corpus.

Vespucci himself could be responsible for any or all of these departures from his other works. It is not credible, however, that he should have filleted out his own favorite themes. The decisive argument against his authorship is that the subjects closest to his heart appear nowhere in the book. There is hardly any material on celestial navigation and nothing on longitude. Nor is there anything about geography, except for one theme that does not appear elsewhere in Vespucci's work: a discussion of Ptolemaic climatic zones.[49] Most remarkably, there is nothing about the novelty of the New World. Even the claim to have perceived the continental nature of the discoveries is omitted from the account of landfall, which in other respects is taken from the manuscript account of the second voyage.[50] The work includes virtually nothing about the ancients or the superiority of observation over authority as a guide to truth. There is much less self-praise than readers of Vespucci's previous output would be schooled or steeled to expect. The compilers did not share Vespucci's priorities. They left out all the learning and arcana that were dear to the magus, like a modern editor dumbing down the work of an author deemed too intellectual for the market.

The *Soderini Letter* is, for the most part, far removed from Vespucci's own words. The editors—whoever they were—did adapt a great deal of material that originated with Vespucci.[51] But I have spent most of my life reading and teaching texts of the period, especially those by explorers, and this text looks, walks, and quacks like a canard. The motive for the imposture is obvious. This was a commercial product, a publisher's project, intended to follow up on the success of *Mundus Novus*. In that respect, it was an abject failure. *Mundus Novus* had been an instant best seller when it emerged from the press in 1504. Twenty-three editions appeared from 1504 to 1506. The *Soderini Letter* never took off in the marketplace.

Toward the end, we get the exceptionally elaborate publisher's tease. The writer has repeatedly referred to a work in progress that he calls "The Four Voyages." "This I have not yet published, because I am so displeased with my own things that I take no delight in those which I have written, even though many are urging me to publish it....[52] On each of my voyages I have noted down the most marvellous things and have brought all into a volume after the manner of a geography; and I entitle it The Four Journeys ... and as yet no copy of it has been published, because I must revise it."[53] Finally, the author explains that he has made no mention of the natives he met on his last expedition, because "I saw so many things that I refrain from telling them, reserving them for my Four Voyages." Presumably, had the *Soderini Letter* been a success, this advertised work would have followed. But it was not. So it never did.

There was, however, a little-known German version of the *Soderini Letter* that appeared in 1509 and was reissued in 1532. Meanwhile, in 1507, adoption by the namers of America, who published a Latin version, saved the text from obscurity. The first compilation of American travels, *Paesi Novamente Retrovati*, published in the same year, became the travel-writing sensation of the age.[54] It more or less killed off independent editions of Vespucci's letters, which, from the midcentury, continued to circulate chiefly in the form of an Italian translation in Ramusio's blockbusting compendium, *Navigationi e viaggi*, published in Venice in 1550. Despite the relative failure of the *Soderini Letter*—or perhaps because of it—Vespucci dominated the market in travel writing between Columbus and Cortés. Half the 124 works on exploration published in that period concerned him.[55]

The *Letter* was the first stage in the making of a legend. Most noteworthy historical figures live on in a long series of fictionalizations; a few have the privilege of launching the process themselves. Once launched, the process is uncontrollable. In the mid–seventeenth century, Girolamo Bartolomei Smeducci dedicated to Louis XIV a poem, replete with allegory, about Vespucci. The explorer becomes a symbolic traveler who goes all over the world but is bound for heaven. Much of his time is spent in Africa, where the devil rules a land "blackened by his vices." Amerigo crosses boreal seas and ranges over the Pacific and Indian oceans. But his pilgrimage is a spiritual one. He seeks Truth. It is hard to think of more inappropriate casting for the shifty ex-spiv.

The Vespucci tradition is surely not yet exhausted. The five hundredth anniversary of the naming of America in 2007 must inject it with new life. Columbus has been the hero of innumerable works, as diverse as a play by Lope de Vega, an epic by Joel Barlow, comic songs by Fats Waller and Irving Berlin, a clutch of awful Hollywood movies, and a British comedy full of smutty innuendo called *Carry On Columbus.* Vespucci is bound for the same sort of treatment. His reinventions did not end with his death; nor did his own ingenuity exhaust the possibilities.

CHAPTER FIVE

PROSPERO PREFIGURED

The New World, 1499–1502 ∘ Amerigo contemplates America

A MERICA MADE a curiously occluded first impression on the man who gave the hemisphere his name.

> *We went on shore and there we found so many trees that it was a very wonderful thing—not only the bigness of them but also the greenness, deep as leaves ever produced, and the sweet odor thereof which emanated from them, for they are all aromatic. They gave such enhancement to the atmosphere that we took great recreation therefrom.*[1]

The most conspicuous feature of the description is its vagueness. There is nothing distinctive about it or specific to the place to which it relates. All is hyperbole and sensuality. The appeal is as much to taste and smell as to visual sensation. Nothing in the description suggests that it was based on real experience. On the other hand, it has all the ingredients of the literary topos known to scholars as that of the *locus amoenus*, the undifferentiatedly agreeable place. Though a long literary pedigree lies behind the description, the immediate precedent, as we shall see in a moment, is Columbus's account of a similar experience.

To get as close as possible to Vespucci's personal response to America, we have to read on, in and between the lines he devoted to the subject. For convenience, it is best to look first at how he saw the physical

environment of his brave new world, and then turn to his impressions
of the people in it.

The Physical Environment

Vespucci had never seen anything like it. Whenever we grapple with the
reports of early explorers of unexperienced environments, we have to
take into account the effects of the strange and new on ill-prepared
minds. Before making landfall, Vespucci endured a sea journey im-
mensely longer than any he had undertaken previously. As far as we
know, he had never been farther at sea than from Florence to Barcelona.
Although both his Atlantic crossings took him along routes already pi-
oneered by previous explorers—Columbus in the first case, Pedro Álvares Cabral in the second—as far as he was concerned, they were
voyages into the unknown. The open ocean was still a novel environment for Europeans, who, before the opening of the New World, rarely
traveled far from land. The Azores, Iceland, and the Canaries were the
only open-sea destinations that formed part of Europe's trading system,
and only a few navigators went that far. The approach to America was
therefore fearsome, unsettling, and inexplicable in terms of most travelers' direct knowledge.

What they saw when they arrived was baffling, especially in the tropical latitudes visited by Vespucci, who knew only Mediterranean land-
scapes, in a relatively dry, temperate part of the world that millennia of
deforestation and intensive farming had transformed. Now he confronted shores where vast, dense, moist forest backed coastal swamps of
palm and mangrove. The work of human hands was evident in places
where ditches, drains, and mounds scarred and pocked the soil. The
coasts he visited housed farming peoples who grew cassava, squash,
peanuts, and cotton on earth platforms dredged from below the water-
line, or in forest clearings fertilized by leaf mold and the ash of burned
trees. But the settlements were small, impermanent, and dwarfed by the
forest. To European eyes, this was raw nature, savage or Edenic, accord-

ing to taste. There were two ways of responding. You could be awed into ineloquence, or you could search your memory for help from what you had read. Vespucci responded in both ways simultaneously.

Amerigo was in a privileged position as a reporter of this environment. Few men had seen more of its coastline by the time he wrote his last recorded impressions, in or about 1503. He did not have the advantage of penetrating far inland. But he waxed rhapsodical in his account of his first voyage when he described a probe into the mouth of the Amazon. The land there was continuously low and the trees "so dense that scarcely a bird could fly between them." The explorers saw "an infinite quantity of birds and parrots so great and of so many varieties that it was a wonder."

> *Some were coloured scarlet, some green and red and lemon-like, and others all green and others black and red, and the song of the other birds that were in the trees was a thing so sweet and melodious that whoever attends to it will often be arrested by its sweetness. The trees are of such beauty and so smooth that we thought we were in the terrestrial paradise. And none of those trees nor their fruits confirmed to those of ours in this region. Along the river we saw many kinds of fish of various forms.'*

Like most of Vespucci's attempts at description, it is maddeningly vague, maddeningly exaggerated, and feebly poetic. He showed signs of bafflement, as he described nothing directly or in detail. It was as if he were peering into an unsettled kaleidoscope where all the vivid colors were in motion. Modern writers have similar problems trying to describe, say, an LSD trip.

His responses already seemed mediated through his reading. Vespucci's attempt owed more to the rhetorical tradition of the *locus amoenus* than to the reality of the New World. The richness and diversity of the colors that spilled from his lines, like jewels from a casket, are reminiscent of the maps of the era, which were decorative rather than informative. Vespucci's description was closely modeled, in particular, on Columbus's awestruck account of the trees he found at the end of his first Atlantic crossing. In the first printed report of his voyage, Columbus described islands

> *full of trees of a thousand kinds, and tall . . . so green and so handsome, as in Spain in May. And some were in flower and some in fruit and others at other stages, according to their kind. . . . And there are six or eight kinds of palm that it is wonderful to behold them for their beautiful diversity . . . as with the other trees and fruits and grasses. There are evergreen woods to wonder at and very large grasslands and there is honey and many kinds of birds and very varied fruits.*[3]

Columbus's unpublished account is also worth bearing in mind, as Vespucci had plenty of opportunity to be briefed privately by the admiral, or to discuss impressions of the New World with him upon his return. Of descriptions of the landscape that survive in his own words, Columbus wrote the first within five days of making land. "I saw many trees that are different from ours . . . and all so diverse that it is the greatest wonder in the world. . . . For example, one branch had leaves like sugar cane, another like mastic, and so on, with five or six different types in a single tree." The trees, it seems, fused before Columbus's eyes like the colors of the birds before Vespucci's. Columbus, too, noticed the fish:

> *The fish are so different from ours that it is a wonder . . . of the finest colours in the world—blue, yellow, red, and every sort of colour—and some are streaked with a thousand tints, and the colours are so fine that there can be no man who would not marvel at it and feel refreshed by the sight.*[4]

He went on to mention the parrots without echoing remarks on the diversity of color. If Columbus did not directly influence the way Vespucci beheld the New World, then both of them struggled for utterance in the same awe and under the same constraints.

So heavily did Vespucci lean on literary sources for his descriptions that readers might be tempted to conclude he had never really been to

America, except for the assertion that follows: "Before we reached shore, fifteen leagues off, we found the water as fresh as in a river. We drank it and filled all the casks we had." At first sight, this looks like another trivial marvel or another warped borrowing from Columbus, who described the freshwater sea at the mouth of the Orinoco in similar terms. But allowing for exaggeration—fifteen leagues would be sixty miles, by Vespucci's reckoning at the time, and the filling of the water casks sounds like a picturesque device—this is a plausible reference to the vicinity of a mighty river mouth.

To well-read people at the time, mighty river mouths had a further connotation. Tradition associated them with the Earthly Paradise, the location of Eden, where four mighty rivers tumbled into the habitable world. By consensus among the learned, the Nile, Tigris, Ganges, and Euphrates all had a common source in Eden, which was located where the Bible said: "eastward." St. Augustine had allowed the possibility that the text should be understood symbolically,[5] but it was not unreasonable to suppose that after the expulsion of Adam and Eve, Eden remained, bereft, where God had put it. Columbus sensed the proximity of paradise. He was, he thought, at the "end of the orient," where most traditions placed Eden. On his third voyage in 1498, when he observed all the traditional signs, he believed, for reasons arising from errors in his readings of the elevation of the Pole Star, that he was sailing uphill—and the consensus was that Eden bestrode a mountain. At the mouth of the Orinoco, the tremendous discharge of fresh water Columbus observed suggested to him the "four rivers" traditionally supposed to have flowed out of Eden.[6]

Vespucci's line about the terrestrial paradise is therefore worth pausing to inspect. It is not purely descriptive, nor is it a casually coined metaphor: It is lifted straight from a tradition to which Columbus was also heir. Vespucci does not seem in this instance to have been directly inspired by Columbus. He felt "as if" he were in paradise, not that he was literally there. His image of Eden derived in part from his other favorite texts: first, from his beloved Dante, who put paradise, allegorically speaking, at the summit of purgatory, represented as a hard mountain to climb. Dante's poem also included a literal geography,[7] which located Eden "in the warmer parts of the world," deep in the southern hemisphere.[8] Mandeville probably also helped to shape Vespucci's image, as he did that of Columbus. Disarmingly, Sir John explained, "Of Paradise I cannot speak properly, for I have never been there," but he described it on the basis of tradition as a moon-high mountain guarded by wilderness and steep ascents. "No one can go there by water, either, for those rivers flow with so strong a current . . . that no craft can sail against them."[9] This at once recalls Columbus's insistence that he had detected the proximity of the Earthly Paradise in the volume of water discharged from the mouth of the Orinoco, but did not expect to be able to get any closer.[10]

When Vespucci mentioned the Earthly Paradise, his purpose was glaringly promotional. He had good reasons—better than literary uninventiveness—for raiding both the tradition of the *locus amoenus* and the lexicon of the Earthly Paradise. In order to attract investors, obtain patronage, hire crews, recruit colonists, and—in every way—advance the project of exploring a western route to Asia, he had to make the lands on the way there seem attractive and exploitable in their own right. He wanted, for instance, to represent the New World as conducive to life and health. "Doctors," he opined, "would find it ruinous to live there."[11] He had a motive for stressing every sign of fertility, exaggerating evidence of harmony and peace. Promotional literature on Venezuela and Brazil demanded particularly intense hard work after Columbus's expectations and promises about nearby islands had proved delusory. So, above all, Vespucci concentrated on features that augured well for commerce.

The only detail he gave about the trees was that all were "aromatic"—that is to say, exploitable in the markets of Europe and China that craved aromatic woods. Such geographical details as the writer vouchsafed, including his assurances of the proximity of the Indian Ocean and his invocation of the Earthly Paradise, with its connotations of Eastern promise, were calculated to promote the same agenda as Columbus: a commercially exploitable Atlantic leading to the riches of the East.

For the kind of picture he had in mind, it is useful to call on one of the engravings that illustrated Columbus's first published report—a work that Vespucci obviously read attentively. The scene is of a rich tropical landscape in which naked, elegantly proportioned natives offer trade goods, including what looks like a pot of the kind used at the time to hold expensive unguents, to seafarers whose oar-driven galley lies offshore. The scene is usually misinterpreted by modern beholders as showing Columbus conversing with the natives. But Columbus did not have any galleys. Indeed, no galley could have crossed the Atlantic. The vessel holds a strange creature of camelid appearance such as did not exist in Europe. The traders, moreover, wear pointed hats of Oriental design. The picture illustrates a specific passage in the report where Columbus speaks—imaginatively—of Chinese and Indian traders frequenting the lands he had discovered from their supposedly nearby harbors. As we have seen, Vespucci's expectations were colored by Columbus's views. He, too, was hoping for a share in the trade of the gorgeous East.

Vespucci's second visit to the New World inspired images much like those of his first. If anything, they made an even closer match with those Columbus transmitted: "This land," Amerigo wrote, "is very pleasant and full of infinite great green trees."[12] The odors were very "gentle and aromatic," the fruits infinite, delicious, and salubrious. The fields produced "many very sweet and good grasses, flowers and roots." And the more the author saw and tasted, "the more I reflect within myself that I am close to the earthly paradise."[13] Unknown spices and drugs abounded.[14] Columbus reported all these features in much the same terms.

"The men of the country," Vespucci added, adverting to one of Columbus's favorite themes, "speak of gold and other very miraculous metals and drugs. But I am one of those of the number of St. Thomas: Time will reveal all."[15] It may seem odd—inconsistent with his promotional agenda—that Vespucci should cast doubt on reports of gold. But this is best interpreted as another rhetorical trick, like that of the art dealer who indemnifies himself against charges of fraud by theatrical confessions of uncertainty about his own attributions. The notoriously dodgy dealer Joseph Duveen, who worked closely with Bernard Berenson in the manipulation of the market in Renaissance paintings in the 1930s, is said to have used the technique to great effect, enticing clients into thinking that his scruples led him to reduce the prices of masterpieces, whereas privately, he was convinced that he was handling forgeries or second-rate studio works. The scruples were all for show. Vespucci similarly boosted his reputation for veracity by feigning skepticism.

As for the fauna of the New World,

> *What can I say of the quantity of birds and of their feathers and colours and songs and variety and beauty (I do not want to spend long on this as no one would believe me)? Who would be able to recount the infinite quantity of wild animals, the great amount of lions, lionesses, cats—not now those of Spain but those of the Antipodes [delli antipoti]—so many wolves reminiscent of Cerberus, baboons and mandrill apes [gatti mamone] of so many kinds and many great serpents? And so many other animals did we see that I believe that so many varieties would not have fitted in Noah's ark.*

The list continues with many other species equally alien to the New World. Again, Columbus resorted to the same strategy, scattering Old World taxonomy around America in a desperate effort to make the unfamiliar intelligible. For vagueness and inaccuracy, the tally might be mistaken as evidence that Vespucci had never been there, except for the final detail: "and of domesticated animals we saw none."[16] This was not strictly accurate. Native villages typically had domestic fowl scrounging for food. But, in the absence of domesticated quadrupeds of the kind familiar to Europeans, it was an educated error.

THE GEOGRAPHICAL APPRAISAL

The passage quoted above includes the second time Vespucci labeled his land as "the Antipodes." In effect, he aligned himself with an interpretation of the New World already popular with humanist geographers. America was to be another name for a landmass classical cosmography had predicted. Indeed, the existence of a second or more landmasses seems to have been an orthodox opinion in antiquity at least until the time of Strabo. Geographers accepted that there might be other continents to match what we might now call Afro-Eurasia, or the Old World—rather as most scientists nowadays endorse the speculation that Earth may not be the only life-sustaining planet. It remained a minority opinion thereafter and never quite disappeared from the repertoire of geographical theories at scholars' disposal. In Spain, the Antipodes appeared on most medieval maps.

From the twelfth century onward, as more and more ancient texts reemerged in the candle glow of scholarship, the possibility that the Antipodes existed was entertained with increasing freedom.[17] A landmass south of the equator would balance and perfect the distribution of land in the northern hemisphere. "For you well know," said Sir John Mandeville to his readers, "that those men who live right under the Antarctic Pole are foot against foot to those who live right below the Arctic Pole, just as we and those who live at our Antipodes are foot against foot."[18] Further or alternatively, the size of the earth seemed to allow for or even demand that an unknown continent might lie in the midst of the ocean, as indeed it did.

The rediscovery of Strabo, as we have seen, sparked debate on the subject among Florentine geographers in the fifteenth century. Controversy received an additional boost in 1471, when the work of Strabo's contemporary Pomponius Mela was printed for the first time. Mela was already influential—more than a hundred manuscripts of the fifteenth century survive—and he now became more so. Pedro Álvares Cabral had a shipboard copy of his book.[19] Mela avoided the term "Antipodes" but speculated on the possibility of what he called the "Antichthon": an "anti-world" in the southern hemisphere, "unknown because of the heat of the intervening expanse"[20] and unexplored but theoretically, at least, habitable.

Mela's speculations compounded those of other texts. For instance, Macrobius, a Byzantine encyclopedist of the late fourth and early fifth centuries, was one of the most widely copied writers in the Middle

Ages, from the twelfth century onward, largely because he was regarded as an authority on the interpretation of dreams. He was not a systematic geographer, but he made many geographical remarks that medieval students took to heart. In particular, he devoted some lines to an attempt to reconstruct Cicero's mental image of the world, and Cicero was a hero for every humanist of Vespucci's era. Macrobius argued for a spherical world divided into numerous habitable but mutually inaccessible zones, separated by impenetrable climates, including the land of the Auteochi, a temperate zone in the southern hemisphere, beyond the torrid zone, and the Antipodes beyond them, across a region of intolerable cold.[21]

A Roman writer of the next generation, Martianus Capella, was, to judge from both allusions and manuscripts, "one of the half dozen and most popular and influential writers of the Middle Ages."[22] His work, called *The Marriage of Mercury with Philology*—a fancifully expressed survey of the traditional school curriculum of his time—was printed in Vicenza in 1499 but was already well known to Vespucci's generation in manuscript versions. The book contains a long excursion on geography that was, in effect, an apologia for Vespucci's methods—the use of instruments for measuring the earth, the same project satirized in *The Ship of Fools*. Martianus's personification of Geometry bears rule, compasses, and globe and claims to be able to measure the firmament and describe the earth. The description that follows insists—reasonably enough—that the climatic zones of the northern hemisphere are reproduced in the southern. Beyond the equator live the Antíokoi. Farther south is a region where the seasons of the northern hemisphere are reversed. Here dwell the Antichthones. The Antipodes, properly understood, are inhabitants of the northern hemisphere on the other side of the world, who have day when we have night and vice versa. Many medieval writers, including Mandeville, adopted this confusing terminology; in effect, Martianus concurred with believers in an inhabited world awaiting discovery in the southern hemisphere. He was also careful to point out that we should not expect the Antipodeans to be creatures like ourselves in reason or appearance.

Vespucci was familiar with the idea of the Antipodes and the possibilities that beckoned there before he saw the New World or penetrated the southern hemisphere. Two main arguments countered these possibilities—or at least the possibility that such lands, if they existed, might be inhabited. First, since the world was supposed to be a perfect sphere, and gravity and the motion of the planet were as yet unknown, it seemed incredible that inhabitants of a southern continent could adhere to the underside of the world without falling off. Second, an unknown continent could not contain any people, because Christ's doctrine, according to scripture, had been proclaimed throughout the earth. No part of the earth, therefore, can have been inaccessible to preachers of the gospel. When Columbus, during his quest for patrons, mentioned the Antipodes as a possible target for his proposed ocean crossing, experts charged with reviewing his plans commented, "St. Augustine doubts it."[23]

Yet as soon as Columbus returned from his crossing, scholars acquainted with the classics immediately hailed his findings as proof that the Antipodes did exist. For anyone who accepted traditional methods of calculating the size of the globe, no other interpretation fitted the facts, as Columbus had clearly not gone far enough to reach Asia. Peter Martyr of Anghiera, Ferdinand and Isabella's court humanist, announced that the discoverer had "returned from the Antipodes," even though the sovereigns had "regarded the things he said as fabulous." In 1497 a preacher in Rome praised the explorer for "taking the name of Christ to the Antipodes, which previously we did not even think existed." Not long afterward, in Florence, Columbus's discoveries were designated as "the world opposite to our own."[24] Columbus did not explicitly endorse that opinion. He did, as we have seen, find and correctly identify proof of the existence of lands of continental dimensions in what we now think of as South America, though he continued for as long as he lived to regard them as lying close to Asia.

In view of the tenacity of the tradition that misrepresents Vespucci as the first man to perceive the New World as a continent, it is important to establish that, on this point, he was merely following his usual mentor. Columbus had already established the fact that he had stumbled on a continent by irreproachable observation on his third voyage in August 1498. Sailing past the mouth of the Orinoco, he deduced that so great a body of fresh water required an enormous river to discharge it, with a hinterland of continental dimensions for it to flow through. He had discovered, he concluded, "another world, . . . an enormous land, to be found in the south, of which at the present time nothing has been known."[25] Again he insisted, "Ptolemy can have had no knowledge of this hemisphere, nor did any of the other ancients who wrote about geography, for it was very much unknown."[26] This is an exact description and characterization of the New World that Vespucci was subsequently said to have been the first to identify. Columbus's views on this point are evidently the source of Vespucci's.

This does not mean that Vespucci never saw the world he was credited with discovering—only that he never saw it with fresh eyes. The continent he proposed, moreover, was not what we now call the Americas. It was strictly a southern-hemisphere affair. For Vespucci, the newfound land of continental dimensions was new and surprising precisely because it lay south of the equator. In other words, it was the fabled Antipodes. He thought that for as long as he beheld it. Did he revise his opinion when he got home and thought about it at leisure? Was the New World of *Mundus Novus* merely the Antipodes? Or was it genuinely a new contribution to geographical theory, unprecedented in ancient and medieval texts? How new was it? New in what sense? As one picks over *Mundus Novus*, the absence of any more references to the Antipodes seems striking. But to me, the notion seems implicit.

The new regions which we found and explored . . . we may rightly call a new world, because our ancestors had no knowledge of them, and it will be a matter wholly new to all those who hear about them. For this transcends the view held by our ancients, inasmuch as most of them hold that there is no continent to the south beyond the equator, but only the sea which they named the Atlantic; and if some of them did aver that a continent there was, they denied with abundant argument that it was a habitable land. But that this their opinion is false and utterly opposed to the truth, this my last voyage has made manifest; for in those southern parts I have found a continent more densely peopled and abounding in animals than our Europe or Asia or Africa, and, in addition, a climate milder and more delightful than in any other region known to us. . . .[27]

To understand what this passage meant, it is important to realize that Vespucci was not only reporting observations, he was entering literary lists, fighting a Battle of the Books, rejoining controversies current in Florence in his boyhood—the controversies ignited by the rediscovery of Strabo, fanned by Toscanelli, and made incandescent by the voyages of Columbus.

He returned to this theme in one of his most puzzling passages. The fullest version—revised after Vespucci had received protests from the recipient of the Ridolfi Fragment about the obscurity of his previous efforts to make it intelligible—is in *Mundus Novus*. Here it occurs after a largely fanciful description of the antipodean sky, where rainbows are white and "innumerable vapours and glowing meteors fly about."[28] The writer reduces the number of stars that denote the Antarctic pole to three, compared with the four previously specified. "After these come two others, the half circumference of which, the diameter, has twelve and a half degrees." The author repeats his former reasons for saying that he traversed a quarter of the circumference of the globe. He goes on:

And by this calculation we who live in Lisbon, thirty-nine and a half degrees north latitude this side of the equator, are with respect to those fifty degrees beyond the same line, south latitude, at an angle of five degrees on a transverse line. And that you may the more clearly understand: a perpendicular line drawn while we stand upright, from a point in the sky overhead, our zenith, hangs over our head; it comes down upon their side or ribs. Thus comes about that we are on an upright line, but they on a line drawn sideways. A kind of orthogonal triangle is thus formed, the position of whose upright line we occupy, but they are the base; and the hypotenuse is drawn from our zenith to theirs.[29]

A diagram illustrates: a right-angled triangle in which the lines that form the angle are labeled, respectively, "They" and "We." The passage is calculated to bemuse with jargon. It is actively misleading, since the zenith of anyone standing upright passes, in the image Vespucci used, straight from head to foot. It reminds me of the story of the two American researchers whose study consisted of giving the same lecture twice, once in intelligible and once in unintelligible language, and testing the reactions of the audience. The unintelligible version was by far the more highly rated. All this passage of *Mundus Novus* seems to mean is that points at any given latitudes ninety degrees apart on the surface of the earth will subtend an angle of ninety degrees at its center. This is a truism utterly unworthy of utterance: the thought of a child masked in the language of a hierophant. Why did Vespucci trick it out with all the nonsense about feet and ribs? It sounds like an attempt to deal obliquely with the vulgar problem of how people on the other side of the world coped with life upside down.

Essentially, Vespucci clung to Columbus's opinion but expressed it forcefully and unequivocally. He endorsed Columbus's view that the land was continental. "In 64 days, we arrived at a new land, which we found to be terra firma."[30] But this was in a letter of 1502 and can hardly be called a remarkable or novel insight. It was not, in other words, because he was a sagacious or uniquely insightful geographer that Vespucci insisted he had found a "new world." As usual, he clung closely to the views, example, and even words of Columbus. He assessed the globe at a somewhat larger size than Columbus had, but still erred on the small side. He endorsed the general proposition on which Columbus's voyages were based: the accessibility of Asia by way of a transatlantic route.

In *Mundus Novus*, in switching the emphasis away from the search for a western route to Asia, and stressing the novelty of the world disclosed by Atlantic exploration, Vespucci was making the best of a bad job. Portugal's eastbound route to the Indian Ocean was functioning well. There was no chance of competing with it by heading west. If the westward enterprise was to continue to attract funding and recruits, its proponents had to recommend it for its own sake.

THE ENCOUNTER WITH PEOPLE

All the early European visitors to the New World spent more time describing the inhabitants than the animals, plants, or landscape. This is understandable. Europeans at the time had barely discovered nature. They acknowledged no category between civilization and wasteland. No European painted a landscape without figures until 1523.

At first, however, as Vespucci approached their shores, the people of the New World remained offstage, indicated only by the smoke of campfires the explorers saw from their vessels.[31] The natives made their next appearance as evidence of Vespucci's cleverness. He had disproved, he said, the error of the ancients: The torrid zone was not uninhabitable. Columbus had ascribed exactly the same achievement to himself; again, Vespucci's dependence on his predecessor seems inescapable. Despite his avowals of the superiority of experience over tradition, Vespucci's material on the inhabitants of the lands he visited owed more to literature than observation.

Although he had plenty to say about them, his observations seem depressingly meager. He did not distinguish between different communities, even though the lands he saw housed varied cultures. Broadly speaking, Vespucci roamed lands inhabited by peoples belonging to three big language groups. Along the northernmost parts of the shores he coasted, when he was with Hojeda, there were Arawaks and Caribs. South of the Amazon, where he spent much of his time on his first voyage and most of it on his second, Tupi speakers predominated. The Arawaks—specifically the Guayquieris of what is now the Venezuelan coast—were a maritime people, pearl fishers and traders, turtle trappers and fish farmers, supreme in canoe building, whose networks covered much of the Caribbean and its southern shores. The Caribs also traded, specializing in the ear ornaments of gold and copper that came overland from the northern Andes to their harbors on the Caribbean coast.[32] But they were specialists in warfare, too, who conducted *razzie* against their neighbors. Carib-Arawak hostility generated tales of cannibalism that Columbus was at first disinclined to believe. The Arawaks were so evidently soliciting the Spaniards' sympathy. When he found evidence of butchered human carcasses in Carib camps, he succumbed to belief that he had found the lands of the fabled anthropophagi.

Incursions by the Tupi added to the stress that caused violence in the region. The Tupi had probably been pushing northward for generations, driving their predecessors deeper into the forest as they advanced up the coast. They had a mixed economy, combining seasonal farming with foraging. The game of the forest was a vital part of their diet. Since Vespucci's visits, change has obscured the realities of their way of life, and he was too awestruck or prejudiced to leave us a clear vision. But with the help of other sources—accounts by explorers who followed him and anthropological and archaeological evidence—we can get close to a visualization of some of the sights that greeted him. A convincingly realistic Tupi village, for instance, appears as an illustration in a map of 1541 by Jean Rotz, one of the splendid school of cartography that worked in Dieppe.[33] By then plenty of sources had reported on the Tupi in detail and with something like accuracy, especially, it must be supposed, the French loggers and traders who frequented the Brazilian coast in the early sixteenth century in search of dyewood. In Rotz's depiction, stockade-fenced longhouses surrounded a ceremonial plaza in a glade stripped of foliage but studded with tree stumps: This was a realistic depiction of what land looked like when the Tupi cleared it for tillage. The trees were felled by burning through the trunk along the line of a ring incised at a suitable height. Some Indians fought off neighbors; some reclined in hammocks; others gathered for a ritual dance. Others, serving European commerce, which did not exist in Vespucci's day, felled timber for dyewood and carried it to canoes by the shore. A few domestic fowl pecked determinedly. Only three parts of the scene corresponded to Vespucci's observations: the hammocks, the longhouses "truly wondrously constructed for people who have no iron or other metal," and a barbecue on which a woman roasted a human leg.

I do not draw attention to the deficiencies of Vespucci's observations in order to denigrate him but to stress the difficulties under which he labored. Other early observers faced the same difficulties with the same effects. Apart from Columbus's, the nearest account, in space or time, was that of Pêro Vaz de Caminha,[34] an officer of Cabral's fleet who wrote the first report home of the expedition's landfall in Brazil. Caminha's encounter occurred on a shore inhabited by Tupi speakers, in a region Vespucci probably did not reach until his second voyage. The similarities among the three writers—Columbus, Vespucci, Caminha, the first responding to people in Caribbean Islands, the second to a mixture of communities in Venezuela and Brazil, the third to an encounter with Tupi—are so striking that they can be explained only in one of two ways. They may be the outcome of a form of collusion: Vespucci surely knew the others' texts and may have followed Columbus out of habit, for he was always in the admiral's shadow. By the time of his second voyage, he had had time and opportunity to know Caminha's thoughts as well, which also would have been informed by prior knowledge of what Columbus and Vespucci had already written. Further or alternatively, the similarities of the three accounts may arise from similarities in the writers' predicaments. All had to struggle to comprehend a bewilderingly novel experience, and all had the same literary models in mind.

Vespucci's first descriptions of the people he encountered closely followed the model Columbus had established. The first thing Columbus noted about native people in the New World—the first thing any European is known to have noticed—was that they were, as he put it, "as naked as their mothers bore them, and the women too."[35] Vespucci's version is similar: The men and women were all naked "as they emerged from their mothers' wombs" and, he added, knew no shame.[36] Caminha's opening observation of the people he met was similar: "They were dark brown and naked, and had no covering for their private parts." Their nakedness, the author emphasized, is no cause of shame to them, no more than "showing their faces." "The innocence of Adam himself was no greater than these people's, as concerns the shame of the body."[37]

Despite this consensus, Florentine savants who read Vespucci's reports in manuscript responded skeptically. Could these people really go around naked all the time? In reply, Vespucci appealed to the authority of experience. With a good deal of bombastic, ill-contained ire, he recapitulated the scale of his voyages and insisted that "in the best part of 2,000 leagues of coast and 5,000 islands, I never saw anyone go clothed."[38] But why was the claim that the natives were naked so controversial?

In part, it was the sort of literary topos that seemed calculated to inspire skepticism. Mandeville had included descriptions of socially naked people among the mirabilia he listed in an almost impossibly remote part of the world—the island in the southern hemisphere he called Lamory, which some other texts identified as Sumatra. Here, he said, "the custom is for men and women to go completely naked . . . for they say that God made Adam and Eve naked and men ought not to be ashamed of what God has made, for nothing natural is ugly."[39] Mandeville's chapter on Lamory is by far the major source of Vespucci's unattributed allusions to the travel writer, and he must have had this passage in his mind when he found naked interlocutors of his own.

More important, nakedness was ideologically charged. Mandeville's supposed encounter with naked people was obviously ironic. He was implicitly chiding the learned of his day for an irrational prejudice in favor of clothes. His argument had an almost heretical frisson, for in Europe, nudism was supposedly a practice of the Adamite heretics, who believed themselves predestined for salvation and therefore incapable of sin. If practiced without concupiscence, nakedness did seem to be a morally superior state. It suggested Edenic innocence. It recalled the classical myth of the Golden Age of silvan virtue before war and avarice disturbed the harmony of the earth. And it was a symbol of the goodness of dependence on God, such as St. Francis of Assisi had famously and spectacularly demonstrated by stripping himself naked in public in the main square of his hometown.

Vespucci was explicit about the models he had in mind when he attempted to interpret the Indians' unashamed nakedness. They dwelled, he said, in an Eden or a Golden Age. That was also the way Castile's court humanist, Peter Martyr of Anghiera, thought. Publicizing Columbus's discoveries in a work published in 1500, he asserted that on

Columbus's islands, "the land belonged to all, just like the sun and water. Mine and thine, the seeds of all evils, do not exist for these people.... They live in a golden age ... in open gardens, without laws or books, without judges, and they naturally follow goodness and consider odious anyone who corrupts himself by practising evil." On his second voyage, after the publication of this work, Vespucci transferred Peter Martyr's judgment almost word for word to Brazil, alleging that they practiced a kind of primitive communism. It was not true. According to a mid–sixteenth century observer who spent a lot of time living with Tupi and who was in other respects highly reliable, every couple had a private garden where the women grew their families' own food.[40] Once again, Vespucci allowed literary models to substitute for real observation. Mandeville, with his usual radical timbre, had already trailed the prospect that explorers would find societies that shared property on the fringes of the world. In his fictional account of the island of Lamory, he wrote, "The land is common property ... each man takes what please him, now here, now there. For all things are common, as I said, corn and other goods, too; nothing is locked up, and every man is as rich as another."[41]

This was subversive stuff. There was a theological implication almost too devastating to acknowledge: Had a state of prelapsarian innocence survived original sin in some hitherto unfrequented paradise? Any suggestion that there were people exempt from original sin challenged the entire basis of Christian morality. And for perplexed humanists, the problem of how to understand the myth of the Golden Age was a burning issue. Was there really an era of morally superior people, such as classical poets sang of, in the past, and if so, did vestiges of it survive beyond the corrosive touch of commerce? If it was just a myth about the past, the Golden Age could become a programmatic utopia—a vision of a possible future in which inequality and injustice would vanish.

After or alongside their nakedness, the natives' pigmentation was the next feature to demand attention from the first observers. Pigmentation was important not because of racism—medieval science did not reckon dark skin in itself as evidence of natural inferiority—but because it raised questions about geographical orthodoxy derived from Aristotle, and therefore cast light on the relative methods of rival epistemologies: observation versus received authority. Aristotle had predicted that similar latitudes would produce similar environments and, in consequence, similar products and people. Since black skin was assumed to be an effect of a tropical climate, people were expected to be black wherever they lived in affected latitudes. But was Aristotle right? Did experience and observation bear him out? These were unnerving questions, for Aristotle, in the estimation of the time, was "The Philosopher"—the ultimate arbitrator of knowledge. Any challenge to his authority was, to the science of the time, as unsettling as a challenge to the veracity of the Bible. Moreover, the color of the skin of the people of the New World, if it could be established, would help to fix the natives' place in the biblical and classical panorama of humankind.

Columbus insisted that the people he found were "neither black nor white, but like the Canary Islanders."[42] That was uncontroversial, because Columbus was—or thought he was—roughly on the latitude of the Canaries when he arrived in the Caribbean. Unfortunately, we do not know what the native Canarians actually looked like, since the depredations of the conquest and the ravages of colonialism wiped them all out, except in romantic imaginations.[43] Most reports at the time of the conquest called them white. By rights, according to Aristotle, the natives at the latitudes in which Vespucci and Caminha operated ought to be black, because that was what people in corresponding latitudes of the Old World looked like. Caminha described them variously as dark brown and red. Pigments with which they daubed themselves, he thought, accentuated the redness. For Vespucci, as ever echoing Columbus, they were neither black nor white but "beige, as it were, or tawny [*come bigio o lionato*]." This image, at least, unanticipated by Columbus, was of Vespucci's own devising. But it was too white for his critics.

When his Florentine correspondent challenged him on the matter, he repeated that the people of the New World had skin rather the color of lions. Again, he appealed to experience. He had seen what he had seen. But to make it credible to learned readers, he had to extemporize a theory to fit. He had three suggestions. The first was that blackness was an effect "of compression of the air and the nature of the land." Africa was the victim of poor soil and hot winds, whereas the lands he had visited were "much more pleasant and temperate and of better compression, causing the people to be white."[44] Second, he opined, black pigmentation was hereditary (though this hardly helped explain how differences of pigmentation arose in the first place). Finally, he claimed that if he had time, he could develop a further hypothesis: that astral influences were different in the Americas and produced different effects. This was, in its way, a remarkable suggestion, not because it contained any shred of scientific insight but because it anticipated one of the themes of the eighteenth-century "Dispute of the New World," which pitted detractors of the climate and environment of the Americas against defenders who regarded the New World as capable of breeding superior fruits, fauna, and men—partly on the grounds that the stars that shone there were more propitious.[45]

Once they got over or around the question of the natives' coloring, the early observers sought terms in which to describe their faces and bodies. As we have seen, explorers expected monsters, and the reading public demanded monsters. The observers were in regions that they thought were at the margins of the inhabited world, where classical and medieval legend had strewn the sciapod, who reclined beneath the shade of his one enormous foot; the cynocephali, or dog-heads; the mouthless folk who took nourishment only by inhaling; Amazons and giants; hairy woodchouses; "anthropophagi and men whose heads do grow beneath their shoulders"—the monsters Othello confronted. In the printed version of Columbus's first report, the writer expressed surprise that he had found no monsters on his islands. But more than titillation was at stake. Monsters, too, bore the deforming weight of ideological controversy. St. Augustine had denied the existence of monstrosities. It is only, he argued, our warped perceptions of beauty that make us deny the perfection of beings unlike ourselves.[46] But after a period of skepticism, monsters clawed their way back into medieval geographies, ethnographies, and bestiaries in increasing numbers from the twelfth century onward, partly, as we have seen, as a result of the rediscovery of classical texts in which monsters were enumerated. Their meaning, more than their existence, was at issue. According to a principle of late-medieval psychology, long accepted but authoritatively laid down in the thirteenth century by Albertus Magnus, perfect reason could dwell only in a perfect body. So monstrosity was a sign of subhumanity. The *similitudines hominis*—monsters resembling the rest of us, though in a grotesque way—were not fully, truly human, but nether links in the chain of being that bound animals and men.

This is why the early observers in the New World were so insistent on the natives' normal physiques. "They are people of gentle disposition and good stature," Columbus insisted. "Of good physique and great heart," affirmed Vespucci. According to Caminha, they were "well formed" with "good, well-made faces and noses. . . . The Lord has given them good bodies and good faces, like good men."[47] He added, however, long and repeated musings on their habits of self-deformation, misshaping their lips by forcing stones into specially cut holes. The compiler of *Mundus Novus* added this detail to Vespucci's account. There was more than mere prurience—there was a political, social, and sexual agenda—in the insistence all the observers shared on the physical perfections of native women. Caminha was most eloquent on this point: "One of the girls was all dyed from top to toe with that paint of theirs, and she certainly was so well made and so rounded, and her private parts (of which she made no privacy) so comely that many women in our own country would be ashamed, if they saw such perfection, that theirs were not equally perfect. None of the men was circumcised, but all just as we are."[48]

Having described the natives' appearance, the observers tried to give readers a sense of what these people were like: their behavior, their manners, their comportment, their degree of civility, their willingness to fraternize with the newcomers. The way the natives responded to their European visitors was critical. It would determine whether they were biddable, docile, and easily exploitable, or hostile and intractable. If the latter, what could be done about it? Could the natives lawfully be conquered or enslaved, or their lands appropriated by colonists? Questions of this sort had long been debated in theory by philosophers and academic lawyers, and some principles had been insecurely established or adumbrated. At the risk of oversimplification, these can be summarized thus: Natural law guaranteed the sovereignty of every political community, but people who offended against natural law forfeited its protection.[49] In the years prior to the encounters in the New World, questions about the juridical status of newly encountered people became increasingly urgent. In the 1430s, the Portuguese prince Henrique—commonly miscalled "Henry the Navigator" by English-speaking writers—established a right of conquest, acknowledged by successive popes, against native peoples of parts of West Africa, on the grounds that they were "wild men of the woods," indomitable by peaceful methods. Presumptively, the right of conquest (which Henry was not really interested in) carried a right of enslavement (in which he was), because the law of the time defined slaves as captives of just war. It was a custom hallowed by antiquity and justified by retribution.

By the time of the New World encounters, the questions that arose were urgent in the minds of the explorers and their readers, for the example of the Canary Islanders was plain before the world. These people, too, had impressed Europeans with their rudimentary material culture—their skin-clad poverty, their pastoral lives, their Stone Age technology—and excited humanist speculations about the survival of the Golden Age. But they had proved ferocious and tenacious in resistance. It had taken nearly a hundred years of warfare to reduce all the islands to obedience. The last bloody campaign ended only in 1496. Throughout the conflict, theologians questioned its justice and intervened to prevent or reverse the enslavement of the islanders.[50]

Columbus was quick to assert that the people he met on his islands were the sort you do business with peacefully. "They obliged us so much that it was a wonder.... They took and gave to us of all that they had with a good will.... They must make good servants, of ready grasp, for I see that they very smartly repeat whatever is said to them."[51] In Vespucci's account, they conversed with the newcomers and entertained them generously—Amerigo does not specify the ingredients of the meal—"and anything asked of them they gave at once—I think more for fear than for love."[52] Both writers, anxious to portray the natives as docile and unthreatening, said that they were timid and fled at the explorers' approach. This scene was captured in the woodcuts that accompanied early editions of Columbus's first published report of his discoveries. In the foreground, the king of Spain sits enthroned on a shoreline pointing across the ocean, beyond which a European flotilla, led by a behatted explorer, lands on a palmy coast where naked, long-haired savages, equipped only with staves, hasten offstage. What looks like a cloud lines in the sky, but really it is a recut image of St. Nicholas, patron of mariners, who frequently appears as the celestial overseer of seaborne adventures in the iconography of the time. The image suited Vespucci's recapitulation so perfectly that the publishers of the Florentine edition of the *Soderini Letter* reproduced it without modification as the frontispiece of the work.

Caminha's experience, as he reported it, was at first slightly different in this respect from that of the other two observers. Later, he reclassified the natives as timid, but that was not his first impression. "They carried bows and arrows in their hands" when he first saw them.

They all came determinedly towards the boat. Nicolau Coelho made a sign to them to put down their bows, and they put them down. But he could not speak to them or make himself understood in any other way because of the waves which were breaking on shore. He merely threw them a red cap, and a linen bonnet he had on his head and a black hat. And one of them threw him a hat of large feather with a small crown of red and grey feathers, like a parrot's. Another gave him a large bough covered with little white beads which looked like seed-pearls. I believe that the admiral is sending these articles to Your Majesty. After this, as it was late, the expedition returned to the ships, without succeeding in having further communication with them, because of the sea.[53]

Though these natives were not the timid creatures depicted in the Columbus engravings, everything about the encounter seems auspicious.

Caminha has met a forthright, polite, and commercial people. Mutual unintelligibility is not an inevitable consequence of cultural incommensurability, merely a side effect of the bluster of the sea. A closer-range encounter with two natives a little farther south confirmed the initial impressions. "One of them made gestures that seemed to indicate there were gold and silver ashore, and that he was willing to buy white rosary beads for gold." At least, "we took it in this sense, because we preferred to. If, however, he was trying to tell us that he would take the beads and the collar as well, we did not choose to understand him, because we were not going to give it to him."[54]

Circumstances forced the observers to change their view and acknowledge that the nature of the natives was more complex than at first appeared. Some native communities reacted with suspicion or hostility to the arrival of strangers. Initially docile people could turn nasty when they learned more about the predatory, greedy objectives of their guests. When Cabral's men began to encounter natives by the hundred, peaceful conventions continued, but Caminha observed them with evidently increasing anxiety. The natives, when asked to retire, did not go very far. Their speech was unintelligible because it was "uncouth." Their habit of disappearing after trade became increasingly disquieting: "I deduce from these facts," Caminha wrote,

> *that they are a savage, ignorant people, and for that very reason they are so timid. For all which, they are healthy and very clean. So that I am even surer that they are like the wild birds or animals whose feathers and hair the air makes finer than when they are domesticated, and whose bodies are as clean, as plump and as beautiful as these could possibly be. Which all makes me suppose that these people lodge in no houses or dwellings. The air in which they are nurtured makes them what they are. We, at any rate, did not see any houses of theirs nor anything resembling such.*[55]

As they distanced themselves from the Portuguese, the natives seemed to Caminha to draw closer to the birds and beasts: They were edging out of the ranks of humankind into an effectively monstrous demimonde, bestial and savage, from which they could justly be retrieved by force.

Vespucci, after initially peaceful encounters, soon met natives who resisted. The explorers—despairing of their lives in the thick of the fray—had to fight them off, inspired by prayer and the rallying cry of a bold but unnamed companion. The episode reads like a heroic interpolation. More serious in its implications for future relations between natives and newcomers was the discovery of cannibals. Columbus had reported such things on his first voyage but was disinclined to believe them until, on his second voyage, he found unmistakable evidence of cannibalism in the lesser Antilles: fugitives who were intended victims of cannibal feasts, and human bodies butchered for the pot. Columbus, however, could draw a distinction between good natives and bad natives. Arawaks were good, Caribs bad. Caribs ate Arawaks, but Arawaks did not eat Caribs. The situation Vespucci found was more complex. His Eden had human serpents. The Golden Age was dappled with darkness. The same people were at once moral exemplars and the incarnations of bestial vice. "And we found they were of a race that are called cannibals, and almost the greater part, or all, of this generation lives on human flesh: and this Your Magnificence can take for certain." The influence of Columbus was again discernible in what Vespucci went on to say. Some of the details the Florentine added could have been pieced together from Columbus's reports—the cannibals, for instance, who made raids in canoes on neighboring peoples, the body parts strung up for cooking. Others were perhaps inventions, perhaps genuine observations. "They do not eat any women, but only keep them as slaves."[56] That does seem to have been the normal practice of the Tupi, whose cannibal feasts were forms of ritual sacrifice of prisoners of war. Enemy warriors were eaten in token of victory and possibly in order to appropriate their prowess by ingesting it. On his second voyage, Vespucci elaborated. The cannibals, he explained, bred with captive women, "and after a while, when diabolic fury overtakes them, they slaughter the mothers and babies and eat them."[57] This graphic episode made it into the printed versions and captured engravers' imaginations. One witness Vespucci claimed to have interviewed had eaten over two hundred victims, "which I believe for sure, and let that suffice."[58]

Mandeville's influence again seems to lurk in the background of the tradition Vespucci's account belongs to. On his island of Lamory, he asserted, "they have an evil custom, for they will eat human flesh more gladly than any other. . . . Merchants bring children there to sell and the people of the country buy them. Those that are plump they eat. Those that are not plump, they feed up and fatten, and then kill and eat them. And they say that it is the sweetest flesh in the whole world."[59] Readers will recall that in other respects, Lamory in Mandeville's imagination was a morally exemplary isle on which, as in Vespucci's New World, innocence and savagery seemed to coexist.

Why these equivocations or, at least, inconsistencies? Why depict the natives as both good and bad? Why the strange synthesis between the natives Columbus had met on his first voyage—timid, peaceful, suggestible—and the ferocious cannibals he encountered on his second? Vespucci's perceptions, like those of Columbus, changed as he went along, visiting a series of different peoples with somewhat varying cultures. In Columbus's case, as he traveled around the Caribbean on his first voyage, two changes unfolded. First, he grew increasingly disappointed, even increasingly desperate, at the paucity of exploitable products or opportunities for commerce. That made him think more and more of the natives as potential slaves. The islands had so little else to offer. On the other hand, when he progressed from small, poor outlying islands to the great central island he called Hispaniola, he noticed an improvement in the wealth and political sophistication of the people he met. Vespucci, too, modified his perceptions along with his expectations. He arrived as a merchant on the lookout for naive traffickers who would sell him cheap pearls and people like those Columbus recorded, with their Edenic environment and innocent ways. By the time he left the New World for good, he had become a writer who needed good copy. Hence his increasing attraction to bizarre and sensational tales. Cannibalism sold. It could evoke comfortable horrors in a snug, smug European readership. It was by far the most effective of all Vespucci's remarks about the natives—the thing readers noticed and remembered. The woodcuts of early editions of his writings all feature scenes of cannibalism, with plausible representations of feathered Tupi nonchalantly turning human carcasses into meals.

Moreover, Vespucci had conflicting agendas. He wanted the natives to be amenable—suitable denizens of the *locus amoenus*—or to evoke the humanists' vision of the Golden Age. He was bound, too, to reflect the literary tradition of the "good pagan"—the moral model who was a reproach to sinful Christians. He also had to make money. Columbus's experience suggested that enslavement of the natives was the only way to do so. So did Vespucci's own experience as an employee of Gianotto Berardi. For reasons we have already encountered, it was necessary to ascribe crimes against natural law to the intended victims of enslavement. Such crimes placed them outside the law's protection and made them seem legitimate targets for coercion and violence.

Finally, it is worth insisting that Vespucci never escaped from perceptions colored by reading. His dependence on literary sources does not mean that his account owed nothing to real observation, only that he selected from his observations to suit his purposes. Most observers rely on memories of what they have read for the means of representing what they have seen in writing: for the language, imagery, and intellectual gloss. The most self-consciously literary of all his passages on the natives he met is an episode Vespucci located in a village fifteen leagues inland on an "island of giants"—an image he probably got from Dante, though it was common enough in late-medieval romances of chivalry. As we have seen, many prefigurations of Don Quixote took to the sea to battle with giants before winning an island realm in a fade-out that usually involved marriage with a princess. When Mandeville placed his ragbag of marvels on islands in the ocean east of China, a land of giants was the least incredible, compared with isles of jewel-eyed basilisks or women who rejoice when their children die. Mandeville's giants closely prefigure Vespucci's. They are naked except for the skins of beasts. They eat raw flesh and drink milk. They have no houses. "They will more readily eat human flesh than any other." They are quick to seize and kill anyone injudicious enough to land.[60]

Vespucci managed to work a combination of all these traditions into his account. The giant women, he said, resembled Penthesilea and the men Antaeus. The women received the explorers with modesty or timidity, but one of them—"certainly," said Vespucci, "a lady of discretion"—invited them to take refreshment. The visitors' first inclination was to kidnap a couple of these prodigies "and make a present of them to our king," but the arrival of a party of male giants thwarted them. A civilized exchange of niceties followed: "We answered them by signs that we were men of peace and that we were travelling to see the world." Although the giants were a literary device, they illustrate how topoi come and go across the frontier between reading and real experience, for later visitors to the Atlantic coasts of South America continued for centuries, by the power of suggestion, to seek and expect meetings with Amerigo's giants—to such an extent that Patagonia acquired a name that literally means "Land of the Bigfooted," and its indigenous people, though not particularly tall, were regularly perceived as gigantic by European visitors.

On his second visit, Amerigo claimed closer acquaintance with the natives. He spent twenty-seven days "eating and sleeping amongst them" and "strove hard to understand their lives and customs." In many ways, the experience confirmed the impressions he gathered on his previous visit to regions farther north. They were, he repeated, naked, well proportioned, and cannibalistic. Their contempt for worldly goods continued to project an impression of innocence, untouched by the root of evil. "They have no personal property, for everything is in common," and "value nothing, not gold or silver or other jewels, only things of feather and bone." Anxieties over these issues fed further disbelief among Vespucci's readers. He answered their doubts by adding interesting details on the subject of the natives' contempt for gold and silver. Skeptics pointed out that he mentioned buying slaves from the natives, who must, therefore, have had some commercial inclinations. But there was no contradiction, Amerigo retorted. "In responding," he began, "I lament the loss of time and the waste of paper and ink."[61] The purchasers, he explained, paid for the slaves with "a little wooden comb or a mirror worth four farthings [*quattrini*]" per head, and thereafter the natives "would not part with such a comb or mirror for all the gold in the world." Their way of life, he insisted, "is more epicurean than stoic or academic." Their only wealth was in personal ornament for games and war, for which they used "feathers and fish-bones and other such stuff." On the pearl fisheries—as Vespucci recalled a few years later—the explorers picked pearls worth 15,000 ducats in Castile, and paid the equivalent of less than 4 ducats for them. Vespucci himself bought 1,000 ducats' worth with a single hawk's bell. As for the guileless vendor, "as soon as he got the hawk's bell he put it in his mouth and was off into the wood, and I did not see him again." Amerigo also made some advance in his reflections on the problem of why people with no obvious political or economic motive should have practiced warfare. "I think they do it to eat each other."[62]

Of Amerigo's new observations, some were morally neutral and well observed. Presumably from Caminha, he picked up the importance of the absence of iron-forging technology. This was a positive feature—because the age of iron followed the Golden Age in the classical model—and equally a negative one, because it suggested cognitive inferiority to people in more technically ambitious societies. On balance, the positive and negative connotations canceled each other out. Vespucci took the opportunity to represent reliance on stone tools as evidence of the natives' technical resourcefulness. Despite having no metal tools, they built stupendous houses big enough to accommodate five or six hundred souls, all living a common life. Other new details in Vespucci's account enhanced its realism without affecting its message. The natives, he now noticed, used hammocks. They sat on the ground to eat meals of fruit, herbs, and fish, though "their meat is mostly human flesh." Because of the fierce creatures of the forest, "they do not venture into the woods except in strength of numbers."

Some of the new points arising from Vespucci's second voyage reflected unequivocal credit on the natives. Their women gave birth without fuss, "unlike our women," ate everything, and returned to work in the fields the same day. This sounds like a variant on the theme of pagan as moral example, as well as an instructive instance of male insensitivity to the pains of motherhood. The men were long-lived. The oldest man Vespucci met was 132 years old (inflated to 150 years in the *Soderini Letter*). That was surely a detail intended to reinforce Vespucci's appraisal of the New World as a salubrious place. It started a tradition. The longevity of the Tupi became a topos, and sixteenth-century writers regularly claimed, on the basis of observation, to have met people over a hundred years old.[63]

But Vespucci added new material that, if not also the fruit of experience, was the outcome of thought and reading. The combined impact was decisive: The natives appeared in a stark, accusing light. Where formerly Amerigo had dwelt on their spontaneous generosity and hospitality, he now saw them as "warlike and cruel." He added, rather implausibly, that they used only missile weapons (*"commessi al vento"*). This was an echo of his well-remembered Petrarch (above, p. 102).[64] They had none of the attributes of sovereignty—no recognizable political order, no organs of government, no institutions of justice. Therefore, they were fair game for European conquerors. "They have no boundaries of kingdoms or provinces; they have no king, nor anyone whom they obey: everyone is his own master. They do not administer justice, because covetousness does not reign among them." What was more, "they have no laws" and, by implication, had no knowledge of natural law; that made them, in principle, liable to enslavement. To say, as Vespucci also said, that "they live according to nature" was ambiguous. It could be read to mean that they observed natural law, but in the catalog of native moral deficiencies in which the remark occurs, it plainly means that they lived instinctively, in the manner of brute beasts, rather than reasoningly. By implication, rational men enjoyed the right of lordship over them by divine license. Caminha, too, thought the natives of the land Cabral discovered had no notion of hierarchy. This was not a perception Columbus shared—at least not in the surviving versions of his observations, almost all of which passed through the editorial hands of Bartolomé de Las Casas, the "apostle" and "protector" of the Indians, who devoted most of his life to an attempt to convince fellow Spaniards of the legitimacy and natural order of the native polities of the New World.

Details of natives' sex lives that Vespucci observed on his second voyage strengthened his criticisms. They did not keep to one wife "but as many as they want, and without much ceremony."[65] Polygamy was perhaps contrary to natural law in the estimation of experts at the time, though opinions differed. Mandeville, with his characteristic satirical edge, produced an ingenious defense of it in his description of Lamory: "In that land . . . all the women are held common to every man. They say that if they were to do otherwise they would sin greatly, because God said to Adam and Eve, *Crecite et multiplicamini et replete terram,* that is to say, 'Increase and multiply and fill the Earth.' And therefore no man says, 'This is my wife,' nor any woman, 'This is my husband.' "[66] Polygamy was not the worst of the sexual offenses Vespucci recorded on his second voyage. He also claimed that the natives institutionalized incest.[67] That, by the common consent of Christian jurisprudence, was a horrendous contravention of natural law.

The last deficiency in Vespucci's list was the natives' alleged lack of religion. This was not necessarily to their disadvantage. Columbus had claimed to notice the same phenomenon but made a virtue of it. One of his first observations was "I believe they will very easily be made Christians, for it seemed to me that they belonged to no religion." "They have," echoed Vespucci, "no faith" and "no knowledge of the immortality of the soul."[68] This was not a disinterested observation. Pope Eugenius IV had forbidden the enslavement under any circumstances of Christians and also of "people on the way to conversion." It had become customary during the conquest of the Canary Islands for missionaries who wanted to protect their potential congregations to claim that they had some inkling of God, by direct revelation, and that pagan piety was evidence of potential Christian piety. It was significant that Caminha observed Tupi dancing and leaping about, apparently in response

to witnessing the explorers celebrate mass.[69] "They seem to be such innocent people," he added, in words that echo almost exactly a view
Columbus had already expressed, "that, if we could understand their
speech and they ours, they would immediately become Christian, seeing
that, by all appearances, they do not understand about any faith. . . . Any
stamp we wish may easily be printed on them."[70] They occupied a well-
favored country, "as temperate as Entre Douro e Minho,"[71] but the
greatest fruit it could yield would be the salvation of the inhabitants. In
an Epiphany painting of the early sixteenth century, commonly attributed to Fernão Vasco, we can see a contemporary mind struggling with
this very problem. In accordance with tradition, of the Three Kings who
present gifts to the Christ child, one is white and one black. The third,
with his light brown skin, feathered headdress, and sparse clothing, is
easily recognizable as a Tupi—perhaps modeled on one of the speci-
mens brought back to Portugal by Vespucci's expedition.

In the end, Amerigo himself found his own contradictory perceptions irreconcilable. "And I could not learn from them why they make
war on each other: for they do not have private property or lordships or
empires or kingdoms, and they do not know what covetousness is—that
is, theft or the lust for power, which seem to me to be the causes of wars
and of every disorderly act."[72] This remark sounds like swanky intellec-
tualization, but shows that Amerigo abandoned or shelved—perhaps as
oversimplified, perhaps as false—his assumption that the natives made
war "to eat each other."

The natives prompted moral reflections and raised huge philosophical questions. Their moral status was a deep-going problem. It suggested questions about the value of civilization compared with savagery:
questions that would absorb philosophers over the next two centuries,
as explorations ranged farther and new cultural encounters multiplied.
Unhappily, the most influential images were not those Vespucci
recorded in his manuscript letters but the elaborations concocted for
the published versions of his voyage: the claim that he saw a father feed-
ing on his own wife and children; his encounter with a cannibal who had
personally ingested three hundred fellow humans; his vivid record of

"salted human meat, hanging from roof-beams, just as we strung up bacons and pork";[73] his horrified contemplation of cannibal women feasting on the severed body parts of one of his companions.

The first known picture based on his description appeared in the map known as Kunstman II in the Bavarian State Library, Munich. On a spit over a blazing fire, a kneeling cannibal turns a figure with head drooping toward the flames. Clearly, the scene was based on Vespucci's writings, but the date is uncertain. The map could derive from a manuscript but is more likely based on one of the printed versions of Vespucci's experiences.[74] An engraving of 1505, probably printed in Augsburg, shows Tupi life as the *Soderini Letter* depicts it: hanging joints and naked women, in feathered headdresses, distributing limbs. One of them gnaws on a human arm from which hand and fingers dangle. German and Flemish versions or extracts of the same text, published in 1509, are illustrated with cannibal scenes. The first shows the murder of one of Vespucci's fellow travelers, the second a cannibal family roasting a human head. Within a few years, painters were even modeling demons in hell on Vespucci's cannibals.[75]

CHAPTER SIX

THE CONJURER'S STAGE

Seville and the World, 1502–2005 ∘ ⟨ *Death and renown*

S OON AFTER GETTING BACK from his second voyage, Vespucci was in Seville, complaining about his luck and bemoaning his treatment at the hands of the king of Portugal. The xenophobic craze had waned in Spain, so Amerigo was free to return anytime, but the date of his arrival in his old hometown is unclear. His fellow Florentine and business associate Piero Rondinelli, in a letter from Seville of October 1502, expected him "in a few days." No other document pinpoints his whereabouts until February 1505, when he was keeping Columbus company, still—or again—in Seville. What was he doing in the meantime?

"MATTERS OF NAVIGATION"

Even if he was the author of both *Mundus Novus* and the *Soderini Letter,* they can hardly have taken long to write. Did Amerigo return to sea? The *Soderini Letter* includes a brief and recognizable—if not very accurate—description of a voyage from Portugal in 1503–04, led by an esteemed and experienced seafarer, Gonçalo Coelho, and calls it Vespucci's fourth voyage.

For what it is worth, the *Soderini Letter*'s account of the voyage can be summarized. The expedition left Lisbon on May 10, 1503. The object was Melaka, "the emporium of all the ships that come from the Gangetic Sea and the Indian Sea."[1] It is entirely credible that Melaka should have been the destination of a Portuguese fleet. Vespucci had it in mind ever since his conversation about the Indian Ocean with the mysterious Guaspare, who had been there. The port commanded a key waterway for trade between India and China, which was, at the time, the richest trade in the world, linking the two most productive economies. The *Soderini Letter*, however, does not seem well informed on the subject by Portuguese standards: Melaka was said to be west of Calicut, something the Portuguese already knew to be false.

Other details of the narrative were equally unreliable. Vespucci was represented as the captain of one of six ships, under an intractable, anonymous admiral, whose headstrong incompetence was stressed almost from the opening lines of the narrative. Three hundred leagues beyond Sierra Leone, and a thousand from Lisbon, after the obligatory storms, the explorers sighted an uninhabited island, two leagues by one, where the flagship foundered and the fleet split up. There is no island in that position, but that has not prevented enthusiasts for the text from hailing this as the record of the discovery of Ascension Island. Vespucci's ship, reunited with one of the others, continued to Brazil and anchored in Todos os Santos, familiar from Vespucci's previous voyage. Despairing of their companion ships, Vespucci and his crew followed the coast to a point eighteen degrees south and thirty-five degrees west of Lisbon, where they "pacified all the natives" and garrisoned a fort with twenty-four Portuguese. If Vespucci had really written this account, the longitude would surely be much inflated, in common with all his well-attested estimates. The explorers returned to Lisbon on June 28, 1504, to find their admiral had not survived; "for thus," added the author sententiously, "God rewards pride."[2]

The voyage—or something like it—did happen; other Portuguese sources confirm that Coelho led an expedition, aborted by disaster, at about the right time. But there is no proof that Vespucci took part in it and no independent record of its itinerary. The most likely explanation for its appearance in the *Soderini Letter* is that the compiler appropriated Coelho's voyage in order to make the number of Vespucci's voyages add up to four—partly because Columbus's four voyages had made the number canonical, and partly because *Mundus Novus* had promised a fourth voyage to Vespucci's public. Once again Columbus seems to have been Vespucci's example and inspiration. It is possible that the *Soderini Letter* is reliable on this matter and that Vespucci did ship with Coelho. But, as we have seen, the letter is a confection that owes little to Vespucci's input and includes many inauthentic borrowings and inventions. It would be rash to rely on its uncorroborated authority.

In late 1504 and early 1505, Vespucci was living in Columbus's house, exchanging commiseration and presumably picking the admiral's brains. In February 1505, according to Columbus, Vespucci left Seville to attend on the king, "summoned on matters concerning navigation."[3] Over the next few months, he received reimbursements from the crown for expenses supposedly incurred in royal service. He also became a naturalized Castilian subject by royal decree.[4] So he had succeeded where Columbus had failed: He had the confidence of the court. Evidently, his salesman's skills had not deserted him. From now on, more or less until the end of his life, a series of documents shows him discharging obligations of responsibility in royal service.

To begin with, he had a commission to supply a fleet that Columbus's old shipmate Vicente Yáñez Pinzón was preparing for the Indies with the aim of reaching "the spicerie."[5] This suggests two conclusions: First, that on the rebound from his service as an explorer in Portugal, Amerigo was willing to return to the relatively humdrum business of a ship's purveyor. Second, at this stage of his life, Vespucci evidently still adhered to a small-world model of the size of the globe and still hoped—unless the king and other correspondents had misunderstood him—that the project of finding a westward route to Asia would be fulfilled. In April 1506 a Venetian informant in Seville even thought that Vespucci would take part in this voyage, with the aim of discovering Melaka.[6] Gonçalo Coelho, as we have seen, experienced frustration in his quest for the same objective, and the *Soderini Letter*, at least, associated Vespucci's name with Coelho's efforts in pursuit of the same goal.

Nonetheless, the fact that Pinzón was bound for "the spicerie" suggests that this time Melaka was not part of the plan. Melaka was an emporium. The center of spice production—especially of the low-bulk, high-value items, such as nutmeg, cloves, and mace, all of which merchants craved—was farther east in the Moluccas, or Maluco, as contemporaries often said. "Melaka" and "Maluco" were easily confused. The *Soderini Letter* seems to confuse them, since in it Melaka is called "an island . . . which is said to be very rich"—a description that evokes the Moluccas but does not fit Melaka. Whatever the destination, Vespucci genuinely seems to have intended to ship on this expedition. He obtained an appointment as captain of one of the vessels at a salary of 30,000 *maravedíes*. Ironically, this is the one fleet for which we have evidence of Vespucci's command of a ship, and it never actually sailed. However, he probably made a good deal out of the transactions for ships and supplies that preceded the abandonment of the mission.

The "matters of navigation" that Vespucci claimed as his pretext for going to court may have been of his own invention, but there was significant demand for expertise in the field. First, there was the vexed question of the whereabouts of the "Tordesillas line." In 1494, in the Treaty of Tordesillas, Portuguese and Castilian negotiators had fixed the boundaries of their countries' zones of navigation in the Atlantic. An imaginary line was drawn on the map—literally drawn, for many early-sixteenth-century maps show representations of it. It ran from pole to pole, 370 leagues west of the Azores. Everything west of the line was Castile's to explore; everything to the east would be Portugal's. Since the science of the time knew no reliable means of measuring distance at sea, the whereabouts of the line was indeterminate and a source of more or less constant friction between the two powers. Even vaguer was the location of the countermeridian: the prolongation of the Tordesillas line on the far side of the globe. Since the planet was generally believed, among the learned, to be a perfect sphere, such a countermeridian must exist. But while the size of the globe was in dispute, no agreed basis was available for deciding where it lay. It was a question of critical importance and incalculable pecuniary value, since it had the potential to determine whether the Spice Islands lay in the Portuguese or the Castilian zone.

The problem was complicated by a tendency that cosmographers of the time found hard to avoid: to exaggerate longitudes and, implicitly, to underestimate the size of the globe. This was apparent in Columbus's and Vespucci's bumbling efforts to work out the longitude of their discoveries. Political self-serving might be expected to play some part, because if the countermeridian of the Tordesillas line were accepted as the line of demarcation between Castile and Portugal on the far side of the world, exaggerated longitudes would be very much to Castile's advantage. The bigger the world, the less likely it would be that such fabled locations as the Moluccas or Melaka or Taprobana or the Golden Chersonese would lie within Castile's sphere. The smaller the world, the more, relatively speaking, Castile would get of it. Shortly after Vespucci's death, a committee of experts, appointed by the monarchs of Castile to supervise negotiations on this point with the Portuguese, wrote candidly about the desirability of manipulating the figures: "We must be sparing with our measurements of distance and assign as little distance as possible to a degree of longitude on the surface of the Earth, because the smaller the distance, the smaller the whole world will be, which will be very much to the service of their Majesties."[8]

It is not clear when the Tordesillas countermeridian was accepted as the basis of Spanish-Portuguese negotiations. The Treaty of Tordesillas is explicitly limited to the western hemisphere. At the time, the chief cosmographer of the Castilian monarchs, the Majorcan scholar Jaume Ferrer, assumed that the Castilian zone extended west from the Tordesillas line all the way "to the eastern edge of the Arabian Sea."[9] The anonymous author of a Castilian memorandum of 1497, whom some scholars identify as Columbus, claimed that the treaty gave Castile exclusive rights "up to the point where there is or shall be a Christian prince in possession"—a point that, in the author's opinion, could be identified with the Cape of Good Hope on the grounds that the cape was then the limit of the king of Portugal's authority.[10] As far as I am aware, no document mentions the countermeridian until just after Vespucci's death, when the crown's instructions to his successor ordered him to determine whether Sri Lanka "was in the part which belonged to Spain" and then to sail on "to the Moluccas [*Maluco*] which falls within the limits assigned to us."[11] The Portuguese, at least privately, seem to have thought the same. An August 30 letter from their chief negotiator to the king places "Maluca" "four hundred leagues on Castile's side of the demarcation line."[12]

The countermeridian had presumably been discussed for some time before it was mentioned explicitly in surviving documents. Portuguese historical tradition puts the problem in the mind of King João II at the very moment when he signed the original treaty.[13] It is hard to believe that Vasco da Gama can have returned from India in 1499 without raising a question in diplomats' minds about where the countermeridian lay. And the repeated negotiations over fixing the location of the line of demarcation in the western hemisphere must have called it to mind.[14]

Second, there was the problem of educating pilots for the voyage to the Indies. When Spanish monarchs responded to petitions, they generally repeated the petitioners' wording. It is possible to reconstruct the arguments Amerigo used on this subject from the language the queen's secretariat used in confirming his new appointment and explaining his duties in a privilege issued to him on August 6, 1508. "We have seen by experience," the document began, immediately invoking Vespucci's characteristic epistemology,

> that because the pilots are not as expert as they need to be, nor sufficiently well instructed in what they must know in order to guide and steer the ships that they navigate on the voyages that take place on the ocean sea to the islands and mainland we possess in the region of the Indies, and because of their deficiency in the knowledge of how to guide and steer, and because of their lack of basic knowledge of how to use the quadrant and astrolabe to measure latitude and of how to make the appropriate calculations, they have made many errors, and the men who sail under their orders have incurred great danger, wherein our Lord has been ill served, and much damage and loss have resulted to our treasury and to the merchants who trade there.

All pilots who wanted to sail to the Indies must "know what it is needful to know of the quadrant and astrolabe, so that, joining practice with theory, they can make use of it in the said voyages."[15] This language obviously came from Vespucci. It matches almost exactly phrases he used in his letters.

The superiority of navigating with instruments was an obsession of his, precisely because he was little experienced in pilotage. He was strong on theory but had not been raised in the craft, like most professional pilots. For those who knew the sea from long experience, it was not necessary to toy with instruments to know your latitude. You could judge it by reckoning the height of the sun or, in the northern hemisphere, that of the Pole Star with the naked eye. Techniques of this sort—of "primitive celestial navigation"—seem almost incredible to mariners reliant on technological gewgaws. In the age of GPS navigation, they have disappeared except among a few traditional navigators in remote regions of the Pacific. Even navigators with modest experience could manage perfectly well in the northern hemisphere—where almost all Spanish voyages at the time were confined—by an alternative technique: timing the passage of the guard stars around the Pole Star and subtracting the result from twenty-four in order to obtain the hours of daylight. Printed tables were available so that you could use this information to read your latitude off them. Columbus used this technique— although, as we have seen, he also delighted in flourishing quadrants before his men in an attempt to convince them of his command of arcana. I suspect that Vespucci used it, too, since his assertions of prowess with navigational instruments reek of affectation. They were part of his projected image as a Renaissance magus with access to a secret art, unattainable by ordinary navigators, and a power over the forces of nature that equipped him to defy the sea.

Finally, there was the problem of chart making. Charts were then luxuries for landlubbers. Real seamen did not normally use them. Faith in charts was an eccentricity of semi-amateurs like Columbus. Experienced navigators on familiar routes simply memorized the way. Alternatively, they relied on sailing directions, orally transmitted or confided by forebears in written form. If they carried charts, they did so chiefly to show passengers the route, or as a general guide to unfamiliar objectives.

Not until well into the seventeenth century did charts become a normal part of shipboard equipment. Indeed, until then there were few charts reliable enough to sail by.[16] Vespucci, however, convinced the landlubbers of the royal council that charts were of critical importance at sea.

He also persuaded at least some of his contemporaries that he was an expert mapmaker, even though no map from his hand has survived— not even the globe he once claimed to be making for Lorenzo di Pierfrancesco de' Medici, which he promised to send to his patron with a Florentine messenger. Columbus, too, promised to make maps and globes to illustrate his voyages. Neither explorer ever seems to have delivered. Still, however dubious his own expertise, Vespucci argued for the establishment of a single "model map" to be amended as new information became available, and to be issued to all pilots sailing to the Indies. "There are maps of many patterns," declared the document of 1508, repeating his arguments, "made by various masters, that have set and located the lands and islands of the Indies that belong to us and that have been newly discovered by our command; and these maps are very different from one another, both in depicting the route and locating the lands, which may cause great inconvenience."

Professional mariners had no time for that sort of talk, and no inclination for the arcana of newfangled nautical technology. But the Castilian court was a landlubbers' world. The monarchs relied on scientific experts, not undereducated seafarers, for advice about policy. They had already confided responsibility for exploiting the New World to an organ of the bureaucracy, especially created for the purpose. A royal decree founded the Casa de Contratación, or House of Trade, on January 20, 1502. It was an institution without strict parallels (though there were precedents in Portugal and in Italian trading cities for some of its functions). From 1503, once all those functions had been specified, it was supreme in the New World—a department of government with responsibility for the administration of justice there and, in effect, the exercise of sovereignty on the crown's behalf. In the lands Spaniards conquered and settled, administration soon passed to specialized tribunals and to the royal council, leaving the Casa with command of the sea. The Casa remained essentially as a board of regulation of trade to and from Spain's American possessions and a supervisory board for expeditions of exploration. Both vocations committed the Casa to acting as a repository of data on geography, hydrography, cartography, and navigation. The security of shipping against the hazards of winds, currents, and dangerous shores demanded the coordination of information that explorers recorded and the training of navigators in the latest intelligence about the New World and the ways thither.[17] For Vespucci, the Casa was a perfect milieu. I imagine him besieging its threshold and haunting its corridors.

Life and Death of a Chief Pilot

By the summer of 1506, Vespucci had convinced the officials of the Casa de Contratación of his indispensability. He was organizing their expeditions, negotiating on their behalf with the king, and reporting— perhaps—on the state of affairs at court during an uneasy period in Castilian politics, characterized by tension between the queen's husband and father.[18] The sometime Mr. Fixit of Medicean Florence had become the factotum of the Casa de Contratación. Most of Amerigo's documented work for 1506 and 1507 was in line with his former labors as a chandler: acquiring grain and turning it into ship's biscuit, buying and lading grease for the ship's yards. Venetian informants continued to believe that Vespucci himself would pilot crafts across the Atlantic, but that does not seem to have been the case. He stayed in Seville, trying to garner wealth. From March 1508, when he received his commission as chief pilot of the Casa de Contratación, he had a salary of 50,000 maravedíes and expenses of 25,000 a year at his disposal.[19] He was still making money out of supplying ships bound for the Indies and reputedly culling more funds from trade on his own account.

It is possible to reconstruct his movements in some detail.[20] The word on the street in July 1508 was that he had orders from the king to fortify the hulls of good Biscayan ships with lead against the termites of the tropics "and go by way of the west to find the lands that the Portuguese found navigating via the east."[21] So at that stage, popular opinion still associated Vespucci with an image of the world essentially similar to that of Columbus, and with an essentially similar project: a westward route to Asia.

The opportunity to make the voyage never arose. Early in 1508, he had formed part of an important mission for the Casa de Contratación. He was among those responsible for delivering a consignment of gold to the royal treasury. His three fellow commissioners were leading pilots. Juan de la Cosa and Vicente Yáñez Pinzón had been shipmates of Columbus's before leading their own expeditions across the Atlantic. Juan Díaz de Solís, the fourth member of the quadrumvirate, had shipped with Alonso de Hojeda. For Vespucci, the trip to court was a chance to lobby on his own behalf and seal an appointment.

He took the chance. "My will and grace," the king told the Casa, "is to take and receive as our chief pilot Amerigo Vespucci, resident of Seville."[22] Moreover, Amerigo was to have a monopoly of instruction in the art of oceanic navigation, charging pilots for his services. He was to have the exclusive right to examine pilots before they could undertake any voyage to the Indies or receive any salary; he alone was to ensure that they were sufficiently instructed in celestial navigation with quadrant and astrolabe. If he ever did this, it was in his own house. There are no records of the instruction or examination of pilots before 1527.[23] Since the knowledge Vespucci had to offer was essentially useless, it was remarkable that he was able to persuade the crown to grant these extraordinary powers and privileges, which were calculated to alienate the professionals they humiliated. It is unlikely that pilots ever would have submitted to Vespucci's lessons.

As if this were not enough, Vespucci was also authorized to supervise the compiling of the "model map" for which he had militated and to compel all pilots to use it on pain of a fine. In effect, he was getting another valuable monopoly, since if the policy were rigorously applied, no sailing could be launched for the New World without an expensive document issued under his control. All pilots returning from the Indies were supposed to report back to him so that the map could be updated.

Clearly, this was not a system likely to work. No model map has survived.[24] No effort to make one commanded general assent; no version could ever be kept up to date.[25] In 1512, shortly after Amerigo's death, the job of creating a *padrón* passed to Amerigo's successor as chief pilot, Juan Díaz de Solís, and to the Florentine's heir and nephew, Giovanni Vespucci. The latter had the sole right to issue copies—the critical aspect, as this was where money was to be made. The royal orders were to "assemble all the pilots you can" and "discuss thoroughly how to make a royal model map of the navigation of all the regions that have so far been discovered that belong to the royal crown" and "after they have all spoken their minds, you shall . . . in mutual accord make jointly between you both a model map on parchment."[26] Evidently, Vespucci died without getting the job done. Instead, he tried to make money on the side by selling maps for his own benefit. On June 15, 1510, the king ordered officials in Seville to exact an oath from Amerigo that "from henceforth he will not again commit or consent to a proceeding so irresponsible and so promiscuous, but will issue maps only to such persons as the monarch or the Casa de Contratación may order."[27]

The other advice Vespucci gave in his capacity as chief pilot was of equally dubious value, except perhaps to himself and his business associates. Shortly after his appointment, the royal council debated whether to channel exports to the Indies through a central clearinghouse or to open the region to free trade. Asked for his views, Vespucci produced a cast-iron case for freedom of trade. There were many destinations in the Indies, a great variety of products, a diversity of points of origin for potential trade, and too much sea to police. He concluded that the crown should regulate trade either by imposing a tax on it—which, in view of the arguments he had mustered, would have the effect of multiplying contraband—or by concentrating it in the hands of selected, privileged merchants, which, for the same reasons, would be impossible.

His exploring days were over. One further prospect of a voyage came to nothing. The day after Amerigo's appointment as chief pilot, he received a further commission in collaboration with Pinzón and Solís: to make a voyage "with the help of our Lord, to the region of the north, towards the west [*a la parte del norte hacia occidente*] . . . in order to discover that strait or open sea which is chiefly to be sought."²⁸ So the "new Ptolemy," who supposedly divined the true nature of America, was still engaged in Columbus's quest and still trapped essentially in Columbus's view of what the world was like. The "strait . . . to be sought" was the putative strait that would lead through or around the New World to Vespucci's old sea of illusion—the "Gangetic Sea," where India, Taprobana, the spiceries, and all the gorgeous East awaited. Columbus had inquired for it in central America, where many mapmakers continued to place it. In search of it, Vespucci had scanned the Atlantic coast of South America. Now it was to be sought in the northwest, where John Cabot had died looking for it. For unknown reasons, perhaps connected with Vespucci's new duties as chief pilot, the proposed voyage was canceled. Solís eventually made a new attempt in 1516 on Vespucci's former trajectory and failed, discovering the River Plate in the process. At last, in 1520, Magellan identified the strait now named after him, though it was too far away and too hard to navigate to be commercially exploitable for the next hundred years.

The job of chief pilot effectively returned Amerigo to a landlubber's life. He had always craved a role as a navigator; now it beached him. His duties did not preclude speculations on the side. He continued to organize the provisioning of expeditions "to the spicery"—clear evidence that he had not abandoned hope that Spanish ships would reach Asia. He was a partner in a scheme in 1509 to colonize the inhospitable coast of Veragua, where Columbus had reported gold. It ended in failure. In his will, Vespucci claimed that the promoter of the scheme owed him twenty-seven gold ducats.

He dictated that will on April 9, 1511. It was not his final testament, but the last version, dictated a few months later, has not survived. The surviving document contains the only available clues about Vespucci's way of life in Seville. In view of his speculations in pearls, maps, and chandlery, we might expect him to be rich. His household, however, was modest. He kept two white male servants. Of five slaves, four were women: two from West Africa, one from the Canaries, and one of unspecified provenance. The Canary Islander had two children, a boy and a girl, called Juanica and Juanico. Whose children were they? The tempting answer, suggested by the scholar who found the will, is Vespucci's. But there are too many possibilities and not enough evidence.[29]

The will contains some curious features. The testator called himself "messer" or "micer" in the notary's spelling, the title a Florentine knight bore (the title his murdered cousin, Piero, had enjoyed); but Amerigo had never been knighted, and Spanish documents never even refer to him as "Don." He wanted to be buried in a Franciscan habit, which was a routine form of piety, but for an unknown reason, he seems to have expected permission to be refused. He stipulated that if the authorities of the church concerned made any demur, he preferred to be buried in the Franciscan church, in any grave, rather than in his first-choice location, the family tomb of his wife's relations. I can think of no satisfactory way to make sense of this as it stands. The objections he anticipated must have been to the tomb, not to the habit. If, as seems probable, María was illegitimate and someone her family was ashamed of, it is likely that Amerigo's aristocratic in-laws would have wanted to keep her and her husband out of their private sepulcher. If this reasoning is right, the nonsense about the habit was a smokescreen to conceal the real reason for Amerigo's exclusion from his wife's family circle.

He left most of his fortune to his wife—including a life interest in their household slaves—and all his clothes, books, and navigational instruments to his nephew and colleague Giovanni, who would soon be inscribed as a pilot in the books of the Casa de Contratación and who devoted most of his energy in subsequent years to spying for the Florentine state, reporting in cipher every scrap of data he could cull on Spanish affairs.[30]

Amerigo professed himself ignorant of whether his mother, brothers, and cousins in Florence were still alive. He left any property he might still have or be entitled to in that city to the survivors among them. Mona Lisa had died in 1507, but Antonio and Bernardo were still alive, and Amerigo must have been in periodic contact with the notary, as he had evidently sent a good deal of Spanish business his way. During Amerigo's years in Seville, Antonio specialized in Spanish business, and his range of clients spread through most important cities in Spain.[31] Girolamo, unmentioned in the will, was by now an inmate of Florence's famous Dominican friary of San Marco, where he died in 1525.

Amerigo died on February 22, 1512. Among his creditors was the estate of Gianotto Berardi, who owed him 144,000 *maravedíes*. The disastrous misjudgment of investing in Columbus shadowed Amerigo to the grave.

He left a creditable reputation. Within a couple of years of his death, Peter Martyr marked him down as a man learned in maps, "who sailed many degrees south of the equator under the auspices and at the expense of the king of Portugal." As we have seen, Sebastian Cabot commended his skill with the astrolabe, and other experts concurred with Giovanni Vespucci in citing Amerigo's views and relying on his expertise.[32] More spectacularly, in effect he bequeathed his name to America. How did that happen?

WHAT'S IN A NAME?

The success of *Mundus Novus* was critical to Vespucci's renown. It was a little blockbuster. In its first two years, editions appeared in quick succession in Florence, Augsburg (the first dated edition in 1504), Venice, Paris, Antwerp, Cologne, Nuremberg, Strasbourg, Milan, Rome, and Rostock. Translations into German, Flemish, and Czech appeared in the same period. Further diffusion followed, thanks to the popular compilation edited by a Vicenzan humanist in 1507, *Paesi novemente retrovati et Novo Mondo da Alberico Vesputio Florentino intitulato* (*Newfound Lands and the New World, so called by Alberic [sic] Vespucci, Florentine*). This was the first publication to give Vespucci the credit for coining the name "New World," even though Peter Martyr had beaten him to the phrase by at least three years, and Columbus had called America an "other world" even earlier. Giovanni Battista Ramusio included *Mundus Novus* in the first volume of his hugely successful compilation, *Navigationi et viaggi* (Navigations and

Voyages), published in Venice in 1550. Together with the *Soderini Letter,* the little book brought Vespucci, as Stefan Zweig said, "immortality from thirty-two pages."[33] On its own, however, *Mundus Novus* could not have induced the world to call the newly described hemisphere after Vespucci. On the contrary, it established an alternative name that many people still prefer. The naming of America happened beyond Amerigo's ken and control.

St. Dié is in the mountains of the Vosges, 800 kilometers—500 miles—from the sea. It is not necessary to be sea-struck to take an academic interest in maritime affairs. Nor is it necessary to be sea-bound to feel sea fever. In 1992 I was teaching a summer course in maritime history for college professors at the John Carter Brown Library in Providence, Rhode Island. One of the participants in the course came from Kansas—which, in North America, is nearly as far as you can get from the sea. I made the obvious joke, but the student assured me solemnly that it was only as a result of moving to Kansas that he had become interested in maritime history. His explanation made psychological sense. People far inland—as far as St. Dié and farther—can feel the call of the sea.

The ruler of the principality to which St. Dié belonged was René II, duke of Lorraine. He inherited enormous ancestral pretensions. His ancestors called themselves kings of Sicily and Jerusalem. Their great adversaries for enjoyment of those titles and for real control of Sicily were the kings of Aragon. Columbus claimed to have fought on behalf of one of René's predecessors in a war against the Aragonese in the early 1470s.[34]

St. Dié had the makings of an academic community: a cathedral chapter, a Benedictine monastery. Under René's ardent patronage, the court of Lorraine attracted an erudite coterie with a strong cosmographical bent. The major project on which scholars there were embarked was a new edition of Ptolemy's *Geography*—the very work that had inspired Vespucci, based on the Greek original. Among the scholars who contributed to work on Ptolemy, the most important was Martin Waldseemüller. He had joined the St. Dié group in 1505 or 1506 at the duke's invitation, apparently because of his accomplishments as a map-maker. He was probably then in his early thirties. Previously, he had lived in Basel, where he learned something about engraving and print-ing, to supplement the humanist curriculum he had absorbed as a stu-dent at Freiburg. Consistently with humanist humor, he gave himself a Greek-sounding pseudonym: Hylacomylus, a punning translation of the meaning of his German surname—"miller of the forest mere." His special skill, in which he displayed great originality and skill, was in de-signing and engraving maps; the cartographic illustrations were to be his special responsibility in the St. Dié group's edition of Ptolemy.

The text, it seems, was to be a collaboration between Waldseemüller and his more distinguished colleague Matthias Ringmann. Matthias was a young man still, probably born in 1482 but already renowned as a poet. His self-ascribed Greek pseudonym was Philesius Vosesigena, pre-sumably in allusion to one of the designations of Apollo, but "Vosges-born." Like Waldseemüller, he was a Freiburg graduate, schooled in the same rather self-indulgent humanism, learned in Greek, and with a *méchant* wit. He was already an admirer of Vespucci. In 1505 he had per-sonally seen a version of the *Mundus Novus* through the press.

Early in 1507 Gauthier (or, as an alternative translation of his name put it, Vautrin) Lud, the effective dean of the community of scholars, announced the arrival of a letter in French from Vespucci to the duke, enclosing a copy of the text we know as the *Soderini Letter.* There is no in-dependent confirmation of the existence of the letter, which may have been a convenient fiction, to justify the incorporation of work the St. Dié circle admired. When a version of the *Soderini Letter* was published at St. Dié, the publishers merely added the duke's name to the existing dedication, without modifying the passages specifically addressed to Soderini. This suggests a deplorably slapdash attitude to a text and casts doubt on Lud's story of how news of Vespucci's career reached St. Dié.

Evidently, the St. Dié community was suckered. They believed the *Soderini Letter* was Vespucci's exclusive work; more fatally, they believed its contents were true. The project of using Vespucci's data to complete Ptolemy's picture of world geography rapidly took shape. The decision was ill considered but pardonable in the circumstances. Ptolemy still had much to offer readers, especially his digest of ancient geographical learning, his counsel on mapmaking, and his project for using a grid of lines of longitude and latitude to map the world. But his world picture was obviously out of date, superannuated by recent discoveries in the Indian Ocean and the New World. Vespucci's text—or rather, the text published under Vespucci's name—seemed to be a ready-made corrective. There is an irony here too delicious to leave unremarked. The fame and honor Vespucci craved were at last secured for him by a fake—the *Soderini Letter*—fabricated by hands other than his own. The great salesman never quite succeeded in selling himself. As with so many authors, it took publishers and publicists to do it for him. The *Soderini Letter* sold him in St. Dié and, from there, on to the world.

Already, the Ptolemy project seems to have been too expensive for Duke René to see through. It was proving too laborious and costly to retranslate the text. The projectors feared a scoop: Ptolemy remained a much loved, much sold text, and the need for an updated edition was widely acknowledged. Ringmann and Waldseemüller therefore resolved on a shortcut. They would publish their introduction to Ptolemy at once, along with a world map that Waldseemüller prepared in order to illustrate the impact of recent discoveries.

The result was the *Cosmographiae Introductio* (*Introduction to Geography*), published in 1507, ostensibly authored by Waldseemüller, with some contributions from Ringmann. Waldseemüller's huge map accompanied it: *Universalis Cosmographia Secundum Ptholoemaei Traditionem et Americi Vespucii Aliorumque Lustrationes* (*Universal Geography According to the Tradition of Ptolemy and the Contributions of Amerigo Vespucci and Others*). It covered nearly three square meters. This was a novel concept: the map as wallpaper.

For coverage of what we now think of as the Old World, Waldseemüller drew heavily on the Martellus map—the same map Amerigo knew from his days in Florence and probably used as the basis for his own world image. Waldseemüller's depiction of the New World was original and evidently represented an attempt to make the best possible sense of the data in the *Soderini Letter*, with help from such materials as the author could garner from other sources: the voyages of Cabral and Pinzón, perhaps, and maps or sailing directions or hearsay fragments based on them. The most original feature of all is the name America, emblazoned over the part of the hemisphere we think of today as Brazil.

Portraits of Ptolemy and Vespucci crown the whole majestic composition, symmetrically positioned, facing each other across the breadth of the world, as figures of equal stature. Vespucci wields dividers. Ptolemy holds a geometer's rule or set square. Together they guard cartouches in which maps of the New and Old worlds appear. There are some curious differences between the main map and the cartouches. In the main map, for instance, there is a strait between North and South America—the strait Columbus had sought in vain and that Vespucci was still dreaming of finding in 1508. In the cartouche that displays America, the coast of South America does not extend below the Tropic of Capricorn, as if Waldseemüller had been in two minds about Amerigo's claims to have gotten so far south.

This huge map was the model for the printed globe segments Waldseemüller issued in the same year, designed to be pasted on a wooden sphere and colored by hand: the world's first printed globe. Here, too, Waldseemüller used the name America to label what is recognizably Brazil. More than a thousand copies of this exceptionally fragile work were printed, though only one has survived.[35] Both maps—the globe segments and the vast wall map—according to a record Waldseemüller proudly made in 1508, were "distributed around the world, not without praise and glory."[36] One wonders what happened to all the copies. It is hard to imagine anyone using them as they were intended. Both were essentially impractical, overambitious experiments.

The text of the *Cosmographiae Introductio* formed, in a sense, an extended commentary on the maps. The big version would surely dominate the study of any scholar injudicious enough to cover a wall with it. It would excite comment from visitors. The version made for a globe would be a novelty in any setting. It would be what decorators call "a conversation piece." The owner would need a crib sheet.

In their text, Waldseemüller and Ringmann were explicit about their reasons for devising the name America: They were paying tribute to Vespucci, proposing for the new continent a feminine version of Americus—Vespucci's Christian name in the learned language of the day—by analogy with the feminine forms of Africa, Asia, and the Latin form of Europa. They described the three continents known to Ptolemy, and continued:

> *Now indeed these regions are fairly well known and Amerigo Vespucci has found another, fourth part, for which I see no reason why anyone could properly disapprove of a name derived from that of Amerigo, the discoverer, a man of sagacious genius. A suitable form would be Amerige, meaning [in Greek] Land of Amerigo, or America, since Europe and Asia have received women's names.*

As we have seen, Vespucci's use of the term "fourth part" was different from the way Waldseemüller and Ringmann read it. In any case, Columbus had beaten him both to the discovery of the landmass and to its identification as a new continent. But the combined impact of *Mundus Novus* and the *Soderini Letter* convinced the authors of the *Introductio* otherwise. Clearly, they never intended the name to apply to the whole hemisphere of the Americas, only to the portion south of the equator, where tradition placed the Antipodes and where Vespucci thought he had found them.

However radical and awkward were the maps that accompanied it, the *Introductio* was a phenomenal success. Four editions appeared in 1507. They kept on coming. And Waldseemüller's maps were too extraordinary—triumphs alike of the mapmaker's art and the printer's craft—to escape the notice and admiration of fellow cartographers. The name America caught on. Some authors preferred "Terra Sanctae Crucis" or variants of "Brazil" or "New World." But even these often incorporated "America." In 1510 Heinrich Glarean, a teacher at Freiburg, made sketches of Waldseemüller's 1507 map, including the name America.[37] A wooden painted globe of 1513–15, known as the Globe Vert, now in the Bibliothèque Nationale in Paris, used the same name twice, once in the northern moiety of the new hemisphere, once in the southern. In 1515 Johann Schöner wrote a *Description of the World* (*Luculentissima quaeda[m] terrae totius descriptio*), published in Nuremberg. Heavily dependent on Waldseemüller's work but acquainted with Vespucci's *Mundus Novus* at first hand, it referred to the western hemisphere as "America or Amerige," while using "New World" as a secondary designation. Vespucci's giants, cannibals, and emphasis on the nudity of Native Americans all featured prominently in Schöner's account. Like Waldseemüller, Schöner made a later retraction: His *Opusculum Geographicum* of 1533 indicted Vespucci as an unjust pretender to the discovery of America.

In 1520 the name America appeared in a book published in Salamanca,[38] although Spaniards generally remained resistant to the name, preferring on the whole to speak of the Indies or the New World until the eighteenth century. In 1520 Peter Apian's printed world map in Vienna showed South America alone as "America Provincia," separated from the northern lands of the hemisphere by a strait. In 1525 a booklet accompanying a map published in Strasbourg[39] listed America as one of the regions of the world; the purported "explanation" is mainly about cannibals, depicted as dog-headed and cleaver-wielding. In 1528, Heinrich Glarean, who, as we have seen, was one of Waldseemüller's early and attentive readers, retained the name of America in his *De Geographia* (*On Geography*), published in Basle and much republished in following years. In 1532 the celebrated publisher Simon Grinaeus in the same city issued a world map, to which Hans Holbein contributed, together with Sebastian Münster, who had made sketches of Waldseemüller's 1507 map as early as 1515.[40] They opted for America Terra Nova (America, the New Land) as their name for the hemisphere. America—plain and simple— was the choice of Maximilian I's court scholar Joachim von Watt on a printed world map of 1534. In 1538 Mercator marked both parts of the American hemisphere with the name America, North and South, respectively, on his influential world map. The tradition was secure, the decision irreversible.[41]

Ironically, Martin Waldseemüller himself tried to reverse it. While his proposed nomenclature spread, he lost confidence in it. He and Ringmann moved to Strasbourg to finish work on their projected edition of Ptolemy, partly because finances were tight in St. Dié and partly because the printing trade there was too small-scale and inefficient to cope with a project as demanding as the new edition of Ptolemy. Ringmann died in about 1511. Waldseemüller lost heart in the work and gave it up. But he continued to produce what he thought were improved world maps. In the next map to survive from his hand, published in 1513, not long after Vespucci's death, he made a critical revision. The land he formerly called America now bore the less catchy name of Terra Incognita (Unknown Land), with an annotation attesting to Columbus's priority in discovery: *hec terra cum adiacentibus insulis inventa est per Columbum Ianuenensem ex mandato regis castellae* ("this land with the adjoining islands was found by Columbus, of Genoa, at the command of the king of Castile").

Martin had realized that claims of priority advanced on Vespucci's behalf were false. Evidently, he now recognized the *Soderini Letter* for the fabrication it was, while accepting *Mundus Novus*—equally correctly, if our analysis of the text was right—as essentially authentic. In his map of 1516, he named Columbus as the first discoverer, Pedro Álvares Cabral as the second, and Vespucci as the third[42]—which was not quite accurate, as Vespucci on his voyage with Hojeda preceded Cabral. South America became "Prisilia"—presumably a corruption of Brasilia or Brasil—or "Terra Papagalli" (Parrot Land). At the same time, Waldseemüller made a further intellectual retreat: North America was relabeled *"terra de Cuba, Asiae partis."* In correcting his overexuberance in favor of Vespucci, Martin had erred at the other extreme, accepting Columbus's wild and probably dishonest claim that Cuba was part of the mainland of Asia. Waldseemüller had begun by placing too much faith in Vespucci. He ended by relying too uncritically on Columbus. He now joined their names as navigators who had added to Ptolemy's account of the world. Strangely, he referred to them as "Lusitanian captains," even though he knew they were Italians by birth and Castilians by naturalization. Presumably, this was the last of his classical affectations, since "Lusitanian" was sometimes used in an extended sense by Roman authors to mean "Iberian."[43]

VESPUCCI AND COLUMBUS

It is time to tackle one of the most debated questions in Vespucci's life: whether he deliberately despoiled Columbus of the honor of his discoveries. Echoes of Columbus's writings resound in Vespucci's own work; we have seen ample evidence of that. The trajectory of Amerigo's life not only intersected with that of Columbus, it largely followed it, from Italy to Spain and across the ocean sea. For much of his life, Amerigo was in thrall to the admiral.

The relationship between the two was complex. In a hearing before a notary in connection with the authentication of Columbus's autograph in 1510, Vespucci testified that he had known Columbus well for twenty-five years, a clear but pardonable exaggeration. He also claimed to know the admiral's handwriting well "because this witness saw him write and sign on many occasions and because he was an officer of the said lord Don Cristóbal Colón and held his books for him." There is no independent confirmation of this claim, but Vespucci's link with Columbus was long and intimate. He spent time in the admiral's household. He depended on Columbus, sometimes for work, sometimes for ideas and information—sometimes, one is tempted to feel, for emotional support.

Columbus, in turn, needed services Vespucci supplied, as Gianotto Berardi's employee, in providing shipping and chandlery for his Atlantic fleets. His enterprise was—so to speak—the siren that lured Gianotto Berardi's business onto the rocks, to Vespucci's near-ruin. On the other hand, Columbus's trailblazing gave Vespucci the inspiration for a new career when his business in Seville failed, and opened up his chance of making a profit from Atlantic pearls. When Vespucci's Atlantic career began, Columbus's ill fortune gave his former chandler the chance to ship with Alonso de Hojeda in infringement of the admiral's monopoly.

So Columbus and Vespucci were locked by mutual dependence. Each benefited from the other's misfortune. Each suffered from the other's success. Likeness bound them. Columbus noticed it, recognizing in the Florentine a fellow sufferer in the cause of exploration. Connections so common and so profound are likely to lead to conflicts of Tweedledee against Tweedledum.

Their characters and opinions had much in common. Vespucci did not share Columbus's messianic religiosity, and was less deeply steeped in chivalry and hagiography, but both were given to romanticization—especially self-romanticization. Both practiced exaggeration that often slipped into mendacity. They shared a basic motivating force: social ambition, focused in Columbus's case on elevation to noble rank and in Vespucci's on fame and honor. They devoted much of their lives to the same project: seeking the East by way of the West. Although Vespucci did not endorse Columbus's estimate of the size of the globe, they coincided in their essential conceptions of geography: a relatively small world, facilitating a western route to Asia and allowing for a new antipodean continent in the ocean sea, south of the equator. Columbus wavered, but they agreed they had found it—or rather, they agreed in identifying what we now think of as South America as a "new" or "other" continent. But did they agree about which of them reached it first?

Columbus's only reference to his rival occurred in a letter to his son, dated in Seville on February 5, 1505, when the writer, old for his years, sick, weary with contrarieties, bent all his failing energies toward his outstanding claims against the Castilian crown. Vespucci carried the letter to its destination. The picture it gave of him is familiar from earlier documents. On the one hand, Amerigo appeared as an amiable fixer, a reliable man of business, in whom Columbus confided. On the other, he was a luckless, guileless victim of other men's depredations—someone with whom Columbus sympathized.

Both images originated with Vespucci himself, who seems to have lost none of the credibility that had already misinformed so many of his admirers and continues to do so. "He always desired to please me," wrote Columbus, and one can almost hear Vespucci's insinuations. "He is very much a man of high standing, but Fortune has been unfair to him, as she has to so many others." Here one can detect the timbre of Vespucci's methods of winning over his interlocutors: Columbus felt hard done by; Amerigo encouraged the feeling and won the approbation we tend to give to those who confirm our self-image. "He goes determined to do all he can for me," Columbus continued, still addressing his son in recommendation of Vespucci. "Find out at court what he can usefully do and work towards it. He will do everything, and will speak for me and put all into effect, and let everything be done secretly so that no one may suspect him." The appeal to secrecy is a common device of those who promise much but intend little. As far as is known, Vespucci never interceded at court on Columbus's behalf, but by vowing to do so, he acquired useful allies in his own interest. Columbus added that he had told Amerigo everything he could about his own affairs. The guest had learned much of Columbus's business and apparently given away nothing about his own. On the basis of this letter, we can assert with some confidence that Amerigo exaggerated the extent to which he was at Columbus's disposal, but it is quite another thing to suppose that he actively planned to cheat the old admiral or deprive him of his good name.

The naming began in innocent error. As we have seen, Waldseemüller genuinely believed at the time that Vespucci had discovered the continent for Europeans. Vespucci was not directly responsible for the delusion. It arose from the *Soderini Letter.* America was a bit like the *Letter:* not a work to which Vespucci laid claim, but one to which others ascribed his name. When Waldseemüller revised his work seven years later, he acknowledged his mistake. Yet the name spread and stuck like an oil slick, extending over the entire western hemisphere and getting fixed in Old World minds. There was something tacky about it at first, but it was sonorous, and the history of America ever since has given it resonance.

That, perhaps, is why Vespucci partisans have never accepted Waldseemüller's retraction and tenaciously vindicate Amerigo's claims—or claims made in his lifetime on his behalf—to be the real discoverer of the New World. There are five main grounds for that claim. First, Amerigo, according to his devotees, was the first to set foot on the continental New World. That is simply false. Next come the assertions that he was first to identify what came to be called America as a land of continental proportions, and first to class it as a new world. Those are contestable notions, and Columbus had superior claims in both respects. Fourth, America is said to be well named because Amerigo explored so much of it—which is a reasonable judgment but has proved hard to justify because of the intractability of the evidence. It has been extremely difficult to say how much of America Amerigo explored, and we cannot ascribe much to his credit for certain. Finally, he publicized the New World more effectively than anyone else. That, at least, is beyond cavil, though even in this he had unsolicited help from the concoctors of the *Soderini Letter* and the authors of the *Cosmographiae Introductio.*

Partisanship depends on alterity. You have to have some other party to disagree with. In Amerigo's case, the others are the devotees of Columbus, who assert, correctly, their own hero's priority in exploration and argue, less decisively, that his views on the nature of his discoveries were not much inferior to those of his rival. The parties began to form in the sixteenth century. Shortly after Vespucci's death, Sebastian Cabot, whose own father, John Cabot, had preceded Amerigo across the Atlantic, and who had some egregious and improbable claims of his own as an explorer to put forward, accused Vespucci of lying to steal the glory of the discoverer of the New World. The agency with the best reason to detach Columbus from the glory of discovering America was the Castilian crown, which was engaged for most of the sixteenth century in a lawsuit with Columbus's heirs over the division of the profits. The background of the lawsuit encouraged Columbus's detractors, but it was not in the state's interests to back Vespucci, either. So he got no help from that quarter. Francisco López de Gómara—Cortés's secretary and celebrant—reported Vespucci's claim to the discovery in noncommital but distinctly standoffish language: "He makes himself out to be the discoverer of the Indies for Castile." Bartolomé de Las Casas, Columbus's devoted first editor, barred no holds. He dismissed Vespucci as a spinner of lies and professed himself astonished that other experts, including Columbus's own son, should have failed to notice the fact. Vespucci "usurped the glory owed to the admiral." The continent should not have been called America but "Columba."[44] "It is well here," Las Casas wrote, "to consider the injury and injustice which that Amerigo Vespucci appears to have done to the Admiral, or that those have done who published his Four Navigations, in attributing the discovery of this continent to himself, without mentioning anyone but himself. Owing to this, the foreigners who write of these Indies in Latin or in their own mother-tongue, or who make charts or maps, call the continent America, as if Amerigo had been the first to discover it."[45]

THE VAGARIES OF REPUTATION

This version of events was never accepted in Florence.[46] In 1598, when the city celebrated solemn and lavish obsequies for Philip II of Spain, Vespucci's image, labeled "Discoverer of the New World in 1497," was affixed to the facade of the church of San Lorenzo, as if to watch and mock the cortege as it passed. It became a matter of honor for Florentines to defend Vespucci's integrity. Elsewhere, his reputation waned. Philip II's own historiographer, Antonio de Herrera, established, with invincible scholarship, the falsehoods of the *Soderini Letter* and blamed Vespucci for them. Most readers followed him. For 150 years the name of America was generally held to be the result of an imposture. The most critical scholars of the era of the Enlightenment, including Voltaire and Robertson, endorsed that orthodoxy.

In 1745, however, a Florentine teenage prodigy, Angelo Maria Bandini, challenged it in a book of profound scholarship. *Vita di Amerigo Vespucci gentiluomo fiorentino* (*Life of Amerigo Vespucci, Florentine Gentleman*) is still a vital work for the study of Vespucci because of Bandini's insuperable research on the Vespucci family tree. It represented a breakthrough in a further respect: Bandini found not only Vespucci's only surviving letter to his father but also the first manuscript version of Vespucci's reports of his voyage. But his obvious commitment to Florentine civic patriotism undermined his objectivity in readers' eyes. His defense, moreover, of Vespucci's claim to be acknowledged as the discoverer of America was based on a mistake: the belief that Columbus had never set foot on the soil of the continental New World.

Bandini became the librarian of the dukes of Tuscany. But this did not mean he was consigned to obscurity. On the contrary, he was an influential figure in the triumph of the Enlightenment in Florence. Increasingly, Florentine Amerigophiles made Amerigo out to be a hero preincarnate of the eighteenth-century cults of reason and science. But for Columbus's cruel intervention, the argument went, the natives of the New World might have been regulated by Florentine republican standards and spared the massacre that ensued. After long gestation, these notions came together in Florence in the late eighteenth century, in a torrent of new studies of Vespucci. The background was threefold.

First, Western intellectuals were engaged in what scholars now call "the Dispute of the New World": a debate launched by pseudo-scientific despisers of everything American, who argued that the entire hemisphere had an environment peculiarly hostile to life, which condemned all the species that lived there—including humans—to inescapable inferiority, compared with their Old World counterparts. Scholars and scientists in Spanish America responded with counter-claims, demonstrating to their own satisfaction that their continent was conducive to every kind of progress and enjoyed every natural advantage—even the astral influences that beamed from American skies were peculiarly benign. Thomas Jefferson refuted the detractors' claims more simply at a Parisian dinner party, by pointing out that he—the only American present—was the tallest person there.[47]

Second, the intellectual world was engaged in an equally fierce debate about the moral consequences of Europe's discovery, conquest, and colonization of the Americas. Denis Diderot, who presided over the making of the *Encyclopédie*—the definitive compendium of Enlightenment thought—denounced imperialism: "Every colony, whose authority rests in one country and whose obedience is in another, is in principle a vicious establishment."[48] Rousseau concurred. Far from benefiting humankind, the discovery of America had encouraged vices of greed, exploitation, and violence. Contact with Europeans had polluted the purity of the "noble savage." Though Rousseau himself never used the phrase and probably did not acknowledge the concept, this was the simplification that took root and spread.[49] In 1782 the Abbé Raynal—a collaborator of Diderot's and Rousseau's—launched in Lyon a famous essay competition on the consequences of the discovery of America for good and ill.

Finally, a new republic was in the making in America, in a revolutionary war. The United States revived the supposed virtues of ancient Rome—virtues that, the reader will recall, Florentine tradition had once embodied. The outcome of the colonists' struggle for independence seemed to its admirers to settle the dispute of the New World. The Declaration of Independence and the U.S. constitution realized in practice the political principles of the Enlightenment: popular sovereignty, the empire of reason, the equality—women and slaves, of course, excepted—of man.

Little over a year after U.S. independence was definitely accomplished, the ambassador of the king of France at the court of Tuscany devised a novel way of appealing to the goodwill of the Florentine elite. In 1785 he offered a prize for the best eulogy of Vespucci at the Tuscan Academy.[50] He stirred a current of interest, a torrent of studies. In 1787 Marco Lastri produced the most comprehensive and representative of the eulogies excited by the ambassador's initiative: Vespucci emerged as "the most glorious of the heroes of the Arno"—which, when one thinks of all the Florentine genius that has flowed since the Middle Ages, was saying rather a lot—because he was "the discoverer of half the world." Vespucci had founded a realm of possibilities: "Who knows what progress of the human spirit awaits to be accomplished by the people of those regions?" Lastri cited Benjamin Franklin and the transactions of the American Philosophical Society of Philadelphia as proof.[51] "A new order of things is born," he concluded, "and to it we owe the origins of the enlightenment of our present philosophy."[52] The following year Adamo and Giovanni Fabbroni presented an essay that represented Vespucci as a preincarnation of the spirit of revolutionary America in a work replete with praise for U.S. independence and bristling with hatred of colonialism and religious intolerance.

From the point of view of scholarship, the most important of the essays was the dullest. Francesco Bartolozzi started off resoundingly enough, with an impressively sagacious comment that prefigured the view every well-informed and right-thinking liberal now takes. The discovery of America was, he said, "a turning-point ever memorable for the history of the peoples of the world," partly because of "the revolution that followed in customs, ways of life, foods" and partly because it was "fatal for the human race. . . . European barbarism" killed many millions of "innocent and harmless savages"; wars of greed and ambition were unleashed, and the transmission of smallpox, with exterminating effects, to unimmunized peoples, accompanied the other evils.[53] After that stirring exordium, Bartolozzi settled down to refute, one by one, on the basis of tedious trivialities, all previous writers on the subject. He disclosed, however, some of the most exciting discoveries ever in Vespucci scholarship: not only the series of letters to Vespucci on which Chapter One of this book is largely based, but also—more significantly in the present connection—the previously unpublished letter Amerigo wrote to Lorenzo di Pierfrancesco de' Medici on his return from Brazil in 1502. Bartolozzi noticed, moreover, that Vespucci alluded in it to "my other voyages" in the plural.[54]

So, by inference, the Brazilian voyage of 1501–02 must have been preceded by at least two others. For Bartolozzi and those who followed him, the fact that this apparently unquestionable autograph confirmed a third voyage was proof that Vespucci had preceded Columbus on the continent of the New World. For Vespucci's detractors, it was yet more evidence of his lies. "He audaciously announced himself to all Europe as the first discoverer of the Continent of the New World," retorted Claret de Fleurieu, the great publicist of French scientific exploration at the time, "and Europe, deluded, gave credit to his assertion without examining it!"[55]

The greatest scholar of the age, Alexander von Humboldt, adopted a more balanced approach, insisting on Columbus's priority but declining to indict Vespucci for bad faith. Humboldt perceptively regarded the *Mundus Novus* and the *Soderini Letter* as the result of "confused editing," perhaps by "inept and untrustworthy friends."[56] Thomas Jefferson found room in his private museum at Monticello for effigies of both Columbus and Vespucci.

The rivalry of their respective eulogists, however, made it hard to accommodate the two explorers. Vespucci's nineteenth-century critics showed as much inventiveness in unimagining Vespucci's voyages as they ascribed to him in imagining them. History and fiction are full of imaginary voyages and exaggerated or misattributed feats of seamanship. The genre was never more popular than in Vespucci's own environment. Armchair travelers made up journeys. Many writers traveled only in their own heads, and those who did travel tended to exaggerate their extent. To please the public, they added mirabilia—tales of wonder, freaks of nature, monsters, unexperienced riches, and inversions of natural order. The real achievements of explorers emulated—and perhaps consciously imitated—the fictions.[57] It is not surprising, against this background, that some of Vespucci's readers doubted or disbelieved every word he wrote. To them, he was a landlubber whose voyages were more fabulous than real; he resembled the "Ruler of the Queen's Navy" in *H.M.S. Pinafore*, who rose to command real seafarers by the prudence of his golden rule: "Stick close to your desk and never go to sea." His reputation arose from mere confidence trickery, unaided by real experience. The vizconde de Santarém effectively rejected everything about Vespucci's activities as an explorer. Emerson famously dismissed him as a "pickle-dealer."[58] In 1894 Sir Clements Markham—a poor scholar himself, but as president of the Hakluyt Society, a powerful force in the world of scholarship—reduced him to a mere "beef-contractor," denying that there was any evidence to qualify Vespucci as a seafarer at all.[59]

So, one way or another, Vespucci was cast as the hero of his own champions and the villain of the rest. He has inspired extremes of odium and adulation. Both are justified, but not for the reasons usually cited.

Vespucci was a hero and, like most heroes, also a villain. But his heroism and villainy were of unusual kinds. The conventional virtues of heroism are partisan. That is what distinguishes them from the virtues of sainthood, which are universal. So one side's hero is always another's villain. Nowadays, in plural cultures and a multicivilizational world, heroism is subversive. Seeking to be fair to all sides, we recoil from conventional heroes and dislike admitting to having them, whereas villains, at least, can usually summon up some of our sympathy.

Amerigo, however, is not easily classifiable in partisan terms. Of course, he was the hero of his hometown of Florence, where the streets were illuminated when news of his accomplishments arrived and where his fellow citizens worked to reburnish his memory whenever the facts seemed to blacken it. But he never managed to become a hero of Italian patriots generally. This cannot simply be because he left home when he was young and never returned. Columbus did the same, but that does not stop Italian-Americans from turning out in hundreds of thousands to identify with him every Columbus Day. Vespucci was too mercurial in his loyalties to become the hero of any national group, as he oscillated between Spain and Portugal and gave wholehearted allegiance to neither.

The qualities we usually associate with heroism are, in any case, morally equivocal. Courage, prowess, perseverance are virtues made for conflict. Sometimes they generate it. They need it to thrive. The same virtues are also commonly associated with obsession. Heroes usually have bloodstained hands. But Vespucci never qualified as a hero of war or empire. Unlike Columbus, he never made sustained war on the natives of the New World; he founded no colonies, captained no expeditions, commanded no fleets. Nor could he be a hero of postcolonial or anti-colonial revisionism. He was deeply mired in the slave trade and involved in some of the characteristically nasty, bloody little encounters with which European history in the Americas began.

Heroes sometimes arise because communities need them as examples in wartime or models of patriotism. Vasari made heroes of painters and Samuel Smiles of engineers; but these were metaphorical heroes, heroes by analogy. Vespucci might, by analogy, qualify as a hero of exploration. As well as his peregrinations along New World coasts, his main claims under this heading are two: first, that he was the original and astonishingly successful practitioner of dazzling feats of celestial navigation, including navigation out of sight of the Pole Star, and the reading of longitude by lunar distances; and second, that the sheer range of his voyages dwarfed those of any rival in his day—particularly by virtue of penetrating to fifty degrees or more south of the equator. These are impressive claims, but, as we have seen, they are false.

So there is no cause to associate Vespucci with, good or bad, except his own. Amerigo's partisans are partisans of nothing except him, united only by their admiration for him. Vespucci partisanship and, along with it, his elevation to heroic status, began in his lifetime among the group of scholars who promoted the name America and hailed him as the greatest of geographers. Now it is the cause of cranky eccentrics who take defiant pleasure in contending with evidence. It is hard to see what still inspires partisans on Vespucci's side: intellectual perversity, perhaps; resentment of Columbus's status, probably; emotional investment in the name of America, certainly. That name makes the ire of Columbus's admirers is understandable. So is the envy of Vespucci's enemies.

As I write, the five hundredth anniversary of the naming of America is approaching. Old controversies about how apposite the name is are sure to be revived. The controversies are about various kinds of entitlement: whether Vespucci deserves the honor done him by the geographers who imposed the name; whether citizens of the United States have unfairly appropriated it; whether Americans in other parts of the hemisphere, or those in self-conscious ethnic minorities—such as now call themselves Native Americans and Afro-Americans—want to go on using it, or would prefer to discard it in postcolonial indignation as a detestable legacy of white dominion. We may be in for a rerun of the five hundredth anniversary of Columbus's discovery, which was hijacked by a debate—unparalleled since Rousseau condemned the consequences of Columbus's work—over the morality of white mischief in the Americas.

Naming is often said to be a kind of magic. Names change natures. They forge communities. They generate myths. They affirm relationships. They establish claims, especially of parentage and proprietorship. They affect perceptions of things named. They attract and repel. They are hard to get rid of. Their effects are almost indelible. They influence behavior, as people try to live up to them. By leaving his mark on the map, Amerigo, the old magus, is still working his magic. Giving the western hemisphere a name has defined it with an outsider's eyes as a single landmass, in spite of all the diversity it contains. Calling it after a Florentine explorer still affects the way we think of its history—with a supposed rupture, a new beginning, for good or ill, occurring when Europeans arrived.

Yet I doubt whether anyone nowadays thinks of Vespucci when they utter the name America. It triggers no reminiscence of the man, precisely because he has been such an obscure, unknowable figure with a hidden, untold life. Any connotations the name might bear with Florence or Florentines, or with wheeler-dealering, or ship's chandlery, or exploration, or cosmography, or astral magic, or mapmaking, or clumsy conjuration with nautical instruments, or any of the other activities Vespucci espoused in the course of his varied life, are unignited, because people do not know about them. How different the effects would be if Columbus's partisans had gotten their way and we spoke of, say, Christopheria instead! Columbus has such an ineluctable presence in history that a hemisphere named after him would never be free of association with him. With every vocalization, images of imperialism, evangelization, colonization, massacre, and ecological exchange would spring to mind. The controversies would be constant, the revulsion upon durable.

America, by comparison, seems a neutral term. And while Vespucci has vanished from the name's aura, new associations have come to color it. Most of those associations have emerged from the history of the country that calls itself America for short: the U.S.A. They are long-term associations with great American virtues: democracy, liberty, republicanism, and the opportunity to pursue dreams. Thanks to these, the name America comes positively charged with the power to evoke proper pride, and no one any longer automatically recalls the way the name started in error induced by fraud—nor how the country was born in rebellion, enlarged by imperialism, and, for too long a time, sustained by slavery. More recently, because of superpower arrogance, corporate greed, corrupt politics, trigger-happy warmongering, ecological irresponsibility, and crass consumerism, to utter "America" unfortunately conjures up other, less happy effects. But the spell is not Amerigo's. History has made him irrelevant to the major resonances of his own name.

If he contributed so little to subsequent history and can be exempted from any share in the effects of the name of America, why read about him? Why write about him? It may be too late to raise that question with any reader who may have been kind enough to get this far. But I have what I think is a good answer.

The Representative Paladin

To me, Vespucci is of interest, even of historical importance, because he was a representative of a strange, world-shaping breed: Mediterranean men who took to the Atlantic, denizens of a calm inner sea who crossed an immense ocean. For generations, they were at the frontier of Atlantic voyaging, leading the way, as if Atlantic-side Europeans could not explore their own ocean without these outsiders' help. I find it hard to believe that without the initiative of Mediterranean participants, the Atlantic we now inhabit—the home sea of Western civilization, across which we traffic in goods and ideas and around which we still tend to huddle for defense—ever would have come to be.

I look back on Vespucci's life from my own little rimlands around the Atlantic's edges: from Massachusetts, where I work, and from my ancestral homeland in Galicia, in northwest Spain—outposts of an Atlantic-spanning life. Because I am by origin thoroughly, unmistakably a

Western European, no one will accuse me of hostile partisanship if I say that we Western Europeans are the dregs of Eurasian history and that our part of the world is the sump into which Eurasian history has drained. We like to congratulate ourselves on how much Western Europe has contributed to the making of Western civilization, and thence to the world, as the world's horizon has broadened and Western traditions have been shared or inflicted across the globe. We might mention, in this connection, the scientific and industrial revolutions, the Enlightenment, romanticism, and other movements of more doubtful provenance or more questionable merit, including the global imperialism that Vespucci's fellow explorers did so much to launch. But these are all fairly recent developments. If we take a longer-term view, extending over several millennia, we can see that most of the great movements that have shaped Europe came from outside—from Asia—and spread from east to west: the arrival of farming and metallurgy and Indo-European languages; the migrations of Phoenicians and Jews, and later of steppe-landers and gypsies; the transmission of ideas and technologies, including the rays from Asia that fell on the "east face of Helikon" and ignited Greek fire in antiquity. The influence of Islam on medieval thought and of Song and Yuan China on Western technology followed.

All these movements swept residues, refuse, and refugees into Western Europe. There my ancestors stared at the ocean for hundreds, perhaps thousands, of years, without ever daring to venture far into it. They exploited it for fishing and for coastal cabotage. Their lack of enterprise seems stunning compared with their counterparts in the Indian and Pacific oceans. In the former, the monsoons facilitated long-range sailings back and forth across the breadth of the ocean and around the coasts of maritime Asia and East Africa for centuries before anyone developed a viable transatlantic route. In the Pacific, by about a thousand years ago, Polynesian voyagers, the world's most skillful seafarers, reached the limits of the technology available to them, crossing the open ocean to colonize the Hawaiian archipelago, Easter Island, New Zealand, and the Chatham Islands—destinations thousands of miles from home to the navigators who found them. Meanwhile, the only ex-

ceptions to Atlantic-rim inertia were those of Norse and Irish navigators, who, taking advantage of the westbound currents that lap the Arctic, and the westerly winds that predominate in the North Atlantic for
the return journey, colonized Iceland from the eighth century, and the
Norse, who continued the effort as far as Greenland and Newfoundland around the turn of the millennium.

"The Rise of the West" is often said to be the great central problem
of modern world history. Viewed from a long-term perspective, the inertia of the West seems more conspicuous and more problematic. Why
did the peoples of Atlantic-side Europe do so little for so long?

When at last communities elsewhere on the Atlantic rim—chiefly in
Spain and Portugal—began to launch ambitious ventures in the fourteenth century, they relied on leadership, investment, and savoir faire
from deep inside the Mediterranean. The men who helped came from
Majorca and, increasingly, as the Majorcan contribution dwindled in
the second half of the fourteenth century, Italy. These lands supplied
navigators, shipwrights, cartographers, financiers who helped to explore
the Azores and the Madeira and Canary archipelagoes in the fourteenth
century and to colonize them in the fifteenth. Until the second half of
the fifteenth century, they were instrumental in Portuguese navigations
in the African Atlantic, which continued to rely on Italian financial
backers in the 1490s, when the Portuguese reached out across the South
Atlantic, toward Brazil and the westerly winds that carried them to the
Indian Ocean.

With very few exceptions, we know almost nothing about most of
these Mediterranean makers of the modern Atlantic, except their
names. But at the very end of the story—when Spain and Portugal were
generating enough navigators of their own to dispense with Italian
frontline help—the cases of Columbus and Vespucci provide us with
the means to know or infer why Italians sought the way west, rather than
staying comfortably in the relatively rich, old, equable Mediterranean.
They were almost the last in the great succession of Italian contributors
to the overseas expansion of late-medieval Iberia. John Cabot's son Sebastian followed his father in England and across the North Atlantic

before turning to serve Spain. One of Columbus's brothers and two or three cousins or nephews joined the admiral in his ventures. Giovanni Vespucci succeeded his uncle in the employ of the Spanish crown. But the times were changing. In Spain and Portugal, homegrown talent and ambition replaced the Italians on voyages of exploration. Even on the financial side, German and, later, French bankers began to compete with—though not replace—Italian participants.

It is vital, therefore, if we are to understand the origin of the Atlantic world, to know what drew or drove Vespucci to take part in it. But Amerigo's legend has obscured the truth. He was not as tradition has represented him: a maker of his own destiny who may or may not have been a captain of ships but was always the captain of his fate. In reality, he was never well enough endowed with wealth or talent to make independent choices. At every stage of his life, every shift in his trajectory, every moment of self-reinvention, he was in flight from poverty and failure. That, I think, was the background of most late-medieval adventurers who abandoned the Mediterranean for the Atlantic. To leave a calm and familiar sea for an ocean of uncertain hazards, ambition may be enough to draw you, but desperation will surely drive you. Not until his life was almost over did Vespucci achieve security and something like the fame and honor his father had schooled him to crave. The fame has remained precarious, the honor spattered with suspicions and reproaches. In retrospect, his life seems a series of wrong choices.

He was up to none of the ambitious roles he adopted. He was too unstudious to be a diplomat, too imprudent to be a great merchant, too incompetent to be a navigator, too ignorant to be a cosmographer. When he played the magus, he relied on sleight of hand to get him by. He seems to fit the fool's cap Sebastian Brant dangled for him. For Alexander Barclay, the Scots author of doggerel inspired by Brant's work, all exploration was folly, because every new discovery was self-undermining evidence of the imperfection of prior efforts. His logic was bizarre, but for Vespucci, struggling to produce a definitive map of the ocean for the Casa de Contratación while the state of knowledge was in maddening flux, Barclay's satire of 1509 was pertinent and timely.

As *Mundus Novus* put it, to "presume to discern the heavens and their majesty and to know more than it should be lawful to know" was "temerity . . . when, in all the long time that has unrolled since the world began, the vastness of the Earth and the things that are therein have remained unknown." We began with lines of Barclay's on the work of Columbus, Vespucci, their colleagues and companions, and their "vain geometry"—or, as we should now say, "geography." We can end with a last home truth of this medieval McGonagall: "Thus it is folly to tend unto the lore / And unsure science of vain geometry / Since none can know the whole world perfitly."

NOTES AND REFERENCES

PREFACE

1. L. Formisano et al., *Amerigo Vespucci: La vita e i viaggi* (Florence, 1991), 69–201. Though I respect and, at some points, rely on Formisano's scholarship, I differ with him radically on many points of interpretation.
2. R. Levillier, *Américo Vespucio* (Madrid, 1966), deploys formidable knowledge that snaps under the author's nutcracker technique. Levillier thought he could reconstruct explorers' itineraries from maps—a fantasy no sound scholar in the field embraced even in his day. G. Arciniegas, *Amerigo and the New World: The Life and Times of Amerigo Vespucci* (New York, 1955), reprinted as *Why America?: 500 Years of a Name* (Bogotá, 2002), has virtues of elegance and evocativeness, but the author's critical faculties go into suspension when he turns to the most delicate and dubious sources. F. Pohl, *Amerigo Vespucci, Pilot Major* (New York, 1944), is the work of an amateurish enthusiast whose understanding of many of the documents he tried to handle was shallow or mistaken.
3. It was not always thus: A. Varnhagen, *Amerigo Vespucci, son caractère, ses écrits (même les moins authentiques), sa vie et ses navigations* (Lima, 1865), argued against the manuscript letters in favor of the authenticity of the published works, with ingenuity so perfect that some readers suspected him of writing in jest.
4. A. Magnaghi, *Amerigo Vespucci: Studio critico* (Rome, 1926).
5. For example, Magnaghi; G. Caraci, *Questioni e polemiche vespucciani*, 2 vols. (Rome, 1955–56); T. O. Marcondes de Souza, *Amerigo Vespucci e as suas viagens* (São Paulo, 1954).

6. Vizconde de Santárem, *Researches Respecting Americus Vespucius and His Voyages* (Boston, 1850), 67.

7. For example, H. Vignaud, *Améric Vespuce* (Paris, 1917); R. Levillier, *América la bien llamada*, 2 vols. (Buenos Aires, 1948); *Américo Vespucio* (Madrid, 1966). G. Arciniegas, *Amerigo and the New World*, relying on assertion, not argument, embraced the authenticity of the published letters. The only other popular biography in the field, by F. Pohl, followed Magnaghi in comprehensively rejecting them. Yet both books adopted an adulatory tone and drew uncritical conclusions. In both, Vespucci played the role of an unblemished hero whose credentials as the discoverer of America were flawless.

8. I. Luzzana Caraci, *Amerigo Vespucci*, Nuova raccolta colombiana, 21, 2 vols. (Rome, 2000).

9. L. D'Arienzo, "Nuovi documenti su Amerigo Vespucci," in *Scritti in onore del profesore P. E. Taviani*, 3 vols. (Genoa, 1983–86), III, 121–73.

10. L. Formisano, *Amerigo Vespucci: Lettere di viaggio* (Milan, 1985); "Vespucci in America: Recuperi testimoniali per una edizione," *Studi di filologia italiana*, 41 (1983), 37–43.

11. M. Pozzi, ed., *Il mondo nuovo di Amerigo Vespucci: Vespucci autentico e apocrifo* (Milan, 1984).

12. C. Varela, *Colón y los florentinos* (Madrid, 1988).

13. Florence, Biblioteca Riccardiana, MS 2649.

PROLOGUE

1. M. P. d'Avezac, *Martin Hylacomylus Waltzemüller: Ses ouvrages et ses collaborateurs* (Paris, 1867), 40.

2. J. Fiske, *The Discovery of America*, 2 vols. (Boston, 1892), I, 132. The academician was Pico della Mirandola.

3. Ibid., 134; D'Avezac, op. cit., 258.

4. Ibid., 91.

5. Ibid., 40–41.

CHAPTER ONE: THE SORCERER'S APPRENTICESHIP

1. D. E. Bornstein, ed., *Dino Compagni's Chronicle of Florence* (Philadelphia, 1986), 3; L. Bruni, *History of the Florentine People*, ed. J. Hankins, 2 vols. (Cambridge,

MA, and London, 2001), I, 8–19, 109; G. Villani, *Croniche,* ed. G. E. Sansone and G. Cura Curà (Rome, 2001).

2. A. Della Torre, *Storia dell'Accademia platonica di Firenze* (Florence, 1907), 772–74.

3. *Letters of Marsilio Ficino,* II (London, 1978), 28–30.

4. Riccardiana, MS 2649, f. 7.

5. E. R. Dodds, *The Greeks and the Irrational* (Berkeley, 1951); K. Dover, *Greek Popular Morality in the Time of Plato and Aristotle* (Berkeley, 1974).

6. L. Martines, *April Blood: Florence and the Plot Against the Medici* (Oxford, 2003), 130–31.

7. F. Yates, *Giordano Bruno and the Hermetic Tradition in the Renaissance* (London, 1964), 12–13.

8. W. Shumaker, *The Occult Sciences in the Renaissance: A Study in Intellectual Patterns* (1972), 18–19.

9. E. H. Gombrich, "Botticelli's Mythologies: A Study in the Neoplatonic Symbolism of His Circle," *Journal of the Warburg and Courtauld Institutes,* 8 (1945), 18; *Letters of Marsilio Ficino,* IV (London, 1988), 61.

10. Quoted in E. H. Gombrich, *Symbolic Images: Studies in the Art of the Renaissance* (London, 1972), 41, 43; *Letters of Marsilio Ficino,* IV, 63.

11. G. Fossi, "Capolavori all'insegna delle vespe: grandi artisti per i Vespucci," in L. Formisano et al., *Amerigo Vespucci: La vita e i viaggi,* 230–41.

12. G. Uzielli, *Paolo del Pozzo Toscanelli* (Florence, 1892), 367–70.

13. B. Toscani, "Lorenzo, the Religious Poet," in B. Toscani, ed., *Lorenzo de' Medici: New Perspectives* (New York, 1993), 89.

14. Luzzana Caraci, I, 13.

15. N. Rubinstein, *The Government of Florence Under the Medici (1434 to 1494)* (Oxford, 1997), 142.

16. G. Arciniegas, *El embajador: Vida de Guido Antonio, tío de Amerigo Vespucci* (Bogota, 1990), 23.

17. Arciniegas, *Amerigo and the New World,* 56.

18. Luzzana Caraci, I, 23.

19. Ibid.

20. Riccardiana, MS 2649, f. 92.

21. Ibid., f. 25.

22. Luzzana Caraci, I, 20.

23. Ibid., 269.

24. K. Lippincott, "The Art of Cartography in Fifteenth-Century Florence," in M. Mallett and N. S. Mann, eds., *Lorenzo the Magnificent: Culture and Politics* (London, 1996), 131–49 (p. 132); see, generally, T. Goldstein, "Geography in XVth C Florence," in J. Parker, ed., *Merchants and Scholars: Essays in the History of Exploration and Trade* (Minneapolis, 1965), 11–32.

25. A. C. de la Mare, *The Handwriting of the Italian Humanists*, I (Oxford, 1973), 106–38.

26. S. Gentile, "L'ambiente umanistico fiorentino e lo studio della geografia nel sceolo XV," in L. Formisano et al., *Amerigo Vespucci: La vita e i viaggi*, 11–45.

27. All measures at the time were approximate, and there were no agreed standards of comparison. Ptolemy presumably thought in terms of Roman miles, which were never standardized; as far as one can tell by comparing contemporaries' calculations for the same distances in different systems of measurement, the Roman mile was a little longer than the Castilian and much shorter than the Portuguese—roughly 1,500, 1,400, and 2,000 meters respectively. See A. Szászdi Nagy, *La legua y la milla de Colón* (Valladolid, 1991).

28. Gentile, 41.

29. Riccardiana, MS 2649.

30. Luzzana Caraci, I, 20.

31. Riccardiana, MS 2649, f. 3.

32. Ibid., ff. 12–13, 54, 62, 161.

33. Ibid., f. 64.

34. Ibid., f. 20.

35. Ibid., f. 19.

36. Ibid., f. 145.

37. Ibid., f. 54.

38. Luzzana Caraci, I, 22–23.

39. Ibid., I, 23.

40. Arciniegas, *El embajador*, 55.

41. J. Coubet, *Louis XI et le Saint-siège, 1461–83* (Paris, 1903), 163.

42. Ibid., 156.

43. Ibid., 164.

44. Ibid., 28.

45. Lorenzo de' Medici, *Lettere*, VI, ed. M. Mallett (Florence, 1990), 100.

46. Martines, 214–20.

47. Ibid., 221–23.
48. E. B. Fryde, "Lorenzo de' Medici's Finances and Their Influence on His Patronage of Art," in E. B. Fryde, ed., *Humanism and Renaissance Historiography* (London, 1983), 145–57.
49. B. Toscani, ed., *Lorenzo de' Medici: Laude* (Florence, 1994), especially pp. 63–66.
50. L. Polizzotto, "Lorenzo il Magnifico, Savonarola and Medicean Dynasticism," in Toscani, *Lorenzo*, 331–55.
51. F. W. Kent, *Lorenzo de' Medici and the Art of Magnificence* (Baltimore, 2004), especially p. 91.
52. J. Beck, "Lorenzo il Magnifico and His Cultural Possessions," in Toscani, 138.
53. Riccardiana, MS 2649, f. 36.
54. A. Brown, *The Medici in Florence: The Exercise and Language of Power* (Florence, 1993), 78.
55. Ibid., 92–96.
56. E. Jayne, "A Choreography by Lorenzo in Botticelli's *Primavera*," in Toscani, 163–77, especially p. 170.
57. Fryde, 152.
58. Brown, 97.
59. J. R. Hale, *Florence and the Medici: The Pattern of Control* (London, 1977), 120.
60. Arciniegas, *Amerigo and the New World*, 56.
61. F. Gasparolo, *Pietro Vespucci, Podestà di Alessandria* (Alessandria, 1892); Arciniegas, *Amerigo and the New World*, 107–8.
62. Arciniegas, *El embajador*, 22.
63. *Silvae*, F. Bausi, ed. (Florence, 1996), 101.
64. Gombrich, *Symbolic Images*, 80–81.
65. Riccardiana, MS 2649, f. 22.
66. I. Masetti-Bencini and M. Howard Smith, *La vita di Amerigo Vespucci a Firenze da lettere inedite a lui dirette* (Florence, 1903), 9–11.
67. Ibid., 86.
68. Ibid., 63.
69. Ibid., 44.
70. Varela, *Colón y los florentinos*, 142–46.
71. Riccardiana, MS 2649, f. 69.
72. Masetti-Bencini and Howard Smith, 85.

CHAPTER TWO: THE PROSPECT FROM EXILE

1. R. Feuer-Toth, *Art and Humanism in Hungary in the Age of Matthias Corvinus* (1990), 68–97.
2. Luzzana Caraci, I, 34.
3. Varela, *Colón y los florentinos*, 17.
4. Ibid., 33.
5. A. Collantes de Terán, *Sevilla en la baja edad media* (Madrid, 1977), 216.
6. Varela, *Colón y los florentinos*, 23.
7. F. Morales Padrón, *La ciudad del quinientos: Historia de Sevilla* (Seville, 1977), 54–55.
8. Collantes de Terán, 78–79.
9. F. Morales Padrón, 19.
10. Collantes de Terán, 103–6.
11. E. Otte, "Los instrumentos financieros," in A. Collantes de Terán Sánchez and A. García-Baquero González, eds., *Andalucía 1492: Razones de un protagonismo* (1992), 159.
12. M. A. Ladero Quesada, *Andalucía en torno a 1492: Estructuras, valores, sucesos* (1992), 53.
13. E. Otte, *Sevilla y sus mercaderes a fines de la edad media* (1996), 67.
14. Collantes de Terán, 139.
15. Ladero Quesada, 154.
16. Ibid., 162.
17. Varela, *Colón y los florentinos*, 25.
18. G. Caraci, *Problemi vespucciani* (Rome, 1987), 152.
19. Luzzana Caraci, I, 31–32.
20. Caraci, *Problemi vespucciani*, 164; Luzzana Caraci, I, 42.
21. F. Fernández-Armesto, "La financiación de la conquista de Canarias durante el reinado de los Reyes Católicos," *Anuario de estudios atlánticos*, XXVIII (1982), 343–78.
22. Varela, *Colón y los florentinos*, 44–45, 96.
23. Ibid., 95–107.
24. L. D'Arienzo, "Un documento sul primo arrivo di Amerigo Vespucci a Siviglia," *Columbeis*, 3 (1988), 19–37.
25. J. Gil and C. Varela, eds., *Cartas de particulares a Colón y relaciones coetáneas* (Madrid, 1984), 66.
26. Varela, *Colón y los florentinos*, 78.

27. Ibid., 77.

28. Ibid., 60.

29. D'Arienzo, "Nuovi documenti su Amerigo Vespucci."

30. A ducat of 375 *maravedíes* was worth 4/7d in English money at the time. So as a crude rule of thumb, one can reckon 1,600 *maravedíes* to the pound.

31. Luzzana Caraci, I, 95.

32. J. Pérez de Tudela et al., eds., *Colección documental del descubrimiento*, 3 vols. (Madrid, 1995–96) II, 873–74.

33. Luzzana Caraci, I, 163; M. Fernández de Navarrette, *Obras*, C. Seco Serrano, ed., 3 vols. (Madrid, 1954–55), I, 181.

34. R. Pike, *Aristocrats and Traders: The Genoese of Seville and the Opening of the New World* (Ithaca, NY, 1966), 1–19.

35. L. A. Vigneras, *The Discovery of South America and the Andalusian Voyages* (Chicago, 1976), 20.

36. D. Ramos, *Las capitulaciones de descubrimiento y rescate* (Valladolid, 1981), 13–52.

37. Riccardiana, MS 2649, f. 67.

CHAPTER THREE: THE STARGAZER AT SEA

1. *Colección documental del descubrimiento*, II, 1179–89.

2. For a cautionary example of abuse of cartographic evidence, see R. Levillier, *América la bien llamada*, I, 93–107, where he proves to his own satisfaction that Vespucci not only made his first voyage to the New World in 1497 but also that on it, he explored the east coast of the continent from Virginia to Costa Rica—though all of the maps the author uses include data gathered much later.

3. Luzzana Caraci, I, 133.

4. Ibid., 268.

5. Ibid., 279.

6. L. Casson, ed., *The Periplus Maris Erythraei* (Princeton, 1974).

7. R. S. Lopez, "European Merchants in the Medieval Indies," *Journal of Economic History*, III (1943), 164–84.

8. Luzzana Caraci, I, 284.

9. Gentile, 37–39.

10. Ibid., 41.

11. Gil and Varela, *Cartas de particulares*, 145.

12. M. Clagett, *Archimedes in the Middle Ages*, 3 vols. (Madison, 1964–78).

13. C. Varela, ed., *Cristóbal Colón: Textos y documentos completos* (Madrid, 1984), 217; G. E. Nunn, *The Geographical Conceptions of Columbus* (New York, 1924), 1–30.

14. P. E. Taviani, *Christopher Columbus: The Grand Design* (London, 1985), 413–27; J.K.W. Willers, ed., *Focus Behaim Globus*, 2 vols. (Nuremberg, 1992), I, 143–66, 217–22, 239–72.

15. Luzzana Caraci, I, 269.

16. Moseley, ed., 127–28.

17. Luzzana Caraci, I, 20.

18. Ibid., 270–71.

19. Gentile, 34.

20. Luzzana Caraci, I, 271.

21. Varela, *Cristóbal Colón*, 311, 319–20.

22. R. Laguarda Trías, *El hallazgo del Río de la Plata por Amerigo Vespucci en 1502* (Montevideo, 1982), 197–204; J. Gil, *Mitos y utopias del descubrimiento, I: Colón y su tiempo* (Madrid, 1989), 150–51.

23. J. W. Stein, "Esame critico intorno all scoperta di Vespucci circa la determinazione della longitudine in mare mediante le distanze lunari," *Memorie della Società Astronomica Italiana*, 21 (1950), 345–53.

24. Sebastian Brant, *The Ship of Fools*, trans. Edwin H. Zeydel (New York, 1944), 220.

25. Ibid., 221.

26. L. Avonti, *Operación nuevo mundo: Amerigo Vespucci y el enigma de América* (Caracas, 1999), 192.

27. Luzzana Caraci, I, 260–61.

28. Ibid., 283.

29. P. L. Rambaldi, *Amerigo Vespucci* (Florence, 1898), 22.

30. Luzzana Caraci, I, 278.

31. Ibid., II, 173.

32. Ibid., I, 278.

33. F. Fernández-Armesto, *The Canary Islands After the Conquest* (Oxford, 1982), 19–20.

34. J. F. Gil, "El rol del tercer viaje colombino," *Historiografía y bibliografía americanistas*, 79 (1985), 83–110; *El libro de Marco Polo* (1986), 146–47; Fernández de Navarrete, II, 247.

35. M. Soares Pereira, *A navegação de 1501 e Americo Vespucci* (Rio de Janeiro, 1984), 23.

36. Luzzana Caraci, I, 282.

37. Soares Pereira, 25.

38. Luzzana Caraci, II, 212–13.

39. Ibid., I, 289.

40. Ibid., 296.

41. According to Laguarda Trías, Vespucci relied on misleading tables to help him calculate his latitude; these would account for the difference between a real latitude attained of twenty-five degrees and the thirty-two degrees Vespucci claimed.

42. Levillier, *América la bien llamada*, II, 273–343, reads cartographic evidence— most of it much too late even to suggest anything about Vespucci's route—to mean that he sailed along the coast from the equator to "about fifty degrees S."

43. *Mundus Novus*, G. T. Northrup, ed. (Princeton, 1916), 11.

44. C. Moseley, ed., *Mandeville's Travels* (Harmondsworth, 1984), p. 128 (translation modified).

45. Luzzana Caraci, I, 295.

46. Ibid., II, 549.

47. G. T. Northrup, ed., *The Soderini Letter* (Princeton, 1916), 18.

48. *Inferno*, XXVI, 97–98.

49. Luzzana Caraci, I, 276.

50. Ibid., 293.

51. Ibid., 279.

52. Ibid., 132.

Chapter Four: THE SPELLBINDER'S BOOKS

1. R. G. Adams, *The Case of the Columbus Letter* (New York, 1939), 7–8.

2. M. Waldman, *Americana: The Literature of American History* (New York, 1925), 7.

3. Pliny, *Natural History*, VII, 7:6, ed. C. Mayhoff (Leipzig, 1885), 2.

4. F. Fernández-Armesto, "Inglaterra y el Atlántico en la baja edad media," in A. Bethencourt et al., *Canarias e Inglaterra a través de la historia* (Las Palmas, 1995), 11–28.

5. D. L. Schacter, ed., *Memory Distortion: How Minds, Brains and Societies Reconstruct the Past* (Cambridge, MA, 1995).

6. E. Calderón de Cuervo, *El discurso del Nuevo Mundo: Entre el mito y la historia* (Mendoza, 1990), 23, 95.

7. *Inferno*, XXXI, 112–45.

8. *Mandeville's Travels*, ed. Moseley, 117.
9. *Inferno*, XXVI, 90–142; Calderón de Cuervo, 99.
10. *Inferno*, XXVI, 137–38.
11. Ibid., 127–29.
12. Petrarch, *Epistolae Familiares*, I, 1.21.
13. T. J. Cachey, "From Shipwreck to Port: Rvf 189 and the Making of the Canzoniere," *Modern Language Notes*, 120 (2005), 30–49.
14. Tacitus, *Germania*, ch. 46.
15. Adam of Bremen, *History of the Archbishops of Hamburg-Bremen*, ed. F. J. Tschan (New York, 1959), 186–229.
16. T. Severin, *The Brendan Voyage* (London, 1978).
17. V. Flint, *The Imaginative Landscape of Christopher Columbus* (Princeton, 1992), 91, 164, 168.
18. E. Benito Ruano, *San Borondón: Octava isla canaria* (Valladolid, 1978).
19. F. Fernández-Armesto, *Before Columbus* (London and Philadelphia, 1986), 184: "Colón y caballerías," in C. Martínez Shaw, ed., *Cristóbal Colón* (Valladolid, 2007).
20. L. Formisano, ed., *Letters from a New World: Amerigo Vespucci's Discovery of America* (New York, 1992), xxiv.
21. D. Ramos, *La primera noticia de America* (Valladolid, 1986).
22. Luzzana Caraci, I, 290.
23. Ibid., 299.
24. Ibid., 297.
25. Ibid., 296.
26. Ibid., 300.
27. Ibid., 309.
28. Ibid., 317–18.
29. *Mundus Novus*, ed. G. Tyler Northrup (Princeton, 1916), 2–3.
30. Ibid., 3–4.
31. Ibid., 5–6.
32. Ibid., 7.
33. Formisano, *Letters from a New World*, xxxv.
34. Ibid., 164–65.
35. These are the arguments of Magnaghi. In dissenting from them, I pay warm tribute to the work of this inspiring scholar, whose many other contributions to Vespucci scholarship are of undimmed brilliance.
36. L. Formisano, "Problemi vespucciani," *Studi di filologia italiana* (1983), 43.

37. L. Formisano, *Amerigo Vespucci: Cartas de viaje* (Madrid, 1986), 40ff.

38. *The First Four Voyages of Amerigo Vespucci . . . from the Rare Original Edition* (*Florence, 1505–06*) (London, 1893), 7–8.

39. Ibid., 8.

40. Ibid., 10.

41. *Mundus Novus*, ed. Northrup, 45.

42. S. Peloso, "Giovanni Battista Ramusio e as cartas do pseudo-Vespucio: os descobrimentos portugueses entre mito e realidade," *Revista da Universidade de Coimbra*, 32 (1985), 89–96.

43. *Mundus Novus*, ed. Northrup, 2–3.

44. Ibid., 20.

45. Ibid., 14–15.

46. Luzzana Caraci, II, 87.

47. *Mundus Novus*, ed. Northrup, 24–25.

48. Ibid., 36.

49. Luzzana Caraci, II, 97.

50. *Mundus Novus*, ed. Northrup, 34.

51. Pozzi, 22.

52. *Mundus Novus*, ed. Northrup, 11–12.

53. Ibid., 17.

54. Luzzana Caraci, II, 361–63.

55. Luzzana Caraci, II, 58, quoting R. Hirsch, "Printed Reports on the Early Discoveries and Their Reception," in F. Chiapelli, ed., *First Images of America: The Impact of the New World* (Berkeley, 1976), II, 537–62.

Chapter Five: PROSPERO PREFIGURED

1. Luzzana Caraci, I, 268.

2. Ibid., 269.

3. Varela, *Cristóbal Colón*, 141.

4. F. Fernández-Armesto, *Columbus on Himself* (London, 1992), 61.

5. *De Civitate Dei*, II, 21.

6. Fernández-Armesto, *Columbus on Himself*, 156–63.

7. *Purgatorio*, IV, 61–96.

8. J. F. Moffitt and S. Sebastian, *O Brave New People: The European Invention of the American Indian* (Albuquerque, 1996), 49–51.

9. *Mandeville's Travels*, ed. Moseley, 184–85.

10. Fernández-Armesto, *Columbus on Himself,* 161–62.

11. Luzzana Caraci, I, 293.

12. Ibid., 290.

13. Ibid.

14. Ibid., 293.

15. Ibid.

16. Ibid., 291.

17. J. Kirtland Wright, *The Geographical Lore at the Time of the Crusades* (New York, 1925), 156–65.

18. *Mandeville's Travels,* ed. Moseley, 128–29.

19. *Pomponius Mela's Description of the World,* trans. F. E. Romer (Ann Arbor, 1998), 28.

20. Pomponius Mela, *Chorographia,* I, 4.

21. Macrobius, *Commentary on the Dream of Scipio,* II, ch. 5.

22. W. H. Stahl, *Martianus Capella and the Seven Liberal Arts,* 2 vols. (New York, 1971–77), I, 55.

23. Fernández-Armesto, *Columbus,* 155.

24. Ibid., 97.

25. *Columbus* (1996), 127–28.

26. Fernández-Armesto, *Columbus on Himself,* 159.

27. *Mundus Novus,* ed. Northrup, 1.

28. Ibid., 11.

29. Ibid.

30. Luzzana Caraci, I, 289.

31. Ibid., 269.

32. A. Szászdi Nagy, *Un mundo que descubrió Colón: Las rutas del comercio prehispánico de los metales* (Valladolid, 1984), 29–99.

33. H. Wolff, ed., *America: Early Maps of the New World* (Munich, 1992), 178.

34. C. D. Ley, ed., *Portuguese Voyages, 1498–1663* (New York, 1947).

35. *Columbus on Himself,* 52.

36. Luzzana Caraci, I, 272.

37. Ley, 58.

38. Luzzana Caraci, I, 296.

39. *Travels,* ed. Moseley, 127.

40. H. Staden, *The True History of His Captivity* (London, 1928), ch. 20.

41. Moseley, 127.

42. Fernández-Armesto, *Columbus on Himself,* 53.

43. F. Fernández-Armesto, *The Canary Islands After the Conquest* (Oxford, 1982), 6–12.

44. Luzzana Caraci, I, 297–98.

45. J. Cañizares Esguerra, "New World, New Stars: Patriotic Astrology and the Invention of Indian and Creole Bodies in Colonial Spanish America," *American Historical Review*, 104 (1999), 33–68.

46. F. Fernández-Armesto, *So You Think You're Human* (Oxford, 2005), 69.

47. Ley, 56.

48. Ibid., 47.

49. M. Wilks, *The Problem of Sovereignty in the Late Middle Ages* (Cambridge, 1964); J. Muldoon, *Popes, Lawyers and Infidels: The Church and the Non-Christian World, 1250–1550* (Philadelphia, 1979).

50. A. Rumeu de Armas, *La política indigenista de Isabel la Católica* (Valladolid, 1969).

51. Fernández-Armesto, *Columbus on Himself*, 52–53.

52. Luzzana Caraci, I, 273.

53. Ley, 42–43.

54. Ibid., 45.

55. Ibid., 52.

56. Luzzana Caraci, I, 273.

57. Ibid., 292.

58. Ibid., 293.

59. *Mandeville's Travels*, ed. Moseley, 137.

60. *Mandeville's Travels*, ed. Moseley, 174–5.

61. Luzzana Caraci, I, 299.

62. Ibid., 300.

63. J. Hemming, *Red Gold: The Conquest of the Brazilian Indians* (London, 1978), 19.

64. Petrarch, *Rerum vulgarum*, frag. XXVIII, 60.

65. Luzzana Caraci, I, 291.

66. *Mandeville's Travels*, ed. Moseley, 127.

67. Luzzana Caraci, I, 291.

68. Ibid., 291.

69. Ley, 50.

70. Ibid., 56.

71. Ibid., 59.

72. Luzzana Caraci, I, 293.

73. Moffitt and Sebastian, 118.

74. C. Sanz, *Mapas antiguos* (Madrid, 1962), 60–61, fig. 9; S. Colin, "Woodcutters and Cannibals: Brazilian Indians as Seen on Early Maps," in Wolff, 174–81, fig. 3 (p. 175).

75. Moffitt and Sebastian, 145–58.

CHAPTER SIX: THE CONJURER'S STAGE

1. G. Tyler Northrup, ed., *Amerigo Vespucci: Letter to Piero Soderini, Gonfaloniere* (Princeton, 1916), 41.

2. Ibid., 44.

3. Luzzana Caraci, I, 135.

4. Ibid., 136–37.

5. Ibid., 142.

6. Ibid., 141.

7. Varela, *Cristóbal Colón*, 311, 319–20; Laguarda Trías, 140–41.

8. Fernández de Navarrete, II, 614.

9. Ibid., I, 358.

10. Varela, *Cristóbal Colón*, 170–76.

11. R. Ezquerra, "Las Juntas de Toro y Burgos," in A. Rumeu de Armas, ed., *El Tratado de Tordesillas y su proyección*, 2 vols. (Valladolid, 1973), I, 155; "La idea del antimeridiano," in A. Teixeira da Mota, ed., *A viagem de Fernão de Magalhães e a questão das Molucas: Actas do II Coloquio Luso-espanhol de historia ultramarina* (Lisbon, 1975), 12–13; Fernández de Navarrete, II, 89; U. Lamb, "The Spanish Cosmographical Juntas of the Sixteenth Century," *Terra Incognita*, 6 (1974), 53.

12. Fernández de Navarrete, II, 87.

13. J. Cortesão, "João II y el tratado de Tordesillas," in *El tratado de Tordesillas*, I, 93–101.

14. A. Rumeu de Armas, *El Tratado de Tordesillas* (Madrid, 1992), 207–9.

15. Fernández de Navarrete, 179–81; J. Pulido Rubio, *El piloto mayor de la Casa de la Contratación de Sevilla* (Seville, 1950), 66–67.

16. F. Fernández-Armesto, "Maps and Exploration," in *History of Cartography*, III, ed. D. Harley (Chicago), forthcoming.

17. E. Schafer, *El Consejo Real y Supremo de las Indias*, I (Valladolid, 2003), 31–47.

18. L. Avonti, *Operación nuevo mundo: Amerigo Vespucci y el enigma de América* (Caracas, 1999), 115–16.

19. Pulido Rubio, 19.

20. Fernández de Navarrete, III, 193–94.

21. Pérez de Tudela, *Colección documental*, I, 178.

22. Pulido Rubio, 461–64.

23. Ibid., 133–34.

24. Ibid., 255–56.

25. D. Harley, ed., *History of Cartography*, iii, forthcoming.

26. Pulido Rubio, 259, 467–70.

27. Varela, *Colón y los florentinos*, 69.

28. Pulido Rubio, 21–22.

29. Varela, *Colón y los florentinos*, 72.

30. Ibid., 80.

31. Ibid., 72.

32. See also Soares Pereira, 58–59.

33. S. Zweig, *Amerigo: A Comedy of Errors in History* (New York, 1942), 31.

34. Fernández-Armesto, *Columbus on Himself*, 20.

35. C. Sanz, *El nombre América: Libros y mapas que lo impusieron* (Madrid, 1959), 61.

36. Ibid., 81.

37. Wolff, 121.

38. Sanz, 81.

39. *Underweisung und Usslegunge der Carta Marina oder die Mer Carte* (Introduction to and Explanation of the Carta Marina or Sea Chart).

40. Wolff, 122.

41. Most of these maps are illustrated in ibid., 30–71.

42. Sanz, 151.

43. Ibid., 73.

44. *Historia de las Indias*, ed. J. Pérez de Tudela and E. López Oto, 2 vols. (Madrid, 1957–61), I, 347.

45. Ibid., II, 42.

46. Raffaella Signori, "Amerigo Vespucci eroe mediceo," in Luzzana Caraci, II, 536–39.

47. A. Gerbi, *The Dispute of the New World* (Pittsburgh, 1973); D. Brading, *The First America* (Cambridge, 1991), 428–62; J. Cañizares Esguerra, *How to Write the History of the New World* (Stanford, 2001).

48. A. Pagden, *European Encounters with the New World from Renaissance to Romanticism* (New Haven, 1993), 141–72.

49. T. J. Ellingson, *The Myth of the Noble Savage* (Berkeley, 2001).

50. R. Pasta, "Nascita di un mito: Il concorso vespucciano dell'Accademia

Etrusca di Cortona," in Formisano et al., *Amerigo Vespucci: La vita e i viaggi*, 252–75.

51. Ibid., 270–71.

52. Ibid., 273.

53. F. Bartolozzi, *Ricerche istorico-critiche circa all scoperte d'Amerigo Vespucci* (Florence, 1789), 3–4.

54. Ibid., 64.

55. C. P. Claret de Fleurieu, "Observations sur la division hydrographique du globe," in *Voyages d'Étienne Marchand* (Paris 1799), 25, cited by Vizconde de Santárem, 102.

56. Alexander von Humboldt, *Examen critique de l'histoire de la géographie du nouveau continent* (Paris, 1836–39), IV, 36; V, 223.

57. J. Goodman, *Chivalry and Exploration, 1298–1630* (Woodbridge, 1998).

58. *English Traits*, ed. D. E. Wilson (Cambridge, MA, 1994), 148.

59. *The Letters of Amerigo Vespucci*, ed. C. Markham (London, 1894), xi.

INDEX

About the author

FELIPE FERNÁNDEZ-ARMESTO is the Prince of Asturias Professor of History at Tufts University, and a Professional Fellow of Queen Mary, University of London. His books on the history of exploration include *Columbus, Before Columbus, Pathfinders,* and *The Times Atlas of World Exploration,* and have won, among other awards, the Caird Medal, the John Carter Brown Medal, and the Premio Nacional de Investigación of Spain's Sociedad Geográfica Española. His other books include *Millennium, Near a Thousand Tables,* and *The World.* His work has appeared in twenty-four languages. His journalism and broadcasts appear frequently in Spanish and British media.